W9-DGC-998

Teenagers and Substance Use

Teenagers and Substance Use

Social Networks and Peer Influence

Deirdre M. Kirke
National University of Ireland, Maynooth

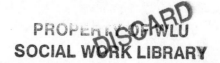

PROPERTY OF WLU
SOCIAL WORK LIBRARY

© Deirdre M. Kirke 2006

All rights reserved. No reproduction, copy or transmission of this
publication may be made without written permission.

No paragraph of this publication may be reproduced, copied or transmitted
save with written permission or in accordance with the provisions of the
Copyright, Designs and Patents Act 1988, or under the terms of any licence
permitting limited copying issued by the Copyright Licensing Agency,
90 Tottenham Court Road, London W1T 4LP.

Any person who does any unauthorised act in relation to this publication
may be liable to criminal prosecution and civil claims for damages.

The author has asserted her right to be identified
as the author of this work in accordance with the Copyright,
Designs and Patents Act 1988.

First published 2006 by
PALGRAVE MACMILLAN
Houndmills, Basingstoke, Hampshire RG21 6XS and
175 Fifth Avenue, New York, N.Y. 10010
Companies and representatives throughout the world

PALGRAVE MACMILLAN is the global academic imprint of the Palgrave
Macmillan division of St. Martin's Press, LLC and of Palgrave Macmillan Ltd.
Macmillan® is a registered trademark in the United States, United Kingdom
and other countries. Palgrave is a registered trademark in the European
Union and other countries.

ISBN-13: 978–1–4039–9238–3 hardback
ISBN-10: 1–4039–9238–X hardback

This book is printed on paper suitable for recycling and made from fully
managed and sustained forest sources.

A catalogue record for this book is available from the British Library.

Library of Congress Cataloging-in-Publication Data
Kirke, Deirdre M.
    Teenagers and substance use : social networks and peer influence / Deirdre
M. Kirke.
        p. cm.
    Includes bibliographical references and index.
    ISBN 1–4039–9238–X
    1. Teenagers—Substance use.   2. Teenagers—Drug use.
    3. Teenagers—Alcohol use.   4. Substance abuse.   5. Peer influence in
    adolescence.   6. Teenagers—Social networks.   I. Title.
    HV4999.Y68K57 2006
    616.8600835—dc22   2006040118

10   9   8   7   6   5   4   3   2   1
15   14   13   12   11   10   09   08   07   06

Printed and bound in Great Britain by
Antony Rowe Ltd, Chippenham and Eastbourne

Contents

v

List of Tables

ix

List of Figures

Acknowledgements

I would like to thank Elsevier for granting permission to reprint Kirke, D. M. (2004) 'Chain reactions in adolescents' cigarette, alcohol and drug use: similarity through peer influence or the patterning of ties in peer networks?' *Social Networks*, 26, 3–28, as Chapter 8, and for granting permission to use large extracts from Kirke, D. M. (1996) 'Collecting peer data and delineating peer networks in a complete network', *Social Networks*, 18, 333–346, in Chapter 7 of this book. I would also like to thank Cambridge University Press for granting permission to include large extracts from Kirke, D. M. (1995) 'Teenage peer networks in the community as sources of social problems: a sociological perspective', from T. S. Brugha (Ed.), *Social Support and Psychiatric Disorder – Research Findings and Guidelines for Clinical Practice*, Cambridge University Press, Cambridge.

My early interest in social network analysis was nurtured while I studied and taught in the Department of Sociology, University College Dublin, and I have enjoyed furthering this interest through research and teaching in the Department of Sociology, National University of Ireland, Maynooth, through my membership of the International Network for Social Network Analysis (INSNA) and through my participation in numerous International Social Network Conferences. Various members of the International Network for Social Network Analysis have been a major source of support and advice to me over the years. I would like to thank especially Frans Stokman, Frans Wasseur, Linton Freeman, Martin Everett, Barry Wellman, Tom Valente and Tom Snijders.

I would like to record my thanks to the Health Education Bureau and the Health Promotion Unit, Department of Health, Dublin, and to an anonymous benefactor, who funded the survey on which this book is based, and to the Reviewers, the Editor, Ms. Jill Lake and Editorial Assistant, Ms. Melanie Blair of Palgrave Macmillan. A special word of thanks goes to the parents in the community who gave their approval, to the teenagers who agreed to be interviewed, and to the interviewers who completed the interviews successfully. My warmest thanks go to my husband, Peadar, and to my daughters, Sandra, Ciara and Karen, who have been a constant source of love and support, and to whom I dedicate this book.

1
Introduction

Over the past ten years or so there has been renewed research interest in understanding the role that peer selection and peer influence play in the increasing similarity in substance use among teenagers. Earlier research had confirmed the importance of peer influence but subsequent research had cautioned that peer influence and peer selection may be involved in the process of teenagers becoming similar in their substance use (Cohen, 1977: 239; Kandel, 1978b: 436; Bauman and Ennett, 1996: 187). The concept peer influence meant that the teenagers and their peers had become similar in their substance use sometime after they had become friends, while peer selection meant that the teenagers were similar (for example, in their use of drugs) before they became friends, in which case peer influence could not have explained their similarity. No definitive results have yet emerged in substance use research to confirm the relative impact of peer influence and peer selection.

This book examines this current research question using research conducted by Kirke (1990; 1995; 1996; 2004) and proposes a new explanation for teenagers' substance use. Complete network data, which were collected in the earlier Kirke (1990) study are used, and new analyses, including the role of gender on chain reactions, retrospective analyses on the timing of the formation of peer ties and the timing of changes in the teenagers' substance use, single and multilevel peer network analyses, and social network analyses, which combine peers, family and community, form the findings reported in this book (see Glossary of Terms). A new explanation for teenagers' substance use is proposed. This chain reaction explanation combines peer selection, the patterning of peer ties in peer networks and peer influence. It builds, therefore, on earlier research which proposed that peer selection and peer influence

1

were involved but adds the important dimension of the patterning of peer ties, which had not been included to date.

This book examines the substance use of teenagers in one working-class community in Dublin, Ireland. The community selected was similar to many other working-class communities in Dublin at the time with most of the population in the manual socioeconomic groups, a high level of unemployment, a large proportion of the population in the under-25-year age group and a large teenage population. This community was quite homogeneous with no geographic, ethnic or religious differences. The community had a population of about 2500 people, living in close proximity to one another, in houses on a number of adjoining roads in one large housing estate. The community was quite self-contained with housing, schools, shops, health services, public houses, cafes and cinema in the vicinity and a bus connection to Dublin city centre, which could be reached in about 30 minutes.

We decided to focus on teenagers of 14–18 years in the expectation that they would be old enough to have had opportunities to use one, or more, of the three substances under study: cigarettes, alcohol or drugs. We also expected that we would get a sufficient number of teenagers who were substance users in that age group and would, at the same time, get a comparative group of non-users, to enable us to examine a range of individual and social network influences. We were also aware that this age group would cover teenagers who were still attending school and others who had already left school.

Teenagers are an important and vibrant section of such a community. They have been born into families in this community. As they are growing up they form friendships with other children and teenagers from other families in the community. These friendships form, what have become known in substance use research as, peer ties and peer groups. At a particular point in the teenagers' life course, usually in the teenage years, substance use becomes a part of their lives. They may have opportunities to use the substances and may resist, or may begin to use. Understanding this transition, and the individual and social network forces influencing the teenagers' substance use, are the foci of this book.

Understanding the teenagers' behaviour, however, requires us to see their individual behaviour in the context of their own attributes, and the social networks in which their lives are embedded. These social networks include their family, school and community, and, most of all, their peer relationships. The best way of getting this overall focus appears to be to collect data on a total population of teenagers in one community, and on a complete network of their peer ties.

Previous research has consistently confirmed that the relationships teenagers have with their peers have an impact on their substance use (Chapter 2). But peer relationships can be explored at different levels of analysis – including the dyad, the egocentric network, the peer group and complete network – and the level of analysis used in research is likely to affect the conclusions reached (Valente, 2003: 11–16). Researchers have examined peer relationships at one of those levels, usually at the level of the dyad or the clique as peer group (Chapter 2). When the clique has been used as a representation of the peer group it has usually included only three to five teenagers. Research has rarely examined teenagers' substance use in peer groups larger than cliques, in complete network data on peer ties, or in multilevel data (Chapter 2).

In this book we use complete network data on a population of teenagers to address the role of their peers, their families and community in their substance use. The research methods used to collect the data are discussed in detail in Chapter 3. The value of using complete network data is that the teenagers' substance use can be placed in the context of their dyadic peer ties, their peer group and the complete network of teenagers in which they are connected by peer ties. The value of covering a population of teenagers is that all of the families of the teenagers and their peers are included because the teenagers become peers to each other. So teenagers' behaviour can be examined in the social context of the families and the community in which they are embedded.

The combined social impact of the social networks of family, community and peers on the teenagers' substance use is examined in this book. By locating the teenagers in the social context in which their lives are embedded, we can examine the impact of that social context on their substance use. We will examine how the families and community, which have produced the teenagers and their peers and have provided the social environment in which they live their lives, also directly influence their substance use. By placing the teenagers' behaviour in the context of their peer ties in a complete network, we can examine the relative impact of peer influence and peer selection on their substance use in a way that has not been possible using dyadic or clique data only. And this book goes further by suggesting a chain reaction explanation which is based on peer selection, the patterning of peer ties and peer influence.

Teenagers' peer data are examined in this book at a variety of levels – including the level of the individual, the dyad, the peer group and the complete network (Chapter 6) – and at multiple levels, combining

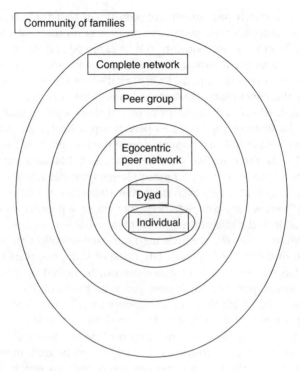

Figure 1.1 Levels of analysis.

individual, dyad and peer group (Chapters 7–9). The levels of analysis are given in Figure 1.1. They range from the level of the individual – when teenagers are asked questions about their own attributes, such as gender or age, or their substance use – to the whole community of families, which comprises the families of the teenagers and their peers covered by the study. Data at the individual level are those produced from the teenagers' answers to questions relating to their own attributes, their substance use behaviour and their families. Dyadic data are formed when teenagers select other teenagers as peers. Each dyad represents one peer tie. The egocentric peer network includes all of the peers named by a teenager and any peer ties they have with each other. The peer group includes any further direct or indirect ties the egocentric peer network members have with other teenagers. Thus, the peer group, as it exists at any particular time, includes all of the peers who might influence the teenagers' substance use at that time. In social network terms these are weak components, which include all of the teenagers and their peers who are connected to each other through peer ties by paths of any distance (Chapter 3; Kirke, 1996: 340). These peer groups are, therefore, distinct from all other peer groups in the complete network and have no peer ties connecting the groups (Chapter 3; Kirke, 2004: 6). The complete network includes all of the peer ties connecting all of the teenagers in the community (Chapter 3; Kirke, 2004: 6). So it includes all of the disparate peer groups and any individual teenagers who were not connected by a peer tie to a peer group at the time of interview and were, therefore, isolates in the community. The community of families includes the population of this community (2500 people approximately) and includes, therefore, the families of all of the teenagers and their peers in this community who were interviewed.

Figure 1.2 illustrates how peer ties between individual teenagers form the different levels of analysis. The example is taken from one all-male peer group (Peer Group 5) in the study. A five-digit identification number is used for each teenager. The first digit indicates the road on which the teenager lives (0–9). The next three digits are the family's identification number and are numbered consecutively along each road, and indicate, therefore how near families live to one another. The final digit indicates the number of teenagers in the family who were interviewed. The figure shows the dyadic peer ties of one teenager (24611) with four other teenagers. The dyadic peer tie between 24611 and 24781 is circled to indicate the dyadic level of analysis. When the peer ties between the four teenagers who have peer ties with 24611 are added, this forms 24611's egocentric peer network and this level is also circled. The direct and indirect peer ties of those in the peer network are added to form the peer group (which includes 61461 and 61481). Analyses in this book focus

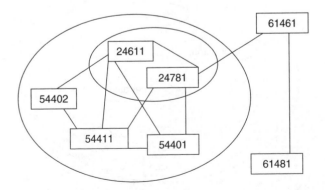

Figure 1.2   Dyads, egocentric peer network, peer group.

on the peer group, rather than the egocentric peer network, because the peer group, as defined here, includes the egocentric peer networks of all members, and all of the interlocks between the egocentric peer networks, and represents, therefore, all of the direct and indirect ties of the teenagers who are members. Thus, it includes all of those who may be in a social position, directly or indirectly, to influence the teenagers' substance use.

A complete network can be visualized by the reader as numerous disparate peer groups, not connected to each other, and some individual isolated teenagers, who have no peer ties in the community (Figure 1.3). The complete network examined in this book includes 35 peer groups, varying in size from 26 teenagers to two teenagers, and 98 isolated teenagers who have no peer tie with another teenager in the population, although almost all of them have at least one peer tie outside the population. The size, composition and the structure, or patterning, of peer ties in the peer groups are discussed in Chapters 6–9. Chain reactions in teenagers' substance use and the role of gender in chain reactions are discussed in Chapters 8 and 9.

Previous research has confirmed associations between a variety of factors and teenagers' substance use. The most important factors have, for many years, been peer influence and the family (Chapter 2). The question of whether peer influence, or the selection of peers who are already similar to the teenagers in their substance use, is more important, arose some years ago (Cohen, 1977: 239; Kandel, 1978b: 436) but has become a major question in substance use research in recent

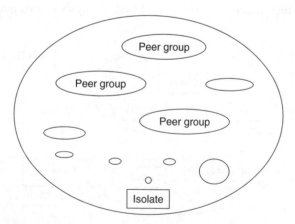

Figure 1.3 A complete network.

times (Bauman and Ennett, 1996: 187). The question being addressed is whether the observed similarity in teenagers' substance use is due to either peer influence or the selection of friends who were already similar in their substance use. In a recent paper it has been demonstrated that both influence and selection are involved in almost every case of a teenager who has used a substance (Chapter 8; Kirke, 2004). It has been suggested in this paper that selection is not necessarily based on similarity in the use of a particular substance, however, but may be based on other similarities, which lead teenagers, or children at an earlier age, to select each other as peers. The selection of these peers links the teenagers into peer groups in which peer influence can flourish (Chapter 8). This book addresses the question of the relative importance of peer influence and selection and proposes a social network explanation, based on peer influence and peer selection, to explain the process at work. The chain reaction explanation proposed includes peer selection, the patterning of peer ties and peer influence which are discussed in Chapter 8, and the role of gender in chain reactions is discussed in Chapter 9.

The conceptual model used in this book includes numerous individual teenagers' attributes, family variables and peer data at different levels of analysis (Figure 1.4). This model includes teenagers' attributes and family variables, which may influence their substance use, and indicates the levels of peer data on which the book focuses. Teenagers' attributes examined include their gender, age, occupational status and their education. The teenagers' substance use and their individual attributes are discussed in Chapter 4. Family variables examined include the teenagers' family circumstances, parental substance use, closeness to parents, parental influence to use substances, parental control of the teenagers' free-time activities, their siblings' substance use and their siblings' influence to use substances. The role of their families in the teenagers' substance use is covered in Chapter 5.

Peer data are examined at the level of individual peers, dyads of teenagers and their peers, peer groups of various sizes, the complete network of peer ties and at multiple levels combining, for example, the levels of the individual, the dyad and the peer group. The role of their peers in the teenagers' substance use is examined in Chapters 6–9. Peer data at the levels of the individual, the dyad, the peer group and the complete network are used in Chapter 6 to examine the selection of peers, the formation of peer groups, and the similarity of teenagers and their peers, in dyads and in peer groups, in their substance use. Changes in their substance use occurring over time, and the role of peer selection and peer influence in those changes, are discussed in Chapter 7.

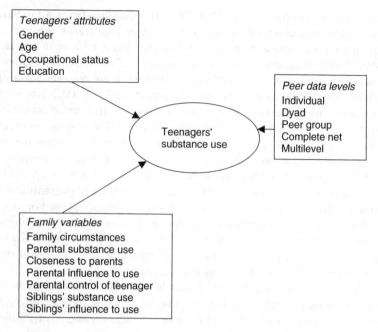

Figure 1.4   Conceptual model.

In Chapter 8, case studies of the three largest peer groups are used to examine the process through which teenagers become similar to their peers in their substance use, and to propose a chain reaction explanation for the similarity which emerges. The relative importance of peer influence, peer selection and the patterning of peer ties in peer groups to the chain reactions in substance use which emerge are examined in Chapter 8 and in Chapter 9 the role of gender in each aspect of the chain reaction process is discussed.

Finally, Chapter 10 examines the substance use of the teenagers by placing it in the context of the social networks in which the teenagers' lives are embedded. These social networks include their peer groups, their families and the community in which they live. This chapter draws together the findings of the book – on the impact of individual teenagers' attributes, family variables and peer network data – to suggest a new theoretical explanation for the teenagers' substance use. This explanation builds on earlier research on the role of peer selection and peer influence on similarity in teenagers' substance use and adds a new dimension, the patterning of peer ties in peer groups. The explanation is based on chain reactions, which result from the selection of peers, the patterning of peer ties and peer influence, and in which gender affects each aspect of the chain reaction process. The book ends with suggestions for future research which, ideally, would use complete network data in a prospective, longitudinal, study.

2
Review of Literature

Introduction

This book reports on the substance use of the teenagers in a working-class community in Dublin. The families in this community were similar in various respects, including socioeconomic status, occupational status, family size, housing, geographic location, ethnic group and religion. More than half of the families had a teenager aged 14–18 years living at home at the time of interview. Teenagers living in families sharing such similarities, and living in such close proximity to one another, would be expected to form peer ties, and they would do so on the basis of other individual similarities, such as age and gender. The peer groups formed from these peer ties would, therefore, be expected to be homogeneous in various respects.

There has also been a widespread belief since the 1970s that peer groups will be homogeneous in their substance use. The source of this homogeneity has been the subject of research for many years now. Research evidence in the 1970s suggested that the homogeneity was based on peer influence. This was followed with some cautionary notes that peer influence may not be the full explanation and that selection may also explain some of the similarity. More recent research has examined the relative importance of peer influence and selection to homogeneity.

Along the way was the methodological difficulty of having appropriate peer data to examine the influence and selection question. Much of the earlier work was on peer dyads and on perceived peer data. This was followed with some analyses of small cliques and more recently with analyses of peer groups and complete networks. The development of social network analysis in the intervening years was crucial. It enabled researchers to identify and analyse peer groups larger than dyads and cliques. It facilitated the exploration of the key questions of whether there was homogeneity in substance use in such peer groups as had been assumed and, if so, whether peer influence or selection were the sources of this homogeneity and how that process worked.

This chapter reviews related research on the peer question, in particular, and on parental influences found to contribute to teenagers' substance use.

Research on peers

Kandel's work, in the early 1970s, was very influential in demonstrating that peer influence was the most important influence on teenagers' substance use at that time. She found that teenagers who had substance-using peers at one point in time were likely to be substance users themselves at a later time point. Thus, peer influence was apparently at work between them. She found that peer influence varied for different substances and was greatest for marijuana use (Kandel, 1978a: 24). When teenagers perceived that their peer group was using marijuana, they were likely to use it too (Kandel, Kessler and Margulies, 1978: 87). When they perceived that their best friends were using illicit drugs other than marijuana they were likely to use those (Kandel, Kessler and Margulies, 1978: 89). Kandel (1980: 270; 1986: 221) also confirmed that female teenagers were more susceptible than male teenagers to peer influence. Kandel's findings were based on longitudinal surveys conducted in public secondary schools in New York State between 1971 and 1973 (Kandel, 1973; 1975) and follow-up surveys later (for example, Yamaguchi and Kandel, 1984a,b). A major strength of her surveys was that substance use data were self-reported by the teenagers and their best school friends, thus avoiding the exaggerations of peer influence likely if perceived peer data were used. The self-reported peer data did not, however, go beyond the dyad. Kandel's explanatory theory was known as adolescent socialization theory (1980: 256). In this theory the two primary agents of socialization, parents and peers, were used to explain teenagers' substance use. When their relative influence was compared, Kandel and her colleagues (Kandel, 1973: 1067; 1974a: 107; Kandel, Kessler and Margulies, 1978: 91; Kandel and Adler, 1982: 295) found that the influence of peers was greater than that of parents, especially for marijuana use.

The importance of peers in influencing other teenagers' substance use has been confirmed by other researchers for drug use (Jessor and Jessor,

1978: 69; Brook, Whiteman and Gordon, 1982: 1160; 1983: 276; Dembo, Schmeidler and Burgos, 1982: 376), for cigarettes, alcohol and drugs (Grube and Morgan, 1986: 77, 104, 126) and for alcohol and drug use (Akers et al., 1979: 638). Burgess and Akers (1966: 131, 145) developed a theory known as social learning theory to explain the process which they observed. This theory was based on social learning principles and, when tested in the 1979 paper, confirmed that the most important sources of influence on teenagers' substance use were their peer group and family (Akers et al., 1979: 638). Like Kandel, they also found that the peer group was the more important of the two.

Very convincing evidence had been produced in these studies that peer influence was the most important influence on teenagers' substance use and that, if teenagers were in a peer group which included substance users, or those perceived to be substance users, they were likely to use those substances too. While there is no direct evidence in these studies that particular peers influenced particular teenagers into taking substances, it was concluded that peer influence had occurred if peers' substance use, or their perceived substance use, preceded (in time) the teenagers' substance use. The findings were influential particularly because they were usually based on longitudinal studies in which changes in the teenagers' substance use and in their peers' substance use could be recorded over time. Some shortcomings of the data were, however, that peer substance use data were rarely self-reported, although perceived peer data had been noted to exaggerate peer effects (Kandel, 1980: 269, 270) and peer group data were not analysed beyond the dyad. Indeed these findings, which were based on similarity in dyads of best friends or similarity in dyads or peer groups based on perceived peer substance use data, led to exaggerated expectations of homophily in peer groups in the substance use of the teenage members.

While providing strong evidence that similarity in teenagers' substance use was due to peer influence, Kandel and Cohen gave evidence which demonstrated that the effect of peer influence on similarity was often exaggerated (Cohen, 1977: 239; Kandel, 1978b: 436). Their point was that the effect was not due only to socialization (peer influence) but also to the selection of peers. Selection suggests that there was similarity between the peers, for example in their drug use, before they chose each other as friends, and socialization (peer influence) suggests that having become friends their similarity in drug use occurred. The evidence indicated that since '. . . both selection and socialization appear to be approximately of equal importance' (Kandel, 1978b: 433) in the marijuana use of friends, the socialization influence of friends explains only half of the similarity. This point must be kept in mind when discussing peer influence which is such an important factor in substance use research. These findings suggest that, when there are similarities in the substance use of teenagers and their peers, only half of the similarity is due to the influence of the peers, the other half is due to the teenagers' selection of peers whose substance use was the same as their own before they formed the peer tie.

The cautionary note about the exaggeration of the impact of peer influence on similarity in teenagers' substance use had been largely ignored until the 1990s. The extent of homophily in peer groups and whether influence or selection explained that homophily could only be properly examined using social network analytic techniques. A major problem at this time was that, although the social network approach and social network methods were undergoing considerable development, few papers had been published applying social network techniques to substance use in teenagers' peer groups, although such research was in progress (Kirke, 1990).

Research on peer groups using a social network approach

The social network perspective provides a very valuable framework for examining the role of peer groups in teenagers' substance use. Social network analysts have a distinctive approach to the study of networks in that they directly analyse the pattern of relationships in networks and examine the impact of that pattern on the actions of individuals in the networks (Wellman and Berkowitz, 1988: 3). Thus, this approach can be used to identify and analyse peer groups, to examine the level of similarity in substance use in them and to examine the impact of the peer group on the individual teenagers' behaviour.

Based on the earlier work by Kandel and others, researchers may have reasonable expectations that teenagers in peer groups would be similar in their substance use. In other words, it would be reasonable to expect a tendency to homophily in peer groups. This is, in part, due to the homophily principle, the tendency for those who are similar in certain respects to form relationships (McPherson and Smith-Lovin, 1987: 370; McPherson, Smith-Lovin and Cook, 2001: 415). It is also, in part, due to the tendency for those who engage in repeated interactions to become more similar to each other over time (Homans, 1950; Collins, 1988: 340). Thus, for example, teenagers of similar age and sex are likely to form peer ties and become members of peer groups. Through their inter-actions in the peer group, they should become more similar, for example in smoking behaviour. Repeated interactions and increasing similarities should strengthen their relationships so that they continue to interact and to increase similarity.

Prior to social network research on peer groups, however, it was not possible to empirically examine the level of similarity in peer groups. It could only be imputed from the dyadic or perceived peer data available. Social network analysts do not assume that similarity will exist in peer groups, although they can reasonably expect that similarity may exist in them. Instead, they use social network analytic techniques to identify peer groups that emerge among teenagers, and examine the behaviour of the teenagers and their peers to assess the level of similarity in the teenagers' behaviour at one point in time or over time. The process which leads to such similarity can then be examined in the context of the peer group. Previous research would suggest that the process at work is selection, whereby teenagers choose each other as friends because they are similar in certain respects, or peer influence, whereby increasing similarity occurs through increasing interaction (Cohen, 1977: 239; Kandel, 1978b: 436).

Pressures towards similarity in the behaviour of individuals in social networks would be expected by social network theorists (Friedkin, 1984: 236; Wasserman and Faust, 1994: 251). These writers would expect similarity to emerge in social networks because of social forces which operate in such cohesive groups. They also suggest that the influences may operate through indirect as well as direct social ties. These views would seem to be particularly relevant to small groups or small peer networks such as egocentric networks or small cliques. Much of the recent research in substance use among teenagers, which will be discussed below, has been on small cliques.

How successful this force for similarity is when operating in larger peer groups is, however, an open question. This question needs to be examined with suitable data on peer groups larger than cliques, and on substance use within them, as it is done in this book. Social network analysts who study the process of diffusion provide a means of understanding how similarity in behaviour could occur in larger groups. As Rogers (1983: 5) explains: 'Diffusion is the process by which an innovation is communicated through certain channels over time among the members of a social system.' When an innovation is being diffused, there is uncertainty due to lack of knowledge about the innovation or the expected outcome. Successful diffusion would depend, therefore, on having others with whom one can communicate about the uncertainties of adopting an innovation (Rogers, 1983: 305; Burt, 1987: 1288; Valente,

1995: 12). As demonstrated in the literature discussed above, uncertainties relating to substance use among teenagers seem to be managed within their peer relationships.

Since the 1980s, researchers have attempted to apply a social network framework to understanding substance use among teenagers and adults. In one of the first social network papers on marijuana use, Barrett and James-Cairns (1980) studied three small groups, of 7, 8 and 10 members respectively, whose members regularly took marijuana together. Each group was studied in its natural environment. The age range was 20–29 years. Their findings showed that peer influence was not a primary reason for initial marijuana use, that, although there were high levels of drug use, members participated more for social than for drug reasons, and that popularity in the group was related to frequency of participation and not to the extent of drug use (Barrett and James-Cairns, 1980: 677, 678, 686). Although their paper was on marijuana use, it was not on teenagers in the early stages of their substance use. Thus, the findings are not directly relevant to teenage substance use. Another limitation was that, although the title of the paper was 'The social network in marijuana-using groups', there was no social network analysis of the structure of the groups. The paper did, however, suggest to other researchers the relevance for future research of a social network approach and the need to analyse the groups directly using social network analytic techniques.

Some of the earliest social network papers on individuals using substances other than marijuana were those of Fraser and Hawkins (1984) and Hawkins and Fraser (1985, 1987). All three papers were based on a study of 106 street drug users, with the 1987 paper covering a follow-up study of 38 of them, who had gone through residential treatment for their drug use. Street drug users meant that they had '. . . long histories of life-styles characteristic of drug use "on the streets", including the sale and use of heroin, other opiates, and amphetamines, as well as barbiturates, cocaine, and hallucinogens'. The mean age was 28.3 years (Hawkins and Fraser, 1985: 7). The authors compiled the respondents' network structures, that is, their egocentric networks, from the self-reports of the 106 street drug users because, as they report, '. . . there is some evidence that people can reliably report their broad network structures . . .' (Fraser and Hawkins, 1984: 89). All peer data were as perceived by the initial respondent. The authors were particularly interested in studying changes in the egocentric peer networks of the sample of street drug users before and after treatment because this was expected to have an impact on relapse into drug abuse after treatment.

The authors found that, following a three-month residential treatment programme, the composition of the peer networks of the participants in the community had changed, although the size of their networks had not. In particular, they found that their peer networks included fewer individuals who favoured drug use and that these changes were a positive step towards the rehabilitation of the drug addicts (Hawkins and Fraser, 1987: 348).

While these papers are of interest in that they used a social network approach, they do not provide an explanation for the initial, and continued, use of substances by teenagers. Teenage substance use covers the searliest stages of use, while these papers cover drug users at much later stages of drug use, which include the use of heroin and cocaine, and involvement in crime. Some of the most helpful contributions of these authors were that they made valuable suggestions for future research. The authors suggested the need for data '... on the levels of deviance commonly found in the networks of conventional people' (Hawkins and Fraser, 1985: 7) and later concluded that 'Future research on the relationships between delinquency or drug use and social influences should focus on the structures, interactions and attachments in the broader personal social networks of individuals rather than be confined to relationships with parents and a few "best friends"' (Hawkins and Fraser, 1985: 11). This advice led to the Kirke (1990) study being conducted in a normal population of teenagers, covering family and all of the teenagers' peers and not just their best friends.

Research by Kirke was designed in the light of these limited social network findings on substance use, none of which tackled the question of teenage substance use directly. It was designed too, at a time when social network methods and computer analytic techniques were undergoing considerable development, and were disseminating slowly across the academic community between the USA, Canada, Australia and Europe. The methods of social network analysis did, however, seem to the author to be most appropriate for examining 'peer groups' and 'peer influence', which previous research had confirmed to be of particular importance in teenage substance use. The research method of the Kirke study has been reported in detail already (Kirke, 1990). That thesis examined the drug use of teenagers in peer groups and examined the sources of similarity in the drug use of the teenagers. It demonstrated that similarity in substance use in peer groups was much lower than was anticipated, that it varied by the size of the peer group, and that peer influence was much less potent than would have been expected from previous research. The findings suggested, rather, that a complex process of peer group and individual influences were at play, which sometimes resulted in changed drug behaviour on the part of the teenager and sometimes did not (Kirke, 1990).

A case study of the formation and development of one peer group of sixteen male teenagers and the diffusion of drug use through that peer group was published in Kirke (1995). That paper demonstrated how changes in peer ties and changes in individuals' drug use over time resulted in other individuals being exposed to drug influence through their peer ties. It also demonstrated how peer influence operated in this peer group to influence some teenagers to use drugs. The method of collecting peer tie data in a complete network was described in Kirke (1996). That paper outlined how accurate peer data could be collected from teenagers about their peer ties, using 2 name generator and 13 name interpreter questions, and how peer groups could be formed from these data using social network analysis.

During this time other papers were published which were applying social network procedures to the examination of patterns of cigarette or alcohol use among school students. These papers focussed on cliques of between three and five members. A paper by Hunter, Vizelberg and Berenson (1991) presented data from the Bogalusa heart study in which they examined the impact of the students' friendship cliques in school on their adoption of tobacco and alcohol use. The study covered 2305 students aged 8–17 years. These writers provided evidence of direct effects from friends who used these substances and indirect effects through imitation of '. . . an admired other's friends' (Hunter, Vizelberg and Berenson, 1991: 91). Results indicated that cliques seemed to form around a preferred behaviour, which was mainly alcohol (1991: 101). This tendency was most marked for females. These findings suggest that selection as well as peer influence were at work. In this study, the number of named friends was confined to three, and each student was asked to report on his or her own use of cigarettes, snuff, chewing tobacco and alcohol. Thus, the substance use data were self-reported and they were linked with the social network data through the analytical process. Unfortunately, this paper reported on only seven cliques of three or more children in which two or more members used tobacco or alcohol. These seven cliques would appear, therefore, to include only about 21 of the students from this very large sample of 2305 students. Thus, much of the potential for an examination of the impact of the patterns of friendship in these schools on the tobacco and alcohol use of the individual students was lost. Concentrating on cliques confined the discussion to a very small number of students. Nevertheless, this paper was valuable in highlighting the importance of examining friendship cliques for their impact on tobacco and alcohol use among teenagers.

A couple of years later Ennett and Bauman (1993) explored this question further. Their purpose was to examine whether the likelihood of adolescents smoking cigarettes varied with their social position among their peers. Social position was determined using the NEGOPY (Richards, 1989) network analysis programme to determine whether the adolescents were clique members, liaisons or isolates. Clique members were adolescents in a group of at least three members, who had most (more than 50 per cent) of their links with other members of the same group, and were all connected by a path entirely within the group. Liaisons were not members of cliques but had at least two links with clique members or other liaisons. Isolates were those who had few or no links with other adolescents. They could be in dyads or tree structures, in which the removal of one link would result in the individual being separated from the rest of the network (Ennett and Bauman, 1993: 229, 230). The study covered 1092 ninth graders who were asked to name their three best friends. From these data the authors identified more than 80 cliques, which usually included about five members. Their findings confirmed that social position was associated with the adolescents' smoking behaviour with isolates being more likely than those in cliques or liaisons to be current smokers (Ennett and Bauman, 1993: 231). In another paper they confirmed that selection and peer influence contributed equally to the homogeneity in cigarette smoking in the cliques (Ennett and Bauman, 1994: 660). In a number of papers around this time, Ennett and Bauman discussed the need to use social network analysis, and ideally complete network data (Ennett and Bauman, 1993: 234), to identify peer groups directly and to examine individual drug use in the context of the peer groups (Bauman and Ennett, 1994: 820; 1996: 191). Their own work had focussed on cliques as peer groups and other researchers followed their example.

The association between social position and smoking has been addressed in a similar way by Michell and Amos (1997) and by Pearson and Michell (2000). Pearson and Michell (2000) examined the association between smoking and drug use and the social position of children in their peer groups. The study covered 150 pupils in one school from whom quantitative data were collected, with more detailed qualitative data collected from 40 pupils. Longitudinal data collected at two time points, one year apart, are discussed in the paper. Pupils were aged 12–13 years in the first year of the data collection. They used the NEGOPY (Richards, 1989) programme but varied the social position categories slightly, dividing the pupils into group members, peripherals to groups and relative isolates. Group members were those defined as such in the NEGOPY programme and by Ennett and Bauman (1993). Peripherals to groups were those who were not members of a group but who had closer linkage to one group than to any other group. Peripherals included isolate type 2s (one reciprocated tie but not a dyad), tree nodes (attaches one or more isolate type 2s, may or may not be attached to a group) or liaisons as defined in NEGOPY. Relative isolates included dyads and isolated tree nodes (that is, not attached to a group) as defined in NEGOPY, isolate type 2s who were attached to tree nodes, and isolate type 1s (no reciprocated tie, sometimes called true isolates) (Pearson and Michell, 2000: 25, 26). They identified 17 peer groups at the first data collection point, and 16 at the second, with about four or five members in each. They found no association between social position and smoking or drug taking when the pupils were aged 12–13 years. One year later they found small differences ($p > 0.05$), with relative isolates being more likely than those in other social positions to have smoked cigarettes ($p < 0.08$) and to have taken drugs ($p < 0.07$) (Pearson and Michell, 2000: 27, 28). These findings are consistent with those of Ennett and Bauman (1993). The longitudinal analysis by Pearson and Michell (2000: 33) indicated that most of the change in behaviour from non-risk-taking to risk-taking (which included smoking cigarettes and drug use) occurred at peer group level. They also demonstrated that the risk-taking peer groups had more peripheral individuals than the non-risk-taking groups, suggesting that they may, in time, be a source of influence or selection to those peripheral individuals (Pearson and Michell, 2000: 33). These findings were confirmed in Pearson and West (2003) when they included a third wave in the longitudinal analysis. These findings confirmed that '. . . there is a significant drift from group non risk-taking into group risk-taking status over time together with a move of peripherals towards risk-taking groups' (Pearson and West, 2003: 69). Their findings also explained, in part at least, the anomalous finding that isolates are more likely than those in other social positions to smoke cigarettes (Ennett and Bauman, 1993) or to smoke cigarettes or take drugs (Pearson and Michell, 2000). Having examined the time spent by pupils in different social positions over the two years of the study, they found that group risk-takers spent the longest time together and that isolate risk-takers spent a longer time in that state (isolate) than did isolate non-risk-takers (Pearson and West, 2003: 67).

Pearson and Michell also reported a gender difference. Girls were more likely to smoke cigarettes, while boys were more likely to take drugs

(Pearson and Michell, 2000: 27–29). In an earlier paper, Michell and Amos (1997) shed some light on why girls would be more likely than boys to smoke cigarettes. Having used NEGOPY to identify groups (that is, cliques), liaisons and isolates, Michell and Amos (1997) examined the association between smoking, gender and the social position of the adolescents in the peer groups identified. In a qualitative analysis of data collected from 36 pupils aged 11 years and 40 aged 13 years, they found that more girls than boys smoked regularly (Michell and Amos, 1997: 1864) and that boys and girls smoked for different reasons. Girls who held positions of high status in their peer groups (popular, attractive, fashionable and spending power to maintain their image) were most likely to smoke. Boys in high status positions were not as vulnerable as girls in similar positions because their wish to smoke and appear 'cool' conflicted with their wish to remain fit for sport.

Fang et al. (2003) also confirmed the findings of Ennett and Bauman (1993: 231) in a study of 1040 school pupils in Beijing, China. They found, also using the NEGOPY definitions of group members, liaisons and isolates, that overall more isolates than group members or liaisons had experimented with smoking. They found, however, that among 10th grade boys the results were reversed, with more group members and liaisons than isolates having experimented with smoking (Fang et al., 2003: 262).

Abel, Plumridge and Graham (2002) highlight some of these difficulties and demonstrate that, when those identified as isolates and liaisons by the NEGOPY programme are regrouped using cluster analysis, different social positions emerge. The social positions they identify, in a school year of 279 pupils aged 13–14 years, are 'popular', 'try-hards', 'ordinary' and 'loners'. 'Popular' members had numerous reciprocated ties and more ties coming to them than they reciprocated. Individuals who had few reciprocated ties but who made numerous unreciprocated ties were described as 'try-hards'. Individuals were described as 'ordinary' if they had one or two reciprocated ties and a few unreciprocated ties coming to or from them. Those who were least well connected were the 'loners', who had no ties or one or two unreciprocated ties (Abel, Plumridge and Graham, 2002: 335). They found that there was an association between these social positions and the smoking behaviour of the pupils, with the 'loners' smoking less than those in the other social positions (Abel, Plumridge and Graham, 2002: 336) contrary to the findings of Ennett and Bauman (1993), Pearson and Michell (2000) and Fang et al. (2003).

Research to date on dyads or cliques has concluded that similarity in the substance use of teenagers is due to either peer influence or selection.

Cohen (1977: 239), Kandel (1978b: 436) and Bauman and Ennett (1996: 187) have confirmed in their research that only half of the similarity in the substance use of teenagers is due to peer influence, while the other half is due to the teenagers' selection of peers, who are already similar to them in their substance use. Haynie (2001) recently addressed the question of peer network structure and adolescents' delinquency. Using the first wave of the Add Health data, which is cross-sectional, she examined the egocentric friendship networks of the adolescents within schools. Data on the friendship ties and on the delinquent behaviour were self-reported by the adolescent and the friend (Haynie, 2001: 1024). Haynie concluded that there was an association between the friends' delinquency and the adolescents' delinquency, and that the association was stronger when the adolescents were located in more central positions in very cohesive networks, and when the adolescents had been named as friends by many others (Haynie, 2001: 1048). While aware that the relative importance of selection and influence could only be adequately examined with longitudinal data, Haynie (2001: 1050) concluded that the findings were more consistent with a peer influence explanation, than a selection explanation, for the similarity in delinquency in the adolescents' peer networks.

While it has been widely acknowledged in research on teenagers, that the peer groups in which they are embedded are a major influence on their substance use, it is important to see the teenagers and their peer groups in the context of the wider community in which they are located. This community is made up of their families. Research, which has focussed on the importance of the family, is discussed below.

Research on parents

Research on the role of parents in their teenage children's substance use suggests that parents may play a positive or negative role in their children's substance use. Some research confirms that parents' own substance use leads to their children's substance use. Other research suggests that parental behaviour may protect their children from substance use.

In some of the earliest research on this topic, Kandel confirmed that parental use of substances at one time point resulted in the subsequent use of substances by their adolescent children. Parental use of hard liquor, that is, spirits, predicted their adolescent children's initiation into hard liquor and to illicit drugs other than marijuana (Kandel, Kessler and Margulies, 1978: 88, 89). Parental use of psycho-active drugs were predictive of later use by their children of illicit drugs other than marijuana (Kandel, Kessler and Margulies, 1978: 89; Kandel, 1978a: 25; Kandel, 1980: 271). The mother's marijuana use led to their child's marijuana use, irrespective of the gender of the child (Newcomb, Huba and Bentler, 1983: 724). In a longitudinal study, Ennett and Bauman (1991: 1706) found a significant association between fathers' beer drinking and the subsequent beer drinking of their adolescent children, but their mothers' drinking was not associated. Bailey, Ennett and Ringwalt (1993: 613, 614) reported significant associations between parents' current smoking and adolescents' lifetime smoking, and between parents' former and current smoking and the adolescents' current smoking. Ennett et al. (2001: 60) reported later that parental use of tobacco led to their children's use of tobacco and alcohol, and parental alcohol use led to increased tobacco use by their children.

Parental support for their children's substance use has been measured by parental attitudes towards drugs and their specific directions to their children about the use of drugs. Parental attitudes to drugs have been reported to influence their children's initiation to marijuana but not to illicit drugs other than marijuana (Kandel, Kessler and Margulies, 1978: 87–89). Parental tolerance of marijuana use and their belief in the harmlessness of various drugs were predictive of subsequent use by their children while their specific rules against use were ineffective (Kandel, Kessler and Margulies, 1978: 87, 89; Kandel, 1978a: 25; Kandel, 1980: 271). Parental attitudes which favoured use were, therefore, accepted by their children but those which rejected use were ignored. Support for their adolescent children's behaviour was shown to affect their children's initiation to marijuana but not initiation to illicit drugs other than marijuana. Ennett and Bauman (1991: 1706) found no association between mothers' or fathers' attitudes to beer drinking and their adolescent children's subsequent use. Findings from Ennett et al. (2001) supported those of Kandel, however, who stated that parental rules against use were ignored. They found that parent–child communication relating to the use of tobacco and alcohol had, at best, no influence on the tobacco and alcohol use of their adolescent children and may have caused some adolescents to increase their use (Ennett et al., 2001: 59).

Bailey, Ennett and Ringwalt (1993: 614) found that family disunion was correlated with adolescents' current smoking. Family disunion was a combination of '. . . family unsupportiveness, lack of shared activities, lack of closeness, tendency to discuss problems with family outsiders, autocratic decision-making, intolerance of differing opinions, and lack of strictness with children . . .' (Bailey, Ennett and Ringwalt, 1993: 609). Barnes, Farrell and Banerjee (1994: 197) confirmed the importance of the quality of parenting in protecting adolescents against alcohol abuse and other deviant behaviours. They found that high levels of parental support, parental monitoring and positive parent–child communication were important in preventing alcohol abuse and other deviant behaviour in their children.

In a review paper, Kobus (2003: 49) also confirmed that some parental practices acted as protective factors against their children's tobacco use. Teenagers were less likely to smoke cigarettes when their parents had an intact marriage, were involved in activities with their children, were supportive of their children, did not smoke themselves and were opposed to smoking.

Research also confirmed that closeness to parents affected their impact on their children's substance use. Lack of closeness between parents and their children has been reported to influence initiation into marijuana (Kandel, Kessler and Margulies, 1978: 87; Kandel, 1978a: 25) and lack of closeness with their fathers influenced their son's marijuana use (Brook et al., 1983b: 208). Lack of closeness between parents and their children was found to be an especially strong predictor of initiation to illicit drugs other than marijuana (Kandel, Kessler and Margulies, 1978: 88, 89; Kandel, 1978a: 25; Kandel, 1980: 271; Brook, Whiteman and Gordon, 1982: 1160, 1161). Brook and her associates examined paternal influences on son's marijuana use. They concluded that paternal factors resulted in the marijuana use of their sons despite control on the mother–son relationship (Brook et al., 1983b: 208). Thus, even when there was a close relationship between mother and son, there was more frequent marijuana use if there was not a close father–son relationship (Brook et al., 1983b: 209). When the relationships between mother–son and father–son were both faulty, there was a synergistic effect producing more marijuana use in the sons, but, when parents had an affectionate marital relationship and the father–son relationship was good, there was a synergistic effect resulting in less marijuana use (Brook et al., 1983b: 209). These findings demonstrate that closeness between parents and their children affects the children's drug behaviour. Specifically, lack of closeness between parents and their children can lead to the adolescent children's use of marijuana and other illicit drugs. If the relationship is close with only one parent, lack of closeness with the other will still lead to marijuana use.

The relative impact of parents and peers

The relative impact of parents and peers on adolescent substance use has been addressed by a number of researchers. Early findings had confirmed that both parents' and peers' substance use influence the adolescents' use. When both influences existed concurrently, however, Kandel found that there was a synergistic effect (Kandel, 1973: 1067, 1069). What this means is that there was a greater likelihood of adolescents, whose parents and peers were drug users, becoming users because the joint effect of the two influences was greater than the sum of each influence operating alone. Brook and her associates also reported a synergistic effect between parental and peer drug use in that adolescents, who were exposed to neither, reported the least amount of drug use (Brook et al., 1982: 1328; Brook, Whiteman and Gordon, 1983: 273).

Assessing the relative influence of parents and peers, it was determined that overall the influence of peers on adolescent drug use was greater than that of parents (Kandel, 1973: 1067; Kandel, 1974a: 107; Kandel, Kessler and Margulies, 1978: 91; Kandel and Adler, 1982: 295) and girls were more susceptible than boys to this influence (Kandel, 1986: 221). Their relative importance differed for different substances. Peers were of greater importance for marijuana use while parents were of greater importance for the use of illicit drugs other than marijuana (Kandel, Kessler and Margulies, 1978: 93; Kandel, 1978a: 24, 25). These findings indicated that peers exerted a greater influence on adolescent drug use than did parents but the influence varied by substance. Bailey and Hubbard (1990: 67) found that the relative influence of parents and peers on adolescents' marijuana use varied with the increasing maturity of the adolescents. Parental attachment was most important for the youngest group in the sixth/seventh grade group, while peer attachment was most important for those in the highest grade group studied (eighth/ninth). In a recent review, Kobus (2003: 49) indicated that research findings, on the relative importance of parents and peers in teenagers' use of tobacco, are mixed. Although numerous studies confirm the greater role of peers than parents, some suggest that the role of parents is greater than, or equal to, the role of peers, while others suggest that their relative importance varies at different stages of tobacco use.

Whether the relative closeness of adolescents to their peers or parents influenced their effect on them was assessed by a number of researchers. Their findings indicated that it was when adolescents were more attached to peers than parents that peer influence was greatest (Kandel, 1978a: 24, 25; Kandel, 1980: 270; Brook, Whiteman and Gordon, 1983: 276). Barnes, Farrell and Banerjee (1994) have confirmed these findings. They found that adolescents who valued their peers' opinions over their parents' opinions on important life decisions were at higher risk of alcohol abuse and other problem behaviours (Barnes, Farrell and Banerjee, 1994: 198).

Conclusion

Research reviewed in this chapter has confirmed the importance of peers and their parents in the substance use of teenagers. Research on peers has confirmed that there is likely to be homophily in the substance use of teenagers and their peers, that is explained, in equal measure, by peer influence and selection (Cohen, 1977: 239; Kandel, 1978b: 436; Bauman and Ennett, 1996: 187). Support for this finding came from dyadic and clique research. The question of the relative importance of peer influence and selection has been addressed by Kirke (2004) and is addressed in this book (Chapter 8), drawing on peer group data, larger than cliques, from a complete network study.

In recent years some researchers, using social network analytic techniques, have examined the influence of the social position of teenagers in their peer groups on their substance use. These researchers have examined the importance of the social positions of clique member, liaison or isolate for cigarette use among teenagers. The findings from clique studies are conflicting and problematic. In particular, it is problematic that some have found that those least well connected (isolates and relative isolates) are those most likely to smoke cigarettes, while others have found that those least well connected (loners) were least likely to smoke. Others have found that girls, in the 'best' social positions in their peer groups, were most likely to smoke cigarettes.

These contradictory findings suggest that researchers might approach the examination of social position and teenagers' substance use with social network data on peer groups larger than cliques. The sample chosen, the definition of peer group used and the number of friends the teenager is allowed to name have profound effects on the size of the peer groups which will ensue and, indeed, on whether some teenagers are seen as liaisons or isolates. Clique data are inadequate as a way of measuring peer groups for a number of reasons. They are unnaturally small because the teenagers are usually only allowed to name a small number of friends rather than all of their friends (Wasserman and Faust, 1994: 256). The criteria for inclusion in the clique are too rigid and exclude some teenagers who have peer ties with clique members. Results from clique studies may exaggerate the level of similarity in behaviour in peer groups because the cliques are so small, while naturally existing peer groups, which would emerge if teenagers were allowed to name all of their friends, may be much larger. Many questions relating to influence and selection cannot be answered using small clique data.

The ideal data to address these questions are complete network data collected from all teenagers and their peers in a particular population. In this type of study the teenagers describe their own substance use behaviour and name their friends in the population. The friends are also interviewed and they describe their own substance use and name their friends in the population. This view is shared by Haynie (2001: 1023), who stated that 'In the best case scenario... all adolescents and friends in the population of adolescents provide this information' and by Ennett and Bauman (1993: 234) who stated that '... the ideal social network analysis would have included complete data from all adolescents and their friends in this population'. Complete network data are used in this book to examine the question of peer influence and selection. Though difficult to produce, ideally changes in the complete network data and changes in the substance use of the teenagers should be recorded in a longitudinal study. The data, on which this book is based, are not longitudinal. They are cross-sectional but have retrospective data on the timing of peer tie development and on initiation into each of the three substances, which can be used in the absence of longitudinal data.

Previous research rarely covered the teenagers' use of all three substances, but it is preferable that data on all three substances be available in the same study as there may be differences in the process of involvement in the different substances. Data on all three substances are discussed in this book.

Research on family influences confirms the importance of parental substance use and parental control of their children's use on teenagers' substance use. In general, if parents use substances their children are likely to do so too, although they may not use the same substances. Parental tolerance of substance use resulted in a more mixed reaction from their children. In some studies parental tolerance led to their children's substance use but parental advice to their children against the use of substances was usually ignored or may even have caused their children to increase their use. Good relationships with parents appear to have a protective effect, preventing children from smoking cigarettes and abusing alcohol. Poor relationships (not close) with parents, on the other hand, led to their children's drug use.

Research findings on the relative importance of parents and peers to teenagers' substance use are mixed and may vary by the maturity of the adolescent and by the level of attachment the teenagers feel to their parents and peers. Research on family influences has been varied and rarely covered the teenagers' use of all three substances. This is problematic as influences may vary between the substances. Also, it seems important to examine the individual teenagers' substance use in the context of their peer groups and the families in which they are embedded, in a single study. These families form the community in which the teenagers' lives are played out.

This book examines the teenagers' use of all three substances in the context of their own attributes, and the social networks of their families and peer groups, in which their lives have become embedded. Data from a cross-sectional, complete network study of one community in Dublin are used to examine the relative importance of peer influence and selection, the role of their families in the teenagers' substance use and variations in individual characteristics of the teenagers. Details of the data and the research methods used to collect them are given in Chapter 3.

3
Research Methods

Introduction

There has been increasing recognition in recent years of the need for a social network approach to the study of the role of peers in teenagers' substance use (Ennett and Bauman, 1993: 234; Bauman and Ennett, 1994: 820; 1996: 191). A number of researchers, including Ennett and Bauman (1993), have examined the importance of the social position of teenagers among their peers to their substance use (Michell and Amos, 1997; Pearson and Michell, 2000; Fang et al., 2003; Pearson and West, 2003). These researchers have, like Ennett and Bauman (1993), focussed on the social position of teenagers in cliques, liaisons and isolates or on a variation of those social positions, group members (in cliques), peripherals and relative isolates (Pearson and Michell, 2000). Clique data include small numbers of teenagers, typically around five. As it has become increasingly clear that it is not possible to address the peer influence and selection question adequately with clique data, researchers have indicated that complete network data are needed to address these questions (Ennett and Bauman, 1993; Haynie, 2001). Ideally the complete network data should be longitudinal.

In this book we use complete network data on a population of teenagers to address the peer influence and selection question. The data were collected to examine the drug question (Kirke, 1990) in particular. Extensive new analyses are added in this book, including multilevel analyses of individual and social network data, the analysis of the use of the three substances by the teenagers, and placing the teenagers' substance use in the context of their wider social networks – including their peers, family and community – in which their substance use behaviour is embedded. The data are cross-sectional, rather than longitudinal, but include retrospective data on the timing of peer tie formation and on the initiation of the teenagers into the use of each substance, which can be used in the absence of longitudinal data. The research methods used to collect these data are described below.

Survey research methods

While most studies of teenagers and substance use focus on school-populations, this study is community-based and covers teenagers in school and out of school. The data were collected in a survey in a working-class community in Dublin. Using the Census of Population (1981; 1986) the community was selected among numerous others which were working-class, had a high level of unemployment, a large proportion of under 25-year-olds in the population, and a projected teenage population of about 400. It had a population of approximately 2500 people and was located in one District Electoral Division (DED) in Dublin County Borough, Ireland. Exact location is not given to protect the anonymity of the community.

Sources of the data

The community: Census of families

The aim of the study was to collect data from 14–18-year-old teenagers because it was anticipated that teenagers of this age would have had opportunities to use the substances being studied. Some would have used one or more of the three substances, others would have used none of them. Users and non-users would be valuable to the study as comparisons could be made between them. In order to identify the hidden population of teenagers of 14–18 years living in this community, we carried out a census of every house in the area. Parents were told the purpose of the study and were asked whether they had teenagers of 14–18 years living in the home and whether the parent would permit the interviewer to speak to the teenagers. The census identified 298 teenagers of the required age (Kirke, 1996: 336).

Population of teenagers

An attempt was made to interview these 298 teenagers. The response rate was 89.6 per cent (267 interviews). There were 25 (8.4 per cent) refusals. Seventeen (5.8 per cent) refusals were from the teenagers themselves, seven (2.3 per cent) were from parents for one teenager in each case, and one sibling (0.3 per cent) refused for another sibling in the family. The six non-contacts included two teenagers (0.7 per cent) who could not be interviewed because of illness, three (1.0 per cent) who were living temporarily outside the study area for the duration of the fieldwork and one person (0.3 per cent) who could not be contacted.

The 31 teenagers not interviewed were from 30 different families (Kirke, 1996: 336). Two teenagers in one family had refused. In 17 of the 30 families at least one other teenager was interviewed. In five of them two teenagers were interviewed. Information on the 22 teenagers interviewed in these 17 families confirms the rate of drug use among them (18.2 per cent) was similar to the rate (16.9 per cent) for the total sample interviewed suggesting that members of these families were no more likely than others in the sample to be deviant in this respect. Information does not exist for the 13 families in which no teenager was interviewed. Those not interviewed were, however, very likely to be similar to those interviewed since they all lived in similar houses and in similar social circumstances in the same DED. Those interviewed were from working-class families with 84 per cent in Social Classes 4, 5 or 6. Census of Population data for the whole population (2500 approximately) in 1986 (one-and-a-half years before interviews were done) shows a similar social class distribution with 74 per cent in Social Classes 4, 5 or 6 (Census of Population, 1986).

The teenagers, when interviewed, gave information about themselves, their families and their peers. Thus, the teenagers' substance use could be viewed in the context of their families and their peer groups. In this way, the study covered the total population of teenagers, the part of the community which their families comprised, and the peer ties these teenagers had within this community and beyond it.

The snowball sample of peers

The other people, outside the population of 14–18-year-olds, with whom the teenagers had peer ties, were either interviewed in the snowball sample or not interviewed at all. When the population coverage of the 14–18-years-olds had been completed, the names of the drug users in the population and the names of all of their peers were known to the author. Since the main focus of the original study was on drug use and the impact of peer ties on such use, it was decided to increase the number of interviews with the named peers through a snowball sampling method. Snowball sampling has been described as a suitable method for collecting network data (Wasserman and Faust, 1994: 33, 34; Barnes, 1972: 23, 24), as particularly suitable for drug studies (Biernacki and Waldorf, 1981: 142), and by Heckathorn (1997: 174) as a suitable method for sampling hidden populations. Snowball sample data are known to be unrepresentative of the population from which they are selected, but that does not present a particular problem for this study. They were not collected to draw inferences about a larger population but simply to provide some added, and very useful, data on some of the teenagers' peer ties which lay outside the initial population chosen for study.

The drug users and a matched sample of current drinkers were chosen from the population interviews. Matching was on age and gender. Although 45 drug users had been identified, only 42 were followed up because 3 had said they would not like to be interviewed again. For each of the 42 drug users and the 42 current drinkers, a list was drawn up on cards of all of the peer ties they had mentioned in the initial interview. The interviewers then returned to the drug users and current drinkers and asked them for the addresses of their peers, who were outside the original study population, so that they could be contacted and interviewed. This method proved very successful in that addresses were given willingly when they were known. From these lists 106 further interviews were attempted and 97 were completed, giving a response rate for the snowball sample of 91.5 per cent. Material from the snowball sample is seldom used in this book. When it is, this is indicated in the text.

Methods of data collection

Data were collected in personal interviews with all respondents in their homes. Great care was taken in the fieldwork of this study in order to ensure a high response rate and a minimum amount of disruption to the families who participated. When more than one sibling was being interviewed in one family, two interviewers interviewed the siblings separately, but at the same time, to minimize the disruption of family life. Fieldwork was completed very quickly, in just six weeks. The result was a very high response rate, which ensured a minimum loss of individual level and social network data.

The pilot study

The author conducted pilot interviews with five teenage drug users living in a different, but similar, DED in Dublin. During these interviews, the questionnaires were tested and a personal approach, aimed at building a relationship of trust with the teenagers, was adopted. After these interviews minor changes were made to the questionnaire and plans were finalized for the training of interviewers, following the format used in the pilot interviews, to ensure an optimum response rate.

Data collection

Six interviewers, who were trained and supervised by the author, completed the interviews. Personal interviews, using structured questionnaires, were conducted with the teenagers in their own homes. The interviewers spoke to the parents first informing them of the purpose of the study, asking them whether teenagers of 14–18 years were living in the home and whether the parent would permit the interviewer to speak to the teenagers. The interviewers then spoke to the teenagers, explained the purpose of the study to them and requested them to participate. Those in the snowball sample were contacted in their homes and asked to participate. The confidential nature of the interview was stressed.

This method of data collection departed from the more usual method adopted in drug studies which has been the use of self-administered questionnaires on anonymous subjects in school (for example, Kandel, 1973: 1067; Shelley et al., 1982: 254; Johnston, O'Malley and Bachman, 1984: 6; Grube and Morgan, 1986: 51) or more recently covering school samples, but naming friends (Ennett and Bauman, 1993: 228; Michell and Amos, 1997: 1862; Pearson and Michell, 2000: 23; Fang et al., 2003: 259). Those methods would have been inappropriate in this study. In particular, a school study would not cover those who had already left school, the range and depth of questioning required a personal approach in which a good rapport was built between interviewer and interviewee, and subjects could not remain anonymous if social network connections were to be made.

It was necessary that the interviewee trust the interviewer with the considerable personal information being requested. Questions on their own substance use and the questions identifying peers, the two sets of questions most central to the study, required a high level of trust which had to be built up before and during the interview. This was also necessary since the respondents were not, in this study, remaining anonymous. It was necessary that their name and address be known to the research team so that contact could be made with them and so that peer connections could be made during the coding and analysis of social network data. In the event, the method adopted in this study worked very well. Evidence of this is the high response rate and the completion of all sections of the questionnaire by almost everyone. Only one respondent did not give the names of all of his peers and one did not give the substance use data.

A potential problem in attempting to collect substance use data, or other personal data, from teenagers in their own homes is lack of privacy for doing the interview. It was anticipated that this problem might arise. Interviewers were trained to conduct the interview as privately as possible, for example in a corner of the room, even if there were others present, but they were asked to record if people were present during interviews. A third party was present for one half (50.6 per cent) of the interviews. Those present included parents, siblings, friends or another person. Having someone present made no difference to the teenagers' acceptance of the interview. Teenagers, whose acceptance of the interview was very positive (74, 27.8 per cent), were equally divided between those who had someone present (37) and those who had not (37). Positive acceptance (126, 47.4 per cent) was also equally divided (64, 62). When teenagers' acceptance was all right (61, 22.9 per cent), they were also equally likely to have someone present (31) or not (30), and those whose acceptance of the interview was negative (5, 1.9 per cent) were also equally divided (3, 2).

The questionnaire

The questionnaire includes sections on the teenagers and their families, relationships with peers, and the teenagers' use of cigarettes, alcohol and drugs. It is reproduced in full in Appendix A, where the exact questions can be consulted. Some points of clarification are given here on questions relating to social networks and substance use.

Social network questions

Questions on the teenagers' relationships with peers produced the dyadic peer data as well as the complete network and peer group data. Peer data were crucial to the purposes of this study and it was desirable that the peer data be as complete as possible, so that peers who might have been involved in the teenagers' substance use would not have been excluded, due to numerical or other restrictions being placed on the collection of peer data. Nevertheless, we also wanted to avoid problems of interviewer or interviewee fatigue (Knoke and Kuklinski, 1982: 33). This was done by adopting a variation of Fischer's (1982b: 36, 37) scheme. His scheme allowed the respondents to name all of the relevant people. He then asked some questions about all of the relationships mentioned and more detailed information on a fraction of them. As a variation of Fischer's scheme, we allowed the respondents to name all of their friends and pals and then asked 13 name interpreter questions about each of those mentioned.

Only two name generator questions were used in the questionnaire. The wording of these questions was designed to get as full a list as possible of all of the friends and pals and to remove any possible ambiguity or confusion in the mind of the respondent about the relationships which should be mentioned. The two name generator questions were: 'Could you tell me first about your friends – starting with your *best friend* – then *boyfriend* or *girlfriend* – then other *good friends* – and then anyone else who is a *friend* of yours?' and 'Will you also tell me the other people of around your age that you *pal around with* (for example, in school or at discos) but who are not as close as friends?' The full list of friends and pals mentioned comprised the teenagers' peers. The interviewer noted each name as it was given.

The question wording avoided some of the known limitations which may be built into name generator questions (Kirke, 1996: 337). A *numerical* limit was not imposed on the number of friends and pals who could be named. The boundary imposed was that the person be someone with whom the respondent spent free-time. A numerical limit has usually been imposed in substance use research on adolescents. Usually the number requested is three best friends (Laumann, 1973; Hunter, Vizelberg and Berenson 1991: 93; Ennett and Bauman, 1993: 231) or their six best friends (Michell and Amos, 1997: 1863; Pearson and Michell, 2000: 24). An exception is a recent study by Abel, Plumridge and Graham (2002: 329) who did not restrict the number but wanted only best friends named. The *intimacy* limit was much less restricted in this study than in other studies which asked respondents to mention only their best friends (Hunter, Vizelberg and Berenson, 1991: 93; Ennett and Bauman, 1993: 231; Michell and Amos, 1997: 1863; Pearson and Michell, 2000: 24; Abel, Plumridge and Graham, 2002: 329). Thus, in the author's study the peer group size was less likely than in other studies to be restricted by numerical and intimacy limitations which are known to restrict network size (Campbell and Lee, 1991: 217).

The name generator questions focussed on current peer ties. Teenagers were asked to record each peer tie existing *at the time of interview*. The imposition of this *time frame* should have enhanced respondent accuracy in reporting ties (Campbell and Lee, 1991: 205). In particular, the potential problem of recall should have been reduced (Knoke and

Kuklinski, 1982: 33). Nevertheless, some research, on university students and other adults, suggests that some friends' names may not be recalled (Brewer, 1993: 335; 2000: 29; Brewer and Webster, 1999: 361).

A *geographic* limit was imposed in this study. While respondents were free to name all of their friends and pals, and information was collected on all of these peer ties, interviews were conducted only with the friends and pals within the DED and with a snowball sample of friends and pals outside the DED.

It has been suggested that some of the problems which can arise in the collection of network data through surveys are the difficulty of recall and interviewee fatigue (Knoke and Kuklinski, 1982: 31–34). Recall has just been discussed. Fatigue may enter in when a very large number of relationships are involved and when numerous questions are asked about each. The author did not wish to confine the number of peers the teenagers could mention, but, in order to reduce interviewee fatigue, the number of questions asked about each peer was kept to a minimum (13 in all) and the overall size of the questionnaire was kept as short as possible. Evidence of this is that almost all, 98.8 per cent, of the interviews were completed in less than one hour ($n = 245$; information not recorded for 22 interviews).

Substance use questions

One other section of the questionnaire which was crucial to the study was the final section which included the questions on smoking, drinking and drug use. The questions covered the teenagers' first and current use of the three substances and the circumstances surrounding both, the kinds of alcohol and the classes of drug taken, the amount, frequency and recency of use and the effects of the use of the substances on the teenagers. All of the data on the substance use of the teenagers and on the substance use of their peers were self-reported by them, thus avoiding the potential exaggeration of peer effects when perceived substance use data are used (Kandel, 1980: 269, 270; Bauman and Ennett, 1996: 188), and the possibility that asking teenagers to tell us about their peers' substance use, while also asking for the names of those peers, might jeopardize the study. Since this was a community study, word could travel fast if the survey was unacceptable for one reason or another. This reasoning was well founded. Word did travel fast around the community but it was positive towards the survey, with friends and pals encouraging each other to take part when one had already done so.

The question arises as to whether self-reported substance use data are valid. There is considerable evidence that they are. It has been confirmed in the drug literature that self-reported drug use data are valid when the respondents remain anonymous (for example, Single, Kandel and Johnson, 1975: 440), and other writers have confirmed that such data are also valid when the respondents are identifiable (Malvin and Moskowitz, 1983: 557) as they were in this study. An important question in this research was the timing of the first use of each substance and there is recent confirmation that such self-reported data are reliable (Johnson and Mott, 2001: 1187).

The self-reported data on the substance use of the teenagers and their peers have been combined with the social network data in this book, and those findings are discussed in Chapters 6–9.

Coding and data analysis

Coding

One coding guide was devised by the author for the individual-level data on the teenagers' attributes, their substance use and all family data. A separate coding guide was devised for the social network data on peer ties. Both guides were used separately. Six research assistants, under the supervision of the author, coded the individual-level data and the author coded all peer tie data.

Data analysis

Statistical Package for the Social Sciences (SPSS) (Nie et al., 1975; Miller et al., 2002) was used to analyse all individual-level data on the teenagers' attributes, substance use data and family data, and dyadic data on peer ties. Results are given in Chapters 4–6.

Social network analysis

The complete network and peer groups

When the teenagers were asked to name all of the people with whom they had peer ties in this population, a complete network of peer ties was produced. A complete network is covered when all relationships existing between all actors within a particular population are identified (Knoke and Kuklinski, 1982: 17). The complete network, therefore, included all of the peer ties between the 267 teenagers interviewed in the population, producing 278 peer ties. Peer ties, which the teenagers had with people outside this population, were not included in the complete network. Thus, although the complete network included all of the peer ties between the teenagers and their peers in the population covered, it included only 28.4 per cent of all 979 peers named by the teenagers.

Covering a complete network has many advantages, especially in substance use studies. The only missing data in the population study were those due to refusals and non-contacts. Thus, the loss of social network data in the complete network can be estimated at 10.4 per cent (Knoke and Kuklinski, 1982: 26). Advantages of covering a complete network are that the naturally existing peer groups of the teenagers can be identified, that data on the peer groups and the individuals (that is, teenagers and their peers) which comprise them can be identified simultaneously (Wellman, 1988: 26), and that the indirect ties can be identified using a social network computer programme. Thus, the possibility of respondent error in providing data on indirect ties is avoided.

Advantages for substance use research include the simultaneous analysis of individual teenagers' substance use and the social network context in which the behaviour is embedded. When the substance use data are added to the naturally existing peer groups, the role of the peer group in the individuals' substance use can be examined. Using complete network data facilitates multilevel analyses, whereby the individual teenagers' substance use can be examined in the context of the peer dyad, the peer group, the complete network and the community in which they live. Complete network data in normal population settings are rare and difficult to obtain, are not available in substance use research, and many researchers have alluded to the need for such data in recent works (Ennett and Bauman, 1993: 234; Haynie, 2001: 1023). They are examined in this book for the contribution they can make to the debate about the relative importance of the selection of peers and peer influence in substance use research.

The peer groups include the teenagers' direct peer ties, that is, the friends and pals named by the teenagers. But they also include their indirect peer ties with other teenagers, that is, the peer ties their friends and pals have. While direct peer ties are known when the teenagers name their friends and pals, indirect peer ties are not immediately obvious and the teenagers were not asked about them.

The dyadic data on each peer tie was used by the social network analysis programme GRADAP (Sprenger and Stokman, 1989) to delineate the complete network and identify the peer groups within it. GRADAP was used to identify 'weak components' and the procedure 'adjacency' to identify who was connected to whom within each weak component. Both processes occurred simultaneously. The delineation of 'weak components' is, in graph theoretic terms, on '. . . simple (undirected) graphs' (Sprenger and Stokman, 1989: 17). The direction of the peer ties is not taken into account when identifying weak components. In social network analysis '. . . a weak component is a maximal weak subgraph' (Harary, Norman and Cartwright, 1965: 405). This means that it is the maximum unique subset of points which are connected, directly or indirectly, to each other by lines (Kirke, 1996: 340). The results of this analysis revealed that a total of 35 'weak components' and 98 teenagers, who had no peer interviewed in the DED, formed the complete network. Note that 'weak components' are based on undirected graphs. Thus, the direction of the lines in the graph are not taken into account. It does not mean that the direction is not known, but that it is not used. What this means for the peer groups is that no account is taken of who named whom as a peer. It is sufficient that one has named the other.

The weak components identified are an excellent representation of teenagers' peer groups, since they include all teenagers connected to each other through peer ties by paths of any length. These 'weak components' are, therefore, peer groups. They varied in size from peer groups of 26 teenagers to 2 teenagers. They included all of the teenagers and their peers who were connected to each other through peer ties by paths of any distance. Each peer group represents the interlocking egocentric networks of each of the individuals in the peer group. Each peer group is distinct from all others. This is because there is no peer tie, however distant, between any of the teenagers in one peer group with any teenager in another. This has particular relevance to substance use research because peer influence can only happen, at any particular time point, within the peer group. Since there are no peer ties, however distant, between peer groups, peer influence cannot occur between groups. Over time, of course, this could change as peer groups change with the formation of new peer ties or the loss of others. These peer groups are examined in this book for their impact on the individual teenagers' substance use as they are the social network context in which their substance use is likely to be embedded.

Data on the complete network and peer groups are discussed in Chapter 6. Data on a selection of the peer groups, combining data at the level of the individual, the dyad and the peer group, are discussed in Chapters 7–9. The figures presented in these chapters were produced using the multidimensional scaling option of KRACKPLOT. Images were exported to a PostScript File and printed using Ghostscript.

Snowball sample of peer ties

Individual teenagers usually have peer ties with more than one individual and many of them may include the same people in their peer ties. Thus, the number of peer ties covered is likely to be much larger than the number of individuals interviewed. Although the total number of individuals interviewed was 267 in the population, this comprised 278 peer ties in the complete network. When the 97 snowball sample interviews were added, the number of peer ties covered increased to 569 (58.1 per cent of all peers named). Snowball sample data are used only in Chapter 7.

Accuracy in network measurement

The author sought to increase the accuracy of the social network data in a number of ways (Kirke, 1996: 343, 344). These included covering a complete network and ensuring a high response rate. The possibility of getting an accurate measure of the peer group structure was maximized by covering a complete network, by having 'free choice', that is, no numerical limit in the number of friends and pals which teenagers could name (Wasserman and Faust, 1994: 47), a relaxed intimacy limit, that is, not just best friends, but ranging from best friend to pal (Wasserman and Faust, 1994: 59). It ensured maximum coverage of the peer relationships and eliminated the considerable problems which might have been encountered had network sampling been used (Granovetter, 1976: 1287–1303; Knoke and Kuklinski, 1982: 26, 27). Complete network data combined with a high response rate of 90 per cent ensured a high level of accuracy in delineating the peer groups of the DED studied. The loss of network data is estimated to be proportionate to the loss of interview data (Knoke and Kuklinski, 1982: 26), so the loss of network data can be estimated to be 10 per cent in the author's study.

Other ways that accuracy in network measurement was increased were by collecting self-reported data from teenagers and their peers, reducing the potential problem of recall – by asking only about current peer ties – and reducing the potential problem of fatigue in interviewees and interviewers – by keeping the number of name generator and name interpreter questions to a minimum and by taking care with the wording of the name generator questions which would provide the network data.

When network data are collected in surveys, the question of the accuracy or reliability of the self-reported data given by the respondents on their network ties arises but it remains very difficult to assess (Wasserman and Faust, 1994: 56–59). One way of assessing this is through '... interviews with alters cited' (Marsden, 1990: 445). The suggestion is that if alters, when interviewed, also acknowledge the relationship claimed by the initial respondents, the relationship is presumed to be genuinely present. In other words, the reciprocation of the relationship is taken as a measure of the accuracy of the data. In the author's study 52.1 per cent of the teenagers' peer ties were reciprocated either within the complete network or by peers interviewed in the snowball sample. This rate is higher than some, and lower than others, quoted by Marsden (1990: 448). The difficulty is that directly comparable peer tie data do not exist and there is no clear guideline on an acceptable level of reciprocation. In the absence of such a guideline, it seems reasonable to suggest that this level of reciprocation is quite high for teenagers' peer ties which are so prone to change over time, that these self-reported peer data can be taken to be more reliable than perceived peer data and than peer data which have not been subjected to a reciprocation measure.

Conclusion

Social network methods have been used in recent years by a number of researchers studying the substance use of teenagers (Ennett and Bauman, 1993; Bauman and Ennett, 1994, 1996; Michell and Amos, 1997; Pearson and Michell, 2000; Fang et al., 2003; Pearson and West, 2003). They have generally focussed on cliques of about five peers. It has become clear to these researchers that many questions relating to teenagers' substance use cannot be answered using small clique data. In particular, it is not possible to address the question of the relative impact of peer influence and selection adequately using small clique data. Recent research has confirmed that complete network data are needed to address these questions (Ennett and Bauman, 1993: 234; Haynie, 2001: 1023) and, in a recent review of the role of peers in adolescent cigarette smoking, Kobus (2003: 37) suggests the need for examining peer influence in the larger social context of the family and neighbourhood.

This book examines teenagers' use of the three substances – cigarettes, alcohol and drugs – in the context of their peer ties, and in the context of the families and community in which their behaviour is embedded. Complete network data on peer ties are used to examine the role of the teenagers' peers in their substance use. Multilevel analyses, which include the levels of the individual, the dyad and the peer group, are used to examine the relative impact of peer influence and selection on the substance use of the teenagers (Chapters 7–9).

The data on which the book is based arise from the original surveys discussed in this chapter, which were designed to examine drug use (Kirke, 1990). The methodology has produced data which are needed to address current theoretical questions relating to teenagers and their substance use, especially the role of peer influence and selection. Extensive new analyses are added in this book, including multilevel analyses of individual and social network data, the analysis of the use of the three substances by the teenagers, and placing the teenagers' substance use in the context of their wider social networks – including their peers, family and community – in which their substance use behaviour is embedded.

The reader should keep in mind that findings presented may be at any one or a combination of levels of analysis. Thus, teenage and family findings are generally at the level of the individual but findings relating to peers may be at the level of the dyad, peer group or complete network, and some findings are presented from a multilevel analysis. To avoid confusion the levels will be indicated in the text. The teenagers and their substance use are discussed in Chapter 4.

4
The Teenagers and their Substance Use

Introduction

This chapter introduces the reader to the teenagers on which this book is based. The chapter provides information on the substances used by the teenagers and how their use varied by their gender, age, occupational status and their education. The concept 'substance use' is used to cover the use of cigarettes, alcohol and drugs, while the concepts 'cigarette use', 'alcohol use' and 'drug use' are used when only that particular substance is being discussed.

The teenagers

The community on which this book is based was chosen for its normality rather than any particular abnormality. The main defining features were that it was working class and had a large enough population of teenagers on which to base a substance use study. The community was not expected to have particular problems with drug use, or other substance use, beyond those of any other working-class area in Dublin at the time. The teenagers living in this community were expected to be living the normal lives of young teenagers. It was against this backdrop of normal living in a normal community that it was expected to reach an understanding of why some teenagers begin to use cigarettes, alcohol or drugs, while other teenagers, living in very similar circumstances, do not. In this chapter, we introduce the reader to the teenagers and the lives they were leading before examining the association between some of the teenagers' attributes and their substance use. The families they were living in and the impact of family variables on their substance use are explored in Chapter 5, while the teenagers' associations with their peers are examined in Chapters 6–9.

The community in which these teenagers lived was located in one large housing estate. There were about 500 houses located on ten different roads, eight of which were parallel with each other (numbered zero to four and seven to nine), with one longer road (number five) linking all eight roads together at the top and another longer road (number six) linking all together at the bottom. The road number is incorporated into the teenagers' identification numbers so that the reader can see, at a glance, whether teenagers who are friends live on the same or different roads (Chapters 1, 6–9). The physical layout of the housing estate ensured that the teenagers had easy access to each others' homes and to their friends in the community. All homes, schools and shops were within walking distance of a maximum of about 20 minutes, and facilities for some leisure pursuits – such as cinema, public houses and sports facilities – were also within walking distance in the surrounding locality. The teenagers' lives were, therefore, generally lived in their community and the surrounding locality. So what were the characteristics of these teenagers?

Gender

There were slightly more female than male teenagers in this community. A total of 139 (52.1 per cent) of the teenagers were female and 128 (47.9 per cent) of the teenagers were male. Gender has usually been found in other studies to be associated with teenagers' substance use, so this will be examined below.

Age

All teenagers in this community between the ages of 14 and 18 years were included in the study in the belief that some of them would have had opportunities to take one or more of the substances – cigarettes, alcohol or drugs – and that some of those, given the opportunity, would have used one or more of the substances. The age of the teenagers is given in Table 4.1. These results confirm that there were teenagers in this community in each year group from 14 to 18 years, with slightly higher proportions in the 16, 17 and 18 year groups. Their mean age was 16.2 years. We will examine below whether their age was associated with their substance use.

Occupational status

By doing a community study, rather than a school study as many other substance use researchers had done, it was expected that some of the

Table 4.1   Age of the teenagers

Age in years	No.	%
14	38	14.2
15	53	19.9
16	57	21.3
17	62	23.3
18	57	21.3
	267	100.0

teenagers would still be at school while others would have left school. This would facilitate an examination of whether education or occupation variables were associated with their substance use. The results confirmed that just over half of the teenagers had already left school (51.3 per cent) and less than half were still at school (48.7 per cent). The results in Table 4.2 also confirm that very many of the teenagers, who had already left school, were unemployed. These teenagers would, therefore, have had lots of free-time to fill during the day and the evening, while other teenagers were busy with school and work. We will see below whether it made any difference to their substance use. One of the difficulties which the unemployed teenagers would encounter is that they would have little money to buy substances, or to follow other leisure pursuits.

The teenagers, who were still at school, attended one of six local schools or schools outside the locality. The schools are identified by a letter, rather than the names of the schools, to ensure the anonymity of the community. The results given in Table 4.3 confirm that more than half of those still at school went to one local school (School A), while smaller proportions of the teenagers went to other schools in the locality or outside it. Even more of those who had already left school had attended School A. There is evidence in Table 4.4 that these teenagers

Table 4.2   Occupational status of the teenagers

Occupational status	No.	%
At school	130	48.7
Employed	69	25.8
Unemployed	68	25.5
	267	100.0

Table 4.3   The schools attended by the teenagers

School code	Teenagers at school (%)	Teenagers left school (%)
School A	56.9	73.7
School B	7.7	3.7
School C	3.1	0.7
School D	2.3	3.7
School E	11.5	6.5
School F	4.7	0.7
Schools outside locality	13.8	11.0
	100.0	100.0
N	130	137

Table 4.4   Education of the teenagers

	Teenagers at school (%)	Teenagers left school (%)
Had done state examination	56.2	70.8
Examination results:		
Honours (all or some)	76.4	60.4
Pass (all or some)	16.7	35.4
Fails only	6.9	4.2
Attitude to school:		
Liked	73.8	62.0
Disliked	16.2	27.8
Other answer	10.0	10.2
School class position:		
One of best students	10.9	11.0
An average student	82.1	83.1
One of the worst students	4.7	5.2
Other answer	2.3	0.7
'Early dropouts'	NA	35.7
Expelled	NA	7.3
N	130	137

were applying themselves while in school. Those who were still at school had done state examinations (56.2 per cent) and had been successful in them (76.4 per cent honours). Most of the teenagers still at school liked school (73.8 per cent) and they generally described themselves as average students (82.1 per cent) or best students (10.9 per cent). More of those who had already left school had done state examinations (70.8 per cent) but fewer of them had obtained honours results (60.4 per cent). Fewer of them had liked school (62.0 per cent) but they described themselves as average students (83.1 per cent) or best students (11.0 per cent). Quite a lot of these teenagers were 'early dropouts' (35.7 per cent), which meant that they had left school before their 16th birthday, and a small number of them had been expelled from school (7.3 per cent).

Education variables have been associated with teenagers' substance use in previous research. Whether the particular school attended or other education variables were associated with the teenagers' substance use in this study are examined below.

Leisure time

So what did the teenagers do with their leisure time? Did they spend time at home with their families or outside the home with friends? The answer is they did both. They spent some evenings at home with their families and some time outside the home with their friends. When asked about the evenings spent at home with their families, their replies confirmed that they usually spent about four evenings at home (mean = 4.1; SD = 1.9) and that they had spent four evenings at home in the week prior to interview (mean = 4.1; SD = 2.1). How they spent their time when at home for an evening is given in Table 4.5. These findings confirm that their main leisure time activity when at home for an evening was watching television or videos, or listening to music (90.1 per cent), while a considerable proportion of the teenagers spent the time studying and reading (27.2 per cent) and many of the teenagers helped with household chores when at home (10.8 per cent).

Table 4.5 Leisure time activities when teenagers at home for an evening[a]

	No.	%
Television/videos/music	209	90.1
Talking/tea with family	4	1.7
Talking/tea with friends	8	3.4
Studying/reading	63	27.2
Helping with household chores	25	10.8
Making or fixing things	9	3.9
Games	7	3.0
Other	17	7.3

[a] Number of teenagers who spent any evening at home was 232; many mentioned more than one activity so number exceeds total and percentages exceed 100.

When asked about meeting their friends, the teenagers' replies confirmed that they met their friends very frequently, about five times a week, and spent their time doing very ordinary things, usually in their community. Some of their main leisure time pursuits together were talking (32.8 per cent), messing or dossing about outside (32.8 per cent), or participating in sport (22.4 per cent). The teenagers' relationships with their peers, and how they passed their leisure time together, are discussed in more detail in Chapter 6.

Suffice to point out here that their lives were those of ordinary teenagers with most of them attending school or work, and spending leisure time at home with their families and outside the home with their friends. Their involvement with the use of the three substances – cigarettes, alcohol and drugs – and the association of the teenagers' own attributes with their substance use are examined below.

Substances used by the teenagers

The results given in Table 4.6 indicate how many of the teenagers had ever used the substances and how recently they had used them. Ever use meant having used the substance at least once in their lifetime and current use meant having used the substance within the month prior

Table 4.6 Substances used by the teenagers

Substance	Ever use		Current use		Never used		N
	No.	%	No.	%	No.	%	
Cigarettes	157	59.0	102	38.3	109	41.0	266[a]
Alcohol	222	83.5	135	50.8	44	16.5	266[a]
Drugs	45	16.9	17	6.4	221	83.1	266[a]
Marijuana	36	13.5	16	6.0			
Inhalants	18	6.8	0	0			
Hallucinogens	6	2.3	0	0			
Cocaine	0	0	0	0			
Heroin	0	0	0	0			
Other opiates	5	1.9	1	0.4			
Stimulants	5	1.9	0	0			
Sedatives	1	0.4	0	0			
Tranquillizers	4	1.5	0	0			

[a] Total is 266 because one teenager did not answer substance use questions.

to the interview. More of the teenagers had ever used alcohol, and were current users of alcohol, than either cigarettes or drugs.

Cigarettes

A total of 157 (59.0 per cent) teenagers had ever smoked cigarettes and 102 (38.3 per cent) were current smokers. The mean number of cigarettes smoked each day by the current smokers was 10.6. A total of 60.7 per cent of the teenagers who were current smokers were smoking at least ten cigarettes each day.

Alcohol

Most of the teenagers (222, 83.5 per cent) had, at some time in their life, taken an alcoholic drink. The teenagers had drunk beer (75.7 per cent), wine (67.6 per cent), cider (62.6 per cent) or spirits (60.8 per cent), and many teenagers had tried two (21.6 per cent), three (22.5 per cent) or even four (33.4 per cent) kinds of alcoholic drink.

Just half of the teenagers (50.8 per cent) were current drinkers. Current drinkers were asked how frequently they had taken alcohol in the past month, and how much and what kind of drink they had taken in their most recent drinking session. These data were used to estimate the amount of alcohol consumed by the teenagers in the past month. To calculate the estimated amount, the number of fluid ounces of absolute alcohol consumed in the most recent drinking session was multiplied by the number of times they had been drinking in the month (Appendix B). In the month prior to interview, 40.3 per cent of the current drinkers were estimated to have consumed at least ten fluid ounces of absolute alcohol. This is equivalent to at least twenty glasses of spirits or 12-and-a-half pints of beer. All of the other teenagers drank less than that.

Drugs

Drugs of abuse have been classified into nine drug classes (Appendix C). These are marijuana, inhalants, hallucinogens, cocaine, heroin, other opiates, stimulants, sedatives and tranquillizers. Marijuana, hallucinogens, cocaine and heroin can only be obtained through illegal channels. Other opiates, stimulants, sedatives and tranquillizers are normally prescribed by doctors. When they are not prescribed and are used for purposes other than medicinal, their use is considered to be abuse. It is their non-medical use that is discussed in this book. Inhalants are products which can normally be bought in shops, supermarkets or garages for various functional uses. They are acquired legally but they are abused when used for psychoactive effects. This study is only concerned with their abuse. The drugs used by the teenagers in this study were marijuana (13.5 per cent), inhalants (6.8 per cent), hallucinogens (2.3 per cent), other opiates (1.9 per cent), stimulants (1.9 per cent), sedatives (0.4 per cent) and tranquillizers (1.5 per cent). None of the teenagers in this study had ever used cocaine or heroin (Table 4.6). Nearly half (46.6 per cent) of those who had tried drugs had tried at least two classes of drugs. A small number of the teenagers had taken as many as three (8.9 per cent), four (2.2 per cent) or five (2.2 per cent) classes of drugs.

Only 17 teenagers (6.4 per cent) were current drug users. The current drug users were using either marijuana (16 teenagers) or other opiates (one teenager). Nearly half (47.1 per cent) (eight marijuana users) of the current users were taking drugs at least once a week while over half of them (52.9 per cent) (eight marijuana and one other opiates) were taking drugs at least once a month but not as frequently as once a week. The current marijuana users were using between one and eight joints on each occasion of use, most using more than two joints. The one person taking other opiates took between one and three tablets on each occasion of use.

Since the number of teenagers, who were ever or current users of specific drugs from each drug class, was so small, all subsequent analyses on drug use in this book group the classes together. Thus, the generic term 'drug use' is used to cover the teenagers' use of drugs from any of the drug classes.

Combinations of substances used

Some teenagers had used more than one of the three substances: cigarettes, alcohol and drugs. Details are given in Table 4.7. These findings indicate that more than half of the teenagers had ever used cigarettes and alcohol and about one-quarter of them were current users of both. Much smaller proportions of the teenagers had ever used combinations of cigarettes and drugs, alcohol and drugs, or all three substances, and even fewer of them were currently using those combinations.

Many other researchers have found associations between teenagers' substance use and these attributes of gender, age, occupational status and education. How these attributes have been associated with each particular substance has varied from study to study. I will examine below to what extent these attributes were associated with the teenagers'

Table 4.7 Combinations of substances used by the teenagers

Combinations of substances	Ever use		Current use		Total No.
	No.	%	No.	%	
Cigarettes + Alcohol	146	54.9	71	26.7	266[a]
Cigarettes + Drugs	41	15.4	12	4.5	266[a]
Alcohol + Drugs	45	16.9	16	6.0	266[a]
Cigarettes + Alcohol + Drugs	41	15.4	12	4.5	266[a]

[a] One teenager did not answer substance use questions.

substance use in my study and how my results relate to previous research.

Teenagers' substance use by gender

Gender has consistently been associated with substance use in previous research but there has been some variation between the substances in some studies. The most consistent association was for drugs where males were more likely than females to have ever used and to be current users (Shelley et al., 1982: 255, ever drug use only; Johnston, O'Malley and Bachman, 1984: 25, 29; Grube and Morgan, 1986: 120, 122; Miller et al., 1983: 30). Male exceeded female rates of ever and current use of alcohol also (Johnston, O'Malley and Bachman, 1984: 25, 29; Grube and Morgan, 1986: 96, 97). Male also exceeded female rates of ever and current of cigarettes in the Grube and Morgan (1986: 72) study but not in the Johnston, O'Malley and Bachman (1984: 25, 29) report in which female rates exceeded male rates. Recent research has reported that girls were more likely to smoke cigarettes, while boys were more likely to take drugs (Pearson and Michell, 2000: 27–29).

The gender composition of the population of teenagers in this study was 139 females (52.1 per cent) and 128 males (47.9 per cent). Statistical tests revealed that, unlike previous research, there was no statistically significant association between the teenagers' gender and either their ever or current use of any of the three substances (Table 4.8). Although the associations were not significant, it is notable that male rates exceeded female rates for all but ever use of cigarettes. But, even for cigarettes, our findings confirmed that more of the males than females were current smokers. These findings were consistent with those of other researchers who found that male rates usually exceeded female rates

Table 4.8   Teenagers' substance use by their gender

Substance	Gender				N	Significance
	Male		Female			
	No.	%	No.	%		
Cigarettes – ever	74	58.3	83	59.7	157	NS
Alcohol – ever	110	86.6	112	80.6	222	NS
Drugs – ever	27	21.3	18	12.9	45	NS
Cigarettes – current	52	40.9	50	36.0	102	NS
Alcohol – current	70	55.1	65	46.8	135	NS
Drugs – current	11	8.7	6	4.3	17	NS
N	127		139			

of use of alcohol and drugs, and they supported those of Pearson and Michell (2000: 27–29), who found that girls were more likely than boys to smoke cigarettes. The role of gender in teenagers' substance use is a rather complex one and is explored further in Chapter 9.

Teenagers' substance use by age

Previous research has consistently found an association between the age of the teenagers and their substance use, with older teenagers being more likely than younger teenagers to have ever used the substances and to be current users of the substances (Shelley et al., 1982: 255, drugs only; Miller et al., 1983: 80, 73, 75, 30; Grube and Morgan, 1986: 64, 88, 113, 65, 92, 116).

The teenagers in this study were aged between 14 and 18 years with a mean age of 16.2 years. A total of 43.9 per cent had taken their first cigarette, 17.1 per cent their first alcoholic drink and 13.3 per cent their first drug before they were 13 years old. The mean age of initiation to cigarettes was 12.5 years, to alcohol was 14.1 years and to drugs 14.5 years. The age of the teenagers was significantly associated with their ever ($p < 0.0019$) and current use of cigarettes ($p < 0.0001$) and with their ever ($p < 0.0014$) and current use of alcohol ($p < 0.0001$), with, in each case, older teenagers being more likely than younger teenagers to be users (Table 4.9). The association between drug use and age was not statistically significant. These findings support those of Grube and Morgan (1986) and Miller et al. (1983), but not those of Shelley et al. (1982).

Table 4.9 Teenagers' substance use by their age

Substance	Age in years						Significance
	14 (%)	15 (%)	16 (%)	17 (%)	18 (%)	N	
Cigarettes – ever	37.8	50.9	56.1	64.5	77.2	157	$p < 0.0019$
Alcohol – ever	64.9	79.2	87.7	82.3	96.5	222	$p < 0.0014$
Drugs – ever	8.1	7.5	19.3	19.4	26.3	45	NS
Cigarettes – current	16.2	24.5	29.8	45.2	66.7	102	$p < 0.0001$
Alcohol – current	21.6	41.5	40.4	56.5	82.5	135	$p < 0.0001$
Drugs – current	0	3.8	7.0	11.3	7.0	17	NS
N	37	53	57	62	57		

Teenagers' substance use by occupational status

There has been a suggestion in the literature that 'early dropouts' from school are more likely to be drug users (for example Shelley et al., 1982: 258; Johnston, O'Malley and Bachman, 1984: 3). Studies of school populations cannot, obviously, examine this question adequately because data are not collected in those studies from those who have already left school. Also data are not available in school studies on the occupational status of those who have left school. In order to examine these issues adequately, this study ensured that data would be collected from teenagers still at school, 'early dropouts' and normal school leavers, and would collect information on the occupational status of those who had left school. More than half of the teenagers (137; 51.3 per cent) had already left school and 49 (35.7 per cent) of them were 'early dropouts'. There was no association between ever or current use of any of the three substances and being an 'early dropout' in this study.

Occupational status was associated with ever cigarette ($p < 0.0005$) and ever drug use ($p < 0.0056$), with those who were unemployed being the most likely users (Table 4.10). Occupational status was also associated with current cigarette ($p < 0.0001$) and alcohol use ($p < 0.0001$), with, in each case, those who were employed being the most likely users. Occupational status is likely to be closely associated with age, however, and it is ($p < 0.0001$) (Table 4.11). When controlled for age, the associations between occupational status and substance use disappeared for all but the 17-year-olds ($p < 0.0005$) for ever cigarette use and the 16-year-olds ($p < 0.0056$) for ever drug use, with, in each case, the unemployed being the most likely users. For current use, the associations disappeared for all

Table 4.10 Teenagers' substance use by their occupational status

Substance	Occupational status			N	Significance
	At school (%)	Employed (%)	Unemployed (%)		
Cigarettes – ever	48.1	62.3	76.5	157	$p < 0.0005$
Alcohol – ever	79.1	87.0	88.0	222	NS
Drugs – ever	10.1	18.8	27.9	45	$p < 0.0056$
Cigarettes – current	21.7	49.3	58.8	102	$p < 0.0001$
Alcohol – current	34.9	66.7	64.7	135	$p < 0.0001$
Drugs – current	4.6	4.3	11.8	17	NS
N	129	69	68		

Table 4.11 Occupational status by age of the teenagers

Category	Age in years					N
	14 (%)	15 (%)	16 (%)	17 (%)	18 (%)	
At school	94.7	83.0	59.6	24.2	1.8	130
Employed	5.3	5.7	26.3	35.5	47.4	69
Unemployed	0	11.3	14.0	40.3	50.9	68
	100.0	100.0	100.0	100.0	100.0	267
N	38	53	57	62	57	

but the 18-year-olds for current cigarette ($p < 0.036$) and current alcohol use ($p < 0.047$), with those who were employed being the most likely users.

Teenagers' substance use by education

A number of studies have suggested an association between substance use and poor academic interest or performance. Jessor and Jessors' findings suggested an association between marijuana use and lack of interest in the goals of school (Jessor and Jessor, 1978: 68), and Kandel reported associations between marijuana and alcohol use, and negative attitudes towards school, low academic aspirations and poor academic performance (Kandel, 1980: 268). Grube and Morgan confirmed lower rates of cigarette, alcohol and drug use among those who were 'bonded' to school (Grube and Morgan, 1986: 82, 108, 130).

While all of the above studies were on school populations, this study had the advantage of being able to collect education data from teenagers still at school and from those who had already left school. Information was collected from the teenagers still at school and from those already left school on the identity of the school they had attended, whether they had done any state examinations, their level of attainment in those examinations, their attitude to school, their school class position and whether they had been expelled from school, and all of these education variables were examined for their association with the teenagers' substance use.

The only two of these variables associated with the teenagers' substance use were, among those who had already left school, having sat a state examination (18-year-olds only) and their attitude to school (all ages). Those who had sat a state examination (18-year-olds only) were more likely to have ever taken alcohol ($p < 0.05$), and those who had disliked school were more likely to be current smokers ($p < 0.0139$). Neither variable was associated with the use of any of the other substances.

Conclusion

In this section, the findings of this study are compared with previous research when comparable results are available, and the implications of this study's findings for understanding and explaining the teenagers' substance use, are drawn out. It should be pointed out at this point that direct comparisons with the findings of other studies are fraught with difficulties. These difficulties are related particularly to methodological differences in sample size, sample composition (for example, in age and social class), question wording and mode of administration of questionnaires. For example, while this study involves total coverage of one working-class population of about 300 teenagers with whom personal interviews, using questionnaires, were conducted in their homes, most other studies of teenage substance use are of school populations of a few thousand pupils who were asked to fill in a questionnaire. Cross-cultural differences also exist. Keeping in mind these methodological and cultural differences, an attempt is made here to compare the findings with those of other studies.

The associations found in previous research between the teenagers' substance use and their attributes of gender, age, occupational status and education were not consistently supported by the findings of this study. Gender was not associated in this study with the ever or current use of any of the three substances, although other research has repeatedly reported that more males than females will have ever used and been current users of drugs (Shelley et al., 1982: 255; Miller et al., 1983: 30; Johnston, O'Malley and Bachman, 1984: 25, 29; Grube and Morgan, 1986: 120, 122) and will have ever used and been current users of alcohol (Johnston, O'Malley and Bachman, 1984: 25, 29; Grube and Morgan, 1986: 96, 97). Male also exceeded female rates of ever and current use of cigarettes in the Grube and Morgan (1986: 72) study but not in the Johnston, O'Malley and Bachman (1984: 25, 29) or Pearson and Michell (2000: 27–29) reports, in which female rates exceeded male rates. Although the individual attribute of gender was not statistically associated with the teenagers' substance use in these findings, the role of gender in the formation of teenagers' social networks, and ultimately in the teenagers' substance use, is considered to be a rather complex one, and is explored further in Chapter 9.

An association between the age of the teenagers and their substance use was found in this study for ever and current use of cigarettes and alcohol, but not drugs. These findings, therefore, supported those of Grube and Morgan (1986: 64, 88, 113, 65, 92, 116) and Miller et al. (1983: 80, 73, 75, 30) for cigarettes and alcohol but did not support their findings, or those of Shelley et al. (1982: 255), which reported a positive association between drug use and age.

When age at leaving school in this study was correlated with the teenagers' substance use, no significant relationship was found between being an 'early dropout' and their ever or current use of any of the three substances. These findings do not support the suggestion in the literature that early dropouts from school are more likely to be drug users (Shelley et al., 1982: 258; Johnston, O'Malley and Bachman, 1984: 3). Studies of school populations cannot, obviously, provide comparable data to those of this study. The statistically significant associations found in this study between the teenagers' occupational status and their ever use of cigarettes and drugs, and their current use of cigarettes and alcohol, were largely explained by the age of the teenagers.

The findings of this study have not supported earlier suggestions in the literature of a negative association between education variables and substance use. Jessor and Jessors' findings suggested an association between marijuana use and lack of interest in the goals of school (Jessor and Jessor, 1978: 68), and, in a review, Kandel reported an association between marijuana and alcohol use and education variables such as negative attitudes towards school, low academic aspirations and poor academic performance (Kandel, 1980: 268). Grube and Morgan confirmed lower rates of cigarette, alcohol and drug use among those who were 'bonded' to school (Grube and Morgan, 1986: 130). This study has examined the association between numerous education variables and the teenagers' substance use. The variables included the school attended, whether the teenagers had done a state examination, their attainment in that examination, their attitudes to school, their school class position, their age at leaving school and whether they had been expelled from school. Because this was a community study rather than a school study, these variables could be examined for those still at school and for those who had already left school. All of the education variables examined, with the exception of two, were not associated with the teenagers' ever or current use of cigarettes, alcohol or drugs. The only variables which were statistically associated were, for those who had already left school, having sat a state examination and attitude to school. Among those who had left school, those who had sat a state examination (18-year-olds only) were more likely than those who had not to have ever used alcohol, and those who had disliked school (all ages) were more likely to have been current cigarette smokers.

In conclusion, of the teenagers' attributes examined, the only attribute which was particularly associated with the teenagers' substance use was their age. And even this attribute was only associated with ever and current cigarette and alcohol use, and not drug use. The associations found between occupational status and substance use were largely explained by age too, with the associations remaining significant only for teenagers in the older age categories for ever cigarette and drug use, and for current cigarette and alcohol use. The age of the teenagers will be discussed again when the composition of the peer groups is being considered in Chapters 6–9. The next chapter will examine the teenagers' substance use by family influences.

5

Teenagers' Substance Use by Family Influences

Introduction

Previous research has consistently found that the two main influences on teenagers' substance use have been their parents and their peers. The influence of peers is examined in Chapters 6–9. In this chapter I examine family influences and include in this parental and sibling influences. Almost all of the teenagers in this community were living with their parents and they had numerous siblings, many of them older than the teenagers. Thus, there was at least some likelihood that the teenagers might be influenced in their substance use by their parents or their siblings. Parental influence includes the role parents play in encouraging their teenage children's substance use and the role they play in discouraging their substance use. Siblings may play similar roles, either helping their younger siblings to use the substances or protecting them from use. This chapter begins with an introduction to the teenagers' families. This is followed by an examination of the impact of various family variables on the teenagers' substance use.

The teenagers' families

Almost all of the teenagers were living with their families in this community. Their parents would have moved to this community early in their marriages and reared their families in the community. Parents would have known each other as neighbours and friends and their small children would have got to know each other as they played with each other in their homes or on the roads of their neighbourhood. Parents, who over the years were neighbours or friends, would have met each other frequently while bringing their children to school, going to the shops or participating in other community-based activities. They would have supported each other over the years when needed. This would be very normal in such a community. Like the teenagers, parents could live out most of their day-to-day lives in the community. Parents would, however, be more likely than the teenagers to have to go outside the community for work and sometimes for leisure.

Most of the parents of the teenagers were alive and living together and providing a caring family life for their families. The families were large but parents and teenagers had close relationships, and parents were involved in their lives providing support, advice and discipline. The teenagers' siblings were an important part of their family life and could have been role models for the teenagers as almost all of them had older siblings. There was a high level of unemployment among these families and this would have put a strain on their financial resources. It did not, however, seem to interfere with a good, close family life with the teenagers studied. Indeed, parental unemployment would have resulted in much more of the parents' time being spent at home, which might have been helpful when rearing teenagers.

Various aspects of their family lives have been found by researchers to be associated with teenagers' substance use. These include family circumstances, parental substance use, closeness to parents, parental influence and control, siblings' substance use and siblings' influence. These family variables are examined below for their impact on the teenagers' substance use.

Teenagers' substance use by family circumstances

Data were collected in this study from a working-class population of teenagers, so very little variation was expected in the family circumstances of these teenagers. Nevertheless, it seemed likely that even small differences in family circumstances might lead to differences in the teenagers' substance use. For example, would the teenagers be more likely to be substance users if their homes were broken, if their parents were unemployed, if they were in the lowest social classes, or if they were in the largest families?

Teenagers' substance use by intact or broken family home

Recent research has reported that teenagers were less likely to smoke cigarettes when their parents had an intact marriage (Kobus, 2003: 49). The findings of this study were that most of the teenagers were from homes in which the parents were alive and living together (230, 86.1 per cent). The other teenagers were from homes in which the parents were separated (7, 2.6 per cent) or in which one parent (29, 10.9 per cent) or both parents (1, 0.4 per cent) had already died. Almost all of the teenagers (98.5 per cent) were living with at least one of their parents. When examined for its association with the teenagers' substance use, the results confirmed that there was no association in this study between being from an intact or broken home and the teenagers' ever or current use of any of the three substances. The findings do not, therefore, support those of Kobus (2003: 49) who found an association for cigarette use.

Teenagers' substance use by employment status of parents

Just over half (51.9 per cent) of the fathers were in employment, while almost half (47.7 per cent) were unemployed, with one father (0.4 per cent) retired (Table 5.1). Just 21.8 per cent of the mothers were in employment and all others were unemployed. While unemployment would have limited the family financial resources, an advantage would have been that most mothers and about half of the fathers would have been at home during the day. Their fathers' employment status was associated with the teenagers' ever use of alcohol ($p < 0.0385$). It was those whose fathers were working, rather than not working, who were more likely to have taken alcohol. The employment status of their fathers was not associated with the teenagers' ever use of cigarettes or drugs or with their current use of any of the three substances. Their mothers'

Table 5.1 Employment status of the teenagers' parents

Employment status	Fathers		Mothers	
	No.	%	No.	%
Employed full-time	120	50.6	53	20.6
Employed part-time	0	0	3	1.2
Self-employed	3	1.3	0	0
Retired	1	0.4	0	0
Unemployed	113	47.7	201	78.2
Total	237[a]	100.0	257[b]	100

[a] Question did not apply to 21 teenagers whose fathers were deceased and to 9 whose fathers were not living in home of the teenager;
[b] Or to 10 teenagers whose mothers were deceased.

employment status was not associated with the teenagers' ever or current use of any of the three substances.

Teenagers' substance use by social class of the family

As explained in Chapter 3, this population was chosen using Census of Population data to select a predominantly working-class area. The findings confirm that this was so. The social class of the family, based on the occupation of the principal wage earner, is given in Table 5.2. The categorization of occupations followed the rules set down in the Census of Population (1986). The occupation of the male head of the household was used if he was gainfully occupied or retired. If he was not, and the female head of the household was gainfully occupied, her occupation was used. If neither parent was gainfully occupied, the occupation of the oldest child in the family, who was working, was used as the indicator of social class for the family (Census of Population, 1986: [iv]). This categorization was very suitable given the high level of unemployment among the parents in this study. Most of the families (84.0 per cent) belonged to the manual social classes of 4, 5 and 6. Just 10.0 per cent were in the non-manual social classes of 1, 2 or 3. No association was found between those in the non-manual and manual social classes and the teenagers' ever use of any of the three substances. This finding was consistent with those of other Irish studies which found no association between the teenagers' ever drug use and their social class (Shelley et al., 1982: 256) and no association between ever smoking, drinking or drug use and the social class of the family (Grube and Morgan, 1986: 73, 101, 123).

Table 5.2   Social class of teenagers' families[a]

Social Class	No.	%
Social Class 1 Higher Professional	2	0.7
Social Class 2 Lower Professional	11	4.1
Social Class 3 Other Non-Manual	14	5.2
Social Class 4 Skilled Manual	115	43.1
Social Class 5 Semi Skilled Manual	64	24.0
Social Class 6 Unskilled Manual	45	16.9
No one working + unknown	15	5.6
Working on a training course	1	0.4
	267	100.0

[a] Classified using the Census of Population Classification of Occupations (Census of Population, 1986).

Social class was associated with current smoking ($p < 0.0420$) with more of those in the manual than non-manual social classes being current smokers. There was no association with current alcohol or drug use. These findings were consistent with those of Grube and Morgan (1986: 101, 123, 73) for current drinking and drug use but not for current smoking since they found no association between social class and the current use of any of the three substances.

Teenagers' substance use by parental substance use

Previous research has confirmed that parental substance use has an impact on the substance use of their teenage children. Kandel, Kessler and Margulies (1978: 88, 89) found that parental use of hard liquor, that is, spirits, predicted their adolescent children's initiation into hard liquor and illicit drugs other than marijuana, and that parental use of psychoactive drugs predicted later use by their children of illicit drugs other than marijuana. Newcomb, Huba and Bentler (1983: 724) also confirmed that mothers' marijuana use led to their children's marijuana use, irrespective of the gender of the children. Ennett and Bauman (1991: 1706) found an association between fathers' drinking and adolescent children's drinking, but their mothers' drinking was not associated. Bailey, Ennett and Ringwalt (1993: 613, 614) and Kobus (2003: 49) reported an association between parents' smoking and adolescent children's smoking. Ennett et al. (2001: 60) also found associations between parental use of tobacco and their children's use of tobacco and alcohol, and between parental alcohol use and their children's tobacco use. These findings suggest that adolescents may be influenced by their parents' substance use, but they may not necessarily use the same substances as their parents.

In order to test the possible association between parental and teenage children's substance use, the teenagers in this study were asked whether, at the time of the interview, their parents smoked cigarettes and drank alcohol. This is referred to as the parents' perceived use. The teenagers were not asked about the recency or frequency of their parents' use nor were they asked whether their parents took drugs.

The teenagers' replies revealed that 52.5 per cent of their mothers and 62.9 per cent of their fathers were perceived to be smokers at the time of the interview. A total of 36.5 per cent of the parents were both perceived to be smokers, while 21.7 per cent were both said to be non-smokers. The findings confirmed that their mothers, fathers or, taken together, their parents' perceived cigarette smoking made no difference to whether the teenagers had ever smoked cigarettes or were current smokers. These findings, therefore, do not support those of Bailey, Ennett and Ringwalt (1993: 613, 614), Ennett et al. (2001: 60) or Kobus (2003: 49), who reported associations between parental and children's cigarette smoking.

Even more of the teenagers' mothers, 67.3 per cent, and their fathers, 84.0 per cent, were perceived to be drinkers. A total of 63.0 per cent of the parents were both perceived to be drinkers, while 11.3 per cent were both said to be non-drinkers. Parental drinking was associated with the teenagers' drinking but results were rather mixed. If their mother, father or parents were perceived to be drinkers, the teenagers were more likely to have ever taken alcohol ($p < 0.0157$, $p < 0.0058$, $p < 0.001$ respectively). These findings support those of Ennett and Bauman (1991: 1706) and Kandel, Kessler and Margulies (1978: 88, 89), who found an association between parental alcohol use and their adolescent children's use. Perceived parental drinking was also associated with the teenagers' current drinking but in the opposite direction. Teenagers, whose mothers ($p < 0.0168$) or parents ($p < 0.0265$) were drinkers, were *less likely* to be current drinkers, and their fathers' alcohol use had no effect on the teenagers' current use.

No questions were asked in this study about the drug use of parents. The data were, however, examined for an association between parental use of cigarettes and alcohol and their teenage children's use of drugs, since previous research had confirmed an association between parental use of hard liquor and the children's use of illicit drugs other than marijuana (Kandel, Kessler and Margulies, 1978: 88, 89). The results showed that there was no association in this study between parental use of cigarettes or alcohol and the ever or current use of drugs by their teenage children.

Teenagers' substance use by closeness to parents

Previous research has confirmed that closeness to parents affects their teenage children's substance use. Lack of closeness between parents and their teenage children has been reported to influence initiation to marijuana and especially to illicit drugs other than marijuana (Kandel, Kessler and Margulies, 1978: 87–89). Lack of closeness to their fathers has been found to influence their sons' marijuana use, and this was so irrespective of the quality of the mother–son relationship (Brook et al., 1983b: 208). There was a synergistic effect when there were good relationships with both parents, resulting in less marijuana use, and a synergistic effect when relationships with both parents were faulty, resulting in more marijuana use (Brook et al., 1983b: 209). Bailey, Ennett and Ringwalt (1993: 614) also reported a relationship between lack of closeness with parents and the adolescent's current smoking.

When asked how close they were to their parents, most of the teenagers were either very close or close to each parent. Nearly all of the teenagers (95.7 per cent) were very close or close to their mother and 86.4 per cent very close or close to their fathers (Table 5.3). A total of 68.5 per cent were very close or close to both parents. Closeness to their mothers, or parents, was not associated with the teenagers' ever or current use of any of the three substances. Closeness to their fathers was associated with ever taking alcohol ($p < 0.0407$) and ever taking drugs ($p < 0.0402$). It was those not close to their fathers who were more likely to have ever taken alcohol and drugs. When gender was controlled, this association remained significant for daughters only, for alcohol ($p < 0.0154$) and drugs ($p < 0.0057$). While this finding is consistent with those of Brook et al., (1983b: 208), who found that lack of closeness to fathers influenced sons' marijuana use, lack of closeness to fathers affected daughters' drug use in this study. While Grube and Morgan (1986: 132) reported an association between drug use and lack of bonding to parents, the findings of this study have found an association only with lack of closeness to fathers. Closeness to their fathers was not associated with the teenagers ever having smoked cigarettes or being current users of cigarettes, alcohol or drugs.

Table 5.3 Whether teenagers were close to their parents

Level of closeness	Fathers (%)	Mothers (%)	Both parents (%)
Very close	54.3	40.3	37.1
Close	41.4	46.1	31.4
Not close	3.9	13.6	3.9
Other answer	0.4	0	0
Total	236[a]	256[b]	229

[a] Question did not apply to 21 teenagers whose fathers were deceased and to 9 whose fathers were not living in home of the teenager, and one teenager did not answer the question.
[b] Question did not apply to 10 teenagers whose mothers were deceased, and one teenager did not give this information.

Teenagers' substance use by parental influence

Parental influence has been measured in previous research by parental attitudes towards substance use and parents' directions to their children about their use. Parental attitudes to drugs have been reported to influence their children's initiation to marijuana but not to illicit drugs other than marijuana (Kandel, Kessler and Margulies, 1978: 87–89). Parental tolerance of marijuana and their belief in the harmlessness of various drugs were predictive of subsequent use by their children (Kandel, Kessler and Margulies, 1978: 87–89; Kandel, 1978a: 25; Kandel, 1980: 271) as parental attitudes which favoured drug use were accepted by their children.

Two variables are used in this study to measure parental attitudes and tolerance of their teenage children's substance use. They do so by measuring the direct involvement of parents in their children's substance use. These variables are taken as evidence of parental influence of their children's substance use in this book. The variables are the teenagers being in the company of their parents for their substance use or having the substance provided by their parents. Information is given in Table 5.4, which confirms that no parent influenced their teenagers' drug use, but a small proportion of parents influenced their teenage children's first and current use of cigarettes and alcohol. These findings suggest that their parents were intolerant of drug use but were slightly more tolerant of cigarette or alcohol use.

Table 5.4   Teenagers' substance use by parental influence

	In company of parents				Provided by parents		
	No.	%	Total		No.	%	Total
First use				*First use*			
Cigarettes	1	0.6	157	Cigarettes	1	0.6	157
Alcohol	15	6.8	221	Alcohol	19	8.6	221
Drugs	0	0.0	45	Drugs	0	0.0	45
Current use				*Current use*			
Cigarettes	4	4.0	101	Cigarettes	8	7.9	101
Alcohol	4	3.0	134	Alcohol	6	4.5	134
Drugs	0	0.0	17	Drugs	0	0.0	17

Parental control of the teenagers' substance use

Previous research has suggested that specific rules laid down by parents against the use of drugs by their teenage children were ineffective as children ignored their parents' rules when they rejected drug use (Kandel, Kessler and Margulies, 1978: 87, 89; Kandel, 1978a: 25; Kandel, 1980: 271). Ennett et al. (2001: 59) also found that parental rules against use of tobacco and alcohol were ignored by their children. They concluded that parental rules had, at best, no influence and may have caused some adolescents to increase their use. A number of measures of parental control were used in this study. These included parents advising their children not to use the substances, trying to control the teenagers' choice of friends and trying to control the teenagers' free-time activities.

Parental advice against substance use

Both parents of most of the teenagers had advised their children not to smoke cigarettes (60.2 per cent), not to drink alcohol (59.4 per cent) and not to take drugs (75.4 per cent) (Table 5.5).

The findings confirmed that parental advice was associated only with ever cigarette and alcohol use, and with current alcohol use. When parents advised against smoking, the teenagers were *more likely* to have ever smoked cigarettes ($p < 0.0392$) supporting the findings of Ennett et al. (2001: 59), who found that parental advice related to tobacco use had, at best, no influence on their adolescent children's use and may have caused some adolescents to increase their use. When fathers advised against alcohol use, the teenagers were less likely to have ever

Table 5.5 Whether parents advised teenagers against substance use

	Fathers (%)	Mothers (%)	Both parents (%)
Cigarettes	66.1[a]	68.4	60.2[d]
Alcohol	66.1[a]	67.6	59.4[d]
Drugs	78.3[b]	80.1	75.4[e]
	N = 236[a]	N = 256[c]	N = 229[d]
	N = 235[b]		N = 228[e]

[a] Question did not apply to 21 teenagers whose fathers were deceased or to 9 whose fathers were not living in home of the teenager, and one teenager did not answer question.
[b] Two teenagers did not answer question on drugs.
[c] Question did not apply to 10 whose mothers were deceased, and one teenager did not answer question.
[d,e] Analysis only on those on whom all necessary information was available.

used alcohol ($p < 0.0068$). When fathers or parents advised against alcohol use, the teenagers were less likely to be current drinkers ($p < 0.0102$ and $p < 0.0014$ respectively). These findings are contrary to those of Ennett et al. (2001: 59), who found that parental advice had no influence on their teenage children's alcohol use. Parental advice was ineffective for all other substance use, including ever and current drug use. These findings support those of Kandel, Kessler and Margulies (1978: 87), who found that parental rules against using drugs are ineffective.

Parental control of choice of friends

Asked whether their parents had ever interfered with their choice of friends, 29.3 per cent of the teenagers said that their mothers had, while 24.2 per cent said that their fathers had. Both parents of 19.2 per cent of the teenagers had objected to friends and at least one parent of 32.8 per cent of the teenagers had objected to their choice of friends. Nearly half of the teenagers (47.1 per cent) never complied with their parents' demands to drop or avoid some friends, while nearly as many always complied (43.7 per cent). The others (9.2 per cent) sometimes complied. When examined, the findings revealed that there was no association between the teenagers having made friends with people whom their parents had advised against, and their ever or current use of any of the three substances. These findings suggest, therefore, that, either the forbidden friends were not a bad influence, or the teenagers were able to withstand the alleged 'bad' influence of those friends.

Parental control of teenagers' free-time activities

When asked about the amount of freedom their parents gave them to do what they wanted with their free-time when they were not at home, most of the teenagers said that they were given a lot (41.7 per cent) or a fair amount (48.9 per cent) of freedom by their fathers, and a lot (44.3 per cent) or a fair amount (50.6 per cent) by their mothers (Table 5.6). A total of 79.8 per cent had been given a lot (36.4 per cent) or a fair amount (43.4 per cent) of freedom by both parents and no one had been given no freedom by both parents. The amount of freedom given by their fathers, mothers or parents was associated with the teenagers' ever drinking ($p < 0.0003$, $p < 0.0001$ and $p < 0.0001$ respectively) and current smoking ($p < 0.0184$, $p < 0.0006$ and $p < 0.047$ respectively). Those receiving most freedom from their fathers, mothers or parents were most likely to have ever taken alcohol and to be current smokers.

Table 5.6 Amount of freedom given by parents to the teenagers

Amount of freedom	Fathers (%)	Mothers (%)	Both parents (%)
A lot of freedom	41.7	44.3	36.4
A fair amount	48.9	50.6	43.4
A little	4.7	8.1	3.5
No freedom	0.4	1.3	0
Total	235[a]	255[b]	228

[a] Question did not apply to 21 teenagers whose fathers were deceased, to 9 whose fathers were not living in home of the teenager, to one teenager who had left home, and one teenager did not answer the question.

[b] Question did not apply to 10 teenagers whose mothers were deceased, and to one teenager who had left home, and one teenager did not answer the question.

These parental variables were unrelated to the teenagers' ever use of cigarettes and drugs and their current use of alcohol and drugs.

Teenagers' substance use by siblings' substance use

All of the respondents, but one, had siblings. The number of siblings the teenagers had ranged from none to eleven. The mean number of siblings was 5.5. It seemed possible that these siblings might have influenced the substance use of the teenagers, especially since 94.7 per cent of the teenagers had older siblings. In order to examine this question, the teenagers were asked whether their siblings smoked cigarettes and drank alcohol. This is referred to as their siblings' perceived use of these substances. Siblings who were interviewed were asked about their own use of drugs.

Most of the teenagers (82.4 per cent) had at least one sibling who was perceived to be a smoker, and even more of the teenagers (89.5 per cent) had at least one sibling who was perceived to be a drinker. Siblings' perceived use of cigarettes and alcohol was associated with the teenagers' ever use of cigarettes ($p < 0.0004$) and alcohol ($p < 0.0008$), and in the expected direction with more teenagers, whose siblings were users, having used themselves. There was no association between siblings' perceived use and the teenagers' current use of cigarettes or alcohol. Siblings who were interviewed in the study reported their own drug use. A total of 152 teenagers had at least one sibling interviewed and 28 (18.4 per cent) of these siblings had used drugs. Siblings' drug use (self-reported) was unrelated to the teenagers' ever or current use of drugs.

Table 5.7   Teenagers' substance use by siblings' influence

	In company of siblings				Provided by siblings		
	No.	%	Total		No.	%	Total
First use				*First use*			
Cigarettes	11	7.0	157	Cigarettes	11	7.0	157
Alcohol	27	12.2	221	Alcohol	17	7.7	221
Drugs	1	2.2	45	Drugs	0	0.0	45
Current use				*Current use*			
Cigarettes	10	9.9	101	Cigarettes	4	4.0	101
Alcohol	9	6.7	134	Alcohol	5	3.7	134
Drugs	1	5.9	17	Drugs	0	0.0	17

Teenagers' substance use by siblings' influence

The findings in Table 5.7 indicate the extent to which their siblings influenced the teenagers' substance use. The criteria of influence were the same as those used for parents, whether the teenagers had been in the company of their siblings or had been provided with the substance by their siblings at the teenagers' first and current use of the three substances. These findings confirm that almost no siblings influenced the teenagers' drug use, and only small proportions of siblings influenced their cigarette and alcohol use. This is interesting considering the proportion of teenagers who had siblings who smoked and drank. It would appear from these findings that, although their siblings smoked cigarettes and drank alcohol, only a small proportion of the teenagers were influenced directly by their siblings in their first use or their current use of the substances.

Conclusion

The findings from this study indicate that the impact of parents on their children's substance use is complex. Parental behaviour, in terms of their own substance use and the controls they put in place to prevent their teenage children using substances, have sometimes had a positive effect resulting in less substance use by the teenagers, other times had no effect on their teenage children's substance use and sometimes had a negative effect, resulting in more substance use by their teenage children. This variation in the impact of parents on their children's substance use is consistent with previous research. This study also examined siblings' substance use and their influence on the teenagers' substance use. The impact of family variables on the teenagers' substance use varied considerably between substances and for ever and current substance use.

The results confirmed that teenagers were *more likely* to have ever smoked cigarettes if their parents had advised against use. These findings do not support those of Kobus (2003: 49), who found that children were less likely to smoke if their parents were opposed to smoking, or Bailey, Ennett and Ringwalt (1993: 613, 614), who found that parental smoking led to their children's smoking, since our results showed no such association. The findings do support those of Ennett et al. (2001: 59), who found that parent–child communication relating to cigarette use had, at best, no influence but may cause some teenagers to increase their use. The teenagers were also *more likely* to have ever smoked cigarettes if their siblings smoked cigarettes. The teenagers were *more likely* to be current smokers if they were in the manual social classes and if they had been given more freedom by their father, mother or parents. Bailey, Ennett and Ringwalt (1993: 609, 614) also found an association between adolescent smoking and parental 'lack of strictness'.

The results confirmed that teenagers were *more likely* to have ever used alcohol if their fathers were employed, if their father, mother or parents drank alcohol, if their father, mother or parents gave them more freedom, if their fathers were not close to their daughters (female teenagers only), and if their siblings drank alcohol. These findings support those of Kandel, Kessler and Margulies (1978: 88, 89) and Ennett and Bauman (1991: 1706), who found an association between parental and adolescent children's alcohol use. Ennett and Bauman (1991: 1706) did not, however, confirm this association for mother's alcohol use. Our findings that teenagers were more likely to have ever used alcohol if parents had given them more freedom to do what they liked in their free-time, is supported by those of Barnes, Farrell and Banerjee (1994: 197), who found that high levels of parental monitoring was likely to prevent alcohol abuse.

Teenagers were, on the other hand, *less likely* to drink if their fathers had advised against drinking alcohol. Thus, the advice of fathers, in particular, seemed to be effective. These findings do not support those of Ennett et al. (2001: 59), who found that parent–child advice against alcohol use was likely to be ineffective or to lead to increased use by their children.

The teenagers in our study were *less likely* to be current drinkers if their mothers or parents drank alcohol. These findings are contrary to previous research which usually found an association between parental drinking and the teenagers' drinking (Ennett and Bauman, 1991: 1706). Teenagers in this study were also *less likely* to be current drinkers if their fathers or parents advised against drinking alcohol. These findings are contrary to those of Ennett et al. (2001: 59), who found that parental advice was likely to be ineffective.

The results confirmed that the only family variable associated with ever or current drug use among the teenagers was that teenage daughters were *more likely* to have ever used drugs if they were not close to their fathers. These findings support those of Brook et al. (1983b: 208), who found a similar association for fathers and sons, while we found the association for fathers and daughters.

Our findings also confirmed that parents and siblings had directly influenced the substance use of the teenagers in this study by being in their company or providing the substance at their first use of the substance or for their current use of the substance. These findings confirmed that parents *never* influenced the teenagers' drug use, that a very small percentage of them influenced their first and current cigarette use and that slightly more of them influenced their first and current alcohol use. Their siblings had *almost never* influenced the drug use of the teenagers, although many of the siblings had taken drugs. A small percentage of the siblings had influenced the teenagers' first use of cigar-ettes and alcohol and even fewer their current use. Comparable findings have not been found but these data will be valuable for comparisons with the influence of peers in subsequent chapters.

Research to date has suggested that the main influencers of teenage substance use were their parents and peers. Data presented in this chapter have confirmed the minimal influence of parents and siblings on the teenagers' drug use, and the mixed influence of parents and siblings on the teenagers' use of cigarettes and alcohol. The role of their peers on the teenagers' use of the three substances is explored in Chapters 6–9 and the relative impact of the role of parents, siblings and peers on the teenagers' substance use is discussed further in Chapter 10.

6
The Role of Peers in Teenagers' Substance Use

Introduction

Previous research has consistently confirmed that their peers are a major source of influence on the substance use of teenagers. Some of the earlier work confirmed an association between teenagers' substance use and the perceived, or self-reported, substance use of their peers. These researchers were usually drawing on dyadic or peer group data. More recent research, with a social network analysis focus, has drawn on data on small cliques to examine the importance of the social position of teenagers in their substance use. Researchers have been in general agreement in recent times that the process of teenagers and their peers becoming similar in their substance use is explained by peer influence or selection, and not by peer influence alone. Thus, some teenagers are influenced by their peers to become similar to them in their substance use, while other teenagers select as peers individuals who are already using the same substances as they are. Recent researchers have been frustrated at the difficulty of adequately examining the relative impact of peer influence and selection using small clique data and they have pointed to the need for complete network data to examine this question adequately (Ennett and Bauman, 1993: 234; Haynie, 2001: 1023).

This chapter uses complete network data to examine questions arising from recent research on social position, similarity in the substance use of peers, and the relative impact of peer influence and selection on increasing similarity. Before doing so, the selection of peers by the teenagers and the formation of the peer groups in the complete network are explained.

Selection of peers

The teenagers in this population formed peer ties with other teenagers in the population and, in doing so, created the complete network which we examine in this book. The population covered is the 267 teenagers interviewed and the complete network is made up of the peer ties existing between these 267 teenagers. Thus, the teenagers are, at once, the population of teenagers and the peers of one another. The teenagers were asked to name all of those they had selected as peers and with whom they were friends and pals at the time of interview. When asked to name their peers (that is, their best friends, boyfriends, girlfriends, good friends, friends and pals), all but two of the teenagers said that they had at least one peer tie (99.3 per cent). The number of peers they named ranged from none (for just two teenagers) to 13, with a mean number of 3.7 peers. Only 169 teenagers (62.3 per cent), however, had at least one peer tie in the population and these formed a total of 278 peer ties because many peers were mentioned more than once. The 98 teenagers, who had no peer ties in the population, remained as isolates in the complete network although all but two of them had peers outside the population covered by the interviews. Complete network data include all peer dyads (278 peer ties), all peer groups (35 peer groups) and all isolates (98 teenagers) in the population covered by the study.

The peer ties were, in general, of long duration, usually since childhood. The mean number of years since the teenagers had selected each other as peers was 7.41 years (SD = 4.96) and they had usually got to know each other even earlier. The mean time lag between getting to know each other and selecting each other as peers was 1.57 years (SD = 3.53). A large proportion of these teenagers had got to know each other because they lived on the same road (43.8 per cent), or on a different road in the neighbourhood (9.8 per cent), and others knew each other since they were babies (6.2 per cent) (for example, their mothers were already friends at that time), since they started in primary school at the age of four years (15.6 per cent), or since they started in secondary school at the age of about 12 years (10.5 per cent) (Table 6.1). These selections were made, therefore, before their teenage years and, for most, before they were at an age to use any of the substances.

These peer ties had continued to the time of interview and the teenagers had very frequent interactions with their peers. The teenagers met each other very frequently, usually about five days of the week (mean 5.23; SD = 2.17), and in the week prior to interview they had met each other on about five days too (mean 5.04; SD = 2.13).

Table 6.1   How peers had first got to know each other

How got to know ...	No.	% of teenagers
Know since we were babies	17	6.2
In primary school	43	15.6
In secondary school	29	10.5
Lives on same road	121	43.8
In neighbourhood	27	9.8
Through a family member	7	2.5
Through a relative	2	0.7
Through a friend	32	11.6
At a disco	6	2.2
Through a sport	7	2.5
Through a hobby	2	0.7
On day trip/holiday	3	1.1
Just met	2	0.7
Peer is cousin	3	1.1
Other way	2	0.7
Cannot remember	2	0.7
Number of dyads	276[a]	>100[b]

[a] No information on 2 dyads.
[b] More than one response given by many teenagers.

Findings on what they did when they met in the previous week confirm that these teenagers simply enjoyed spending time together doing quite ordinary things, usually in their community. Many had spent the time talking (34.7 per cent), others spent the time messing or dossing around together outside (32.8 per cent), some participated in sport (22.4 per cent), others watched television, a video or listened to the radio or to music (10.4 per cent). Some went for a walk (10.0 per cent), went to a disco (9.3 per cent) or visited each other (8.8 per cent). Others played cards (8.5 per cent), went shopping (8.1 per cent) or visited other friends or pals (5.8 per cent). A few went drinking (3.9 per cent), met at work or school (3.5 per cent), engaged in a hobby or attended a club (2.0 per cent). A few went to the cinema (2.0 per cent) or did something else (7.3 per cent) (percentages total to more than 100 per cent because many of them did more than one thing when they met) (Kirke, 1996: 339, 340).

One third of the peer ties were best friends (35.3 per cent), 28.4 per cent were good friends, 18.7 per cent were friends, just 3.2 per cent were boyfriends or girlfriends, and 14.4 per cent were pals. The peer ties were most likely to be between teenagers of the same sex ($p < 0.0001$).

Table 6.2   Age mix in peer ties

Age of peer (years)	Age of teenager				
	14 years (%)	15 years (%)	16 years (%)	17 years (%)	18 years (%)
14	32.1	18.0	13.8	10.4	0
15	30.2	36.1	24.1	9.0	7.7
16	18.9	23.0	20.7	23.9	25.6
17	15.1	16.4	22.4	40.3	23.1
18	3.8	6.6	19.0	16.4	43.6
	53	61	58	67	39
Percentage	100	100	100	100	100

A total of 89.2 per cent were same sex peer ties (54.7 per cent were male; 34.5 per cent were female). They were also likely to be between teenagers of similar age ($p < 0.0001$). Nevertheless, teenagers had not formed peer ties with others of the exact same age as might be expected and, since even small variations in age may be important to peer influence in substance use, the age mix in dyads is given below (Table 6.2). These findings confirm that, while there is a tendency for the teenagers to form peer ties with someone of the same age, the peers they select may be up to four years older than them or may be up to three years younger than them.

Formation of peer groups and the complete network

Over the years, since these peer ties were formed between the teenagers, they had gradually linked the teenagers into peer groups of various sizes. The size and pattern of ties in these peer groups would have gradually changed during the years as new ties were formed and old ties dropped. Peer ties which were dropped over this time were unfortunately not recorded. But the peer ties which had endured had formed the complete network as it existed at the time of interview. In the complete network, there were many teenagers who had not made a peer tie with someone in this population but they had peer ties with others outside the population. These would have been individuals who were outside the age range 14–18 years or outside the geographical area covered by the study.

When the social network analysis was conducted on these peer ties the analysis revealed that 35 'weak components' and 98 individual teenagers, who had no peer ties within the teenage population, formed the complete network. Although forming part of the complete network, these 98 individuals remained as isolates in all further analysis of the complete network. These weak components are an excellent representation of the naturally existing peer groups in this population of teenagers (Kirke, 2004: 6). The method of delineating these peer groups has already been outlined (Chapter 3; Kirke, 1996). The peer groups include all of the teenagers and their peers who are connected to each other, directly or indirectly, by peer ties through paths of any distance. Thus, each peer group is distinct from all others. There are no direct, or indirect, peer ties between them. The relevance of identifying weak components as peer groups is that it is only within these peer groups, and not between them, that peer influence may occur, at any particular point in time. To put this point another way, it is only within peer groups that there will be a social force towards similarity in the substance use of peers. Over time, peer groups could change in size and in the patterning of their ties and this would allow for opportunities for peer influence to also change (Chapters 7–9) but this is not an issue in this chapter.

The size and number of peer groups are given in Table 6.3. There is huge variation in the number of peer groups of different sizes. Other than in the dyadic peer groups in which there is no interlock, each peer group represents the interlocking egocentric networks of the teenagers in that peer group. Thus, Peer Group 1, which has 26 teenagers, includes the peer ties of each of those 26 teenagers and all of the interlocks that occurred between their peers (Chapter 8). Nearly half (48.6 per cent)

Table 6.3 Size and number of peer groups in the complete network

Peer group size (teenagers)	Number of peer groups	%
26	1	2.9
22	1	2.9
21	1	2.9
10	1	2.9
7	3	8.6
4	2	5.5
3	9	25.7
2	17	48.6
	35[a]	100.0

[a] These 35 networks include 169 individual teenagers with a total of 278 peer ties between them.

of the peer groups have only two teenagers in each. Another 25.7 per cent of the peer groups have three teenagers in each. There are a small number of four and seven-teenager peer groups and just one each with 10, 21, 22 and 26 teenagers. Some of the reason for this variation in size is that these peer groups are the naturally existing peer groups among the teenagers in this complete network. There is considerable fragmentation of the complete network. This fragmentation would be reduced by adding information from other peer ties outside the complete network, but this would spoil the integrity of the complete network.

While the size of the peer groups is important for the analysis of the teenagers' substance use, the patterning of the ties in these peer groups is also important. The patterning of ties varies over time as new members join and new interlocks occur. The patterning observed in these peer groups is that which existed at the time of interview. The patterning of ties varied considerably across peer groups (Chapters 7–9; Appendix D) and the importance of this will be discussed in Chapter 10. For now, the analysis centres on whether teenagers who are members of peer groups or are isolates are more likely to use substances, as other researchers have suggested.

Teenagers' substance use by their social position

In recent years, researchers have adopted a social network approach to examining the association between the social position of teenagers in relation to their peers and their substance use. This research has usually focussed on cliques of between three and five members (Hunter, Vizelberg and Berenson, 1991; Ennett and Bauman, 1993; 1994; Bauman and Ennett, 1994; 1996; Michell and Amos, 1997; Pearson and Michell, 2000; Fang et al., 2003; Pearson and West, 2003). Cliques were defined as peer groups in this research. Most of these researchers examined cigarette use only (Ennett and Bauman, 1993; 1994; Michell and Amos, 1997; Abel, Plumridge and Graham, 2002; Fang et al., 2003), while some examined the teenagers' use of cigarettes and alcohol (Hunter, Vizelberg and Berenson, 1991) and some cigarettes and drugs (Pearson and Michell, 2000). None has examined the use of all three substances.

All of these researchers have focussed on the association between the social position of teenagers among their peers and their substance use. In doing so, they did not take into account the substance use of the peers in those social positions. Most of these researchers have used the programme NEGOPY (Richards, 1989) to determine whether the adolescents being studied were clique members, liaisons or isolates, and examined whether the adolescents' substance use was likely to vary depending on their social position among their peers. The definition of clique remained similar in many of these studies (Ennett and Bauman, 1993; Michell and Amos, 1997; Pearson and Michell, 2000; Fang et al., 2003). These researchers adopted the definition used in NEGOPY to define clique members, as adolescents in a group of at least three members, who had most of their links with other members of the same group and were all connected by a path entirely within the group.

Researchers adopted some variations, however, of the definition of liaison and the definition of isolate given in NEGOPY. Ennett and Bauman (1993), Michell and Amos (1997) and Fang et al. (2003) used the NEGOPY definition of liaisons, as those who were not members of cliques but had at least two links with clique members or other liaisons. Pearson and Michell (2000) adopted a variation of this and called them peripherals to groups (Chapter 2).

Ennett and Bauman (1993), Michell and Amos (1997) and Fang et al. (2003) adopted the NEGOPY definition of isolate, that is, those who had few or no links with other adolescents, and could be in dyads or tree structures in which the removal of one link would result in the individual being separated from the rest of the network. Pearson and Michell (2000: 25, 26) changed the NEGOPY definition of isolate and called them relative isolates (Chapter 2). Abel, Plumridge and Graham (2002: 335) regrouped liaisons and isolates into categories of popular, try-hards, ordinary and loners. The loners were least well connected, with no ties or one or two unreciprocated ties.

Findings on the association between social position and substance use vary across these studies. One of the central findings has been that isolates were more likely than clique members or liaisons to be current smokers and that this association was significant in four of the five schools studied (Ennett and Bauman, 1993: 231). These findings were confirmed by Fang et al. (2003: 262) for most of the school pupils covered in their study in China, but they found the reverse situation among 10th grade boys, among whom peer group members and liaisons were more likely to have smoked cigarettes. Abel, Plumridge and Graham's (2002: 336) findings did not support those of Ennett and Bauman (1993: 231). They found, on the contrary, that loners, that is, those who were least well connected, were those least likely to smoke (Abel, Plumridge and Graham, 2002: 336). Pearson and Michell (2000: 27) found no association between social position, and smoking and drug taking among 12–13-year-olds, but found small differences one year later with relative isolates being more likely than those in other social positions to smoke cigarettes ($p < 0.08$) and to take drugs ($p < 0.07$). This size of difference ($p > 0.05$) would have been accepted as not significant in most other studies, and in mine.

In the same paper which highlighted the association between social position and current smoking, Ennett and Bauman (1993: 234) stated that '. . . the ideal social network analysis would have included complete data from all adolescents and their friends in this population' and that such data may have resulted in different findings. They were also aware that limiting the adolescents' choices to three best friends may have underestimated the total number of friendship links and may have distorted the true structure of the school networks (Ennett and Bauman, 1993: 234). The question of whether there is an association between the social position of teenagers among their peers and their substance use is examined here using the complete network data collected in the Dublin study. Teenagers had been allowed to name all of their friends and pals, so the size of the peer groups was not restricted as it had been by researchers who had allowed their respondents to name only three best friends (for example, Ennett and Bauman, 1993: 228, 229). Peer groups in this study are not cliques, as they were in earlier studies. They are the naturally existing peer groups of the teenagers and their peers in this complete network of teenagers. The peer groups discussed here are of various sizes, only some as small as cliques. There are 35 peer groups in all, varying in size from 26 to 2 teenagers. As explained in Chapter 3, the peer groups were delineated by identifying 'weak components' using the Gradap programme (Sprenger and Stokman, 1989: 17). They include all of the teenagers and their peers who are connected to each other through peer ties by paths of any distance (Kirke, 1996: 340). This definition of peer group is important for a substance use study, since it includes in the peer group all peers who might influence the substance use of the teenagers in those groups. Thus, in this complete network, if a teenager has even one peer tie, that dyad formed a peer group, and the teenager would not have been labelled an isolate. And liaisons do not exist in the complete network. There are no liaisons between peer groups because, by definition, weak components, that is, peer groups, include all peer ties between the teenagers, whatever the distance between them. Peer groups in this study, then, would include those who would have been assigned as clique members or liaisons in other studies. Only teenagers who have no peer tie in the complete network are labelled as isolates in the Dublin study. Comparing them with those labelled as isolates in other studies is problematic because the definition of isolate, used in other studies, includes individuals who have few peer ties with individuals who have no peer ties.

Comparisons can be made, nevertheless, between the findings of this study on the association between social position and the teenagers' substance use. In this study, the social position of the teenagers is based on their membership of a peer group or being an isolate. The findings were that there was no association between the social position of the teenagers in this study, based on them being in a peer group of any size, or being an isolate, and their ever or current use of cigarettes, alcohol or drugs (Table 6.4). When the peer groups were divided into larger peer groups (six or more teenagers), smaller peer groups (five or fewer teenagers), and the tests were repeated, there was still no association between the teenagers being in a large peer group, a small peer group, or being an isolate, and their ever or current use of any of the three substances.

These findings confirm that complete network data do produce different results to those obtained in other studies. The findings of this study do not support those of researchers who found an association

Table 6.4   Substance use of the teenagers by their social position in the complete network

Substance use	Member of Peer group (2–26 members) (%)		Isolate (%)	Significance $p < 0.05$
Cigarettes – ever	57.7		61.2	NS
Alcohol – ever	83.9		82.7	NS
Drugs – ever	19.0		13.3	NS
Cigarettes – current	35.7		42.9	NS
Alcohol – current	50.6		51.0	NS
Drugs – current	8.3		3.1	NS
	N = 168		N = 98	

	Peer group (6+ members) (%)	Peer group (2–5 members) (%)	Isolate (%)	Significance $p < 0.05$
Cigarettes – ever	56.6	59.4	61.2	NS
Alcohol – ever	82.8	85.5	82.7	NS
Drugs – ever	20.2	17.4	13.3	NS
Cigarettes – current	34.3	37.7	42.9	NS
Alcohol – current	48.5	53.6	51.0	NS
Drugs – current	8.0	8.7	3.1	NS
	N = 99	N = 69	N = 98	

between social position and the substance use of teenagers. They do not support those of Ennett and Bauman (1993: 231), who found that isolates were most likely to have been current smokers, or Fang et al. (2003: 262), who found that isolates were most likely to have smoked cigarettes, except among the 10th grade boys among whom isolates were least likely to have smoked. Neither do they support the findings of Abel, Plumridge and Graham (2002: 336), who found that loners, those least well connected, were least likely to have smoked cigarettes. Our findings come closest to those of Pearson and Michell (2000: 27), who found no association between social position and smoking and drug taking among 12–13-year-olds, and a small association one year later, which was not significant at $p < 0.05$, but at $p < 0.08$ for cigarettes and $p < 0.07$ for drugs, with isolates more likely to be the users. We would have considered such results not significant and would have described them as such. The conclusion here is that, when complete network data are examined, the results do not support the claim that social position is associated with teenagers' substance use.

Similarity in substance use in dyads

Research since the 1970s has been very influential in demonstrating the importance of peer influence in teenagers' substance use (Jessor and Jessor, 1978: 69; Kandel, 1978a: 24; 1980: 269; Akers et al., 1979: 644; Dembo, Schmeidler and Burgos, 1982: 376; Brook, Whiteman and Gordon, 1983; 276). While there was no direct evidence in this literature that particular peers had influenced particular teenagers into using the substances, there was evidence from the longitudinal research that teenagers, whose peers had taken the substances at one point in time, were likely to have taken similar substances at a subsequent point in time. On the basis of these findings, the inference drawn was that their peers had influenced the teenagers into substance use (Kirke, 2004: 3, 4). Numerous researchers have confirmed an association between teenagers' substance use and that of their peers. Kandel (1978a: 24) found that the association varied for different substances and was greatest for marijuana use. When teenagers perceived that their peer group was using marijuana, they were likely to use it too and when they perceived that their best friends were using illicit drugs other than marijuana they were likely to use those (Kandel, Kessler and Margulies, 1978: 87, 89). Kandel also found that female teenagers were more susceptible than male teenagers to peer influence (Kandel, 1980: 270: 1986: 221). A strength of Kandel's data was that data on best friend dyads were self-reported, but other peer data were not. The importance of peer influence has been confirmed by other researchers for drug use (Jessor and Jessor, 1978: 69; Brook, Whiteman and Gordon, 1982: 1160; 1983: 276; Dembo, Schmeidler and Burgos, 1982: 376), for cigarettes, alcohol and drugs (Grube and Morgan, 1986: 77, 104, 126), and for alcohol and drug use (Akers et al., 1979: 638).

Although these researchers placed particular emphasis on the importance of peer influence in explaining the growing similarity in the substance use of teenagers and their peers, Kandel (1978b: 436) and Cohen (1977: 239) did warn around this time that the role of peer influence on the increasing similarity may be exaggerated if the selection of peers, who were already similar in their substance use, was not taken into account. They confirmed that influence and selection were of equal importance. This point has been taken up by recent researchers and is discussed below.

When dyadic data were used to examine similarity in the substance use of the teenagers and their peers in this study, the findings confirmed that teenagers were likely to be similar to their peers in their ever use of cigarettes ($p < 0.042$), and in their current use of cigarettes ($p < 0.0001$), alcohol ($p < 0.012$) and drugs ($p < 0.036$). Thus, teenagers were more likely to use these substances when their peers did. These findings, based on cross-sectional data, could not confirm influence over time. The findings, nevertheless, confirmed associations found by Dembo, Schmeidler and Burgos (1982: 376), Brook, Whiteman and Gordon (1983: 276; 1982: 1160) and Jessor and Jessor (1978: 69) for drug use, Grube and Morgan (1986: 77, 104, 126) for cigarettes, alcohol and drugs, and Akers et al. (1979: 638) for alcohol and drug use. There was some variation across the substances as Kandel (1978a: 24) had also found, since there was no association in this study between the teenagers and their peers for ever alcohol and ever drug use.

Kandel and her colleagues had reported that the level of closeness between teenagers and their peers affected their susceptibility to peer influence in drug use. They reported that closeness to peers and extensive involvement with them in activities preceded initiation to marijuana (Kandel, Kessler and Margulies, 1978: 82, 87, 88; Kandel, 1978a: 25; 1980: 270) but it was one relationship, which was not close, to a school friend who used the drug, which preceded the teenager's use of illicit drugs other than marijuana (Kandel, Kessler and Margulies, 1978: 89, 90). In this study we combined the use of all drugs for our analyses because the rate of drug use was so low (16.9 per cent for ever use and 6.4 per cent for current use), current drug users used only marijuana or other opiates, and no person in this study had ever used heroin or cocaine, which are the main 'illicit drugs other than marijuana' in drug studies. Our findings confirmed that teenagers and their peers were more likely to be similar in their current drug use if they were close than not close. These findings, therefore, confirmed those of Kandel and her colleagues that closeness was associated with similarity in drug use. Our findings also confirmed that teenagers and their peers were more likely to be similar in their current alcohol use if they were close than not close. Closeness did not, however, affect similarity in current smoking.

Previous research has concluded that peer influence has occurred when similarity in the substance use of teenagers and their peers increased over time. While this conclusion may be well founded, we took the view that it would be better to ask teenagers to tell us who had provided them with the substances and with whom they had taken the substances. When the teenagers answered that their peers had been involved in either, or both, of these two ways, we took these replies as confirmation that peer influence had occurred. The findings given in Table 6.5, based on individual teenagers' replies, confirm that at their first use, and in their current use, of the respective substances, large proportions of the teenagers were influenced by their peers. At their first use, a large proportion of the teenagers were provided with their first cigarette and first drug by their peers, and a smaller proportion were provided with their first alcoholic drink by their peers. For each substance, even more of the teenagers took their first cigarette, their first alcoholic drink and their first drug with their peers. Thus, even if their peers had not provided the substance, the teenagers joined their peers for the use of the substance. When currently using the substances a large

Table 6.5 Teenagers' substance use by peer influence

	In company of peers				Provided by peers		
	No.	%	Total		No.	%	Total
First use				*First use*			
Cigarettes	131	83.5	157	Cigarettes	111	70.7	157
Alcohol	160	72.4	221	Alcohol	69	31.2	221
Drugs	40	88.9	45	Drugs	28	62.2	45
Current use				*Current use*			
Cigarettes	88	87.1	101	Cigarettes	26	25.7	101
Alcohol	130	97.0	134	Alcohol	47	35.1	134
Drugs	15	88.3	17	Drugs	10	58.8	17

proportion of the teenagers was provided with drugs by their peers, and a smaller proportion was provided with cigarettes and alcohol. Again, a much larger proportion of teenagers currently used each substance with their peers. Nearly all of the teenagers currently drank alcohol with their peers, very high proportions currently smoked cigarettes and currently used drugs with their peers.

The earlier work by other researchers drew attention to the import-ance of peer influence and to peer group influence, although peer groups were not examined directly in those studies. An increasing recogni-tion in the research community of the value of the social network perspective for examining peer groups led to research efforts to delin-eate peer groups and examine their role in teenagers becoming similar in their substance use.

Similarity in substance use in peer groups

In recent years researchers have examined the level of similarity in substance use in cliques and how this level of similarity can be explained. Hunter, Vizelberg and Berenson (1991: 101) found that similarity in smoking and alcohol use in the seven cliques studied was due to the direct and indirect influence of friends and to cliques forming around a preferred behaviour, which was mainly alcohol use (1991: 101). Thus, their findings suggest that peer influence and selection were at work in the similarity they observed in cliques. Ennett and Bauman (1994: 660) also confirmed that peer influence and selection were at work. They reported that peer influence and selection contributed equally to the similarity in smoking observed in the 80 cliques studied by them (Ennett and Bauman, 1994: 660). The findings of Pearson and Michell (2000: 33) confirmed that peer influence was also at work within the cliques studied because they found that most of the change in smoking and drug use occurred within the peer groups. They also reported that there were more peripherals to the risk-taking groups than to the non-risk-taking groups, suggesting that the groups may be a source of influence or selection to those peripherals at a later time point. Pearson and West (2003: 69) confirmed this in a later paper on a third wave in the longit-udinal analysis. They reported that there were changes in risk-taking, that is, cigarette and drug use, within the peer groups, confirming peer influence, and peripherals became members of the risk-taking groups, confirming selection. These findings support the earlier findings of Kandel (1978b: 436) for marijuana use and Cohen (1977: 239) for cigar-ette smoking and alcohol use, who confirmed that half of the similarity found in the substance use of teenagers was due to peer influence, while the other half was due to selection. Haynie (2001: 1048) examined the association between friends' delinquency and adolescents' delinquency with cross-sectional data, and found that the association was stronger when the adolescents were located in more central social positions in very cohesive networks and when the adolescents had been named by many others. She concluded that her findings were more consistent with a peer influence explanation, than a selection explanation, for the similarity in delinquency in the adolescents' peer networks. Urberg, Degirmencioglu and Tolson (1998: 703), on the other hand, concluded that selection may play a stronger role than influence in the similarity of peers, since the adolescents in their study were similar on numerous variables, including cigarette and alcohol use, before becoming friends.

The findings on similarity in substance use in the peer groups in this complete network are given in Table 6.6. These findings confirm that there are ever cigarette and ever alcohol users in most of the peer groups (30; 85.7 per cent and 34; 98.1 per cent respectively) and ever drug users in less than half of them (16; 45.7 per cent). There are current cigarette smokers in 20 (57.1 per cent), current alcohol drinkers in 30 (85.7 per cent) of them, and current drug users in just 8 (22.9 per cent) peer groups. If we are measuring similarity in these peer groups, however, a minimum of two teenagers must have used, or be currently using, the same substance in any particular peer group. Otherwise, no change in substance use has occurred which could be attributed to peer influence or selection. Peer groups with a minimum of two teenagers using each substance can be observed in Table 6.6. There are 21 (60 per cent) such peer groups for ever cigarette smoking, 31 (88.6 per cent) for ever alcohol use and just six (17.1 per cent) for ever drug use. Peer groups with at least two current users of the substance are much fewer, with 15 (42.9 per cent) for current cigarette smoking, 19 (54.3 per cent) for current alcohol and just 4 (11.4 per cent) for current drugs. Thus, there is some similarity among teenagers in these peer groups in their substance use and similarity is much higher in many of the peer groups. Some peer groups have full similarity with all teenagers in the peer group having ever used the substance. For example, all ten teenagers in Peer Group 4 have ever used alcohol, and all four teenagers in Peer Group 9 have ever smoked cigarettes. Based on previous research, the assumption would be that the similarity observed was due partly to peer influence and partly to peer selection.

But these data are cross-sectional, so change in substance use within the peer groups cannot be attributed to peer influence or selection based

Table 6.6 Peer groups by size and number of teenagers using substances

Peer Group Id. No.	Size of group No. of teens	Teens' ever use			Teens' current use		
		Cigarettes No.	Alcohol No.	Drugs No.	Cigarettes No.	Alcohol No.	Drugs No.
1	26	14	22	7	6	15	3
2	22	12	19	1	8	10	1
3	21	13	15	4	7	8	0
4	10	9	10	5	8	6	3
5	7	2	6	0	0	3	0
6	7	4	6	2	4	5	1
7	7	2	4	1	1	1	0
8	4	1	3	1	0	2	0
9	4	4	3	0	2	1	0
10	3	1	2	1	0	1	0
11	3	2	3	1	1	2	0
12	3	3	3	1	3	2	0
13	3	2	2	0	0	1	0
14	3	1	3	0	0	0	0
15	3	1	3	0	0	2	0
16	3	2	2	0	0	2	0
17	3	3	3	2	3	3	2
18	3	2	3	0	1	1	0
19	2	2	2	0	2	2	0
20	2	1	1	0	0	1	0
21	2	1	2	0	0	0	0
22	2	0	2	0	0	1	0
23	2	1	2	0	1	1	0
24	2	2	2	1	2	1	0
25	2	0	1	0	0	1	0
26	2	1	1	0	0	0	0
27	2	2	2	0	2	2	0
28	2	0	0	0	0	0	0
29	2	0	2	1	0	2	0
30	2	2	2	2	2	2	2
31	2	2	2	0	2	1	0
32	2	0	2	0	0	0	0
33	2	2	2	0	2	2	0
34	2	1	2	1	1	2	1
35	2	2	2	1	2	2	1
Totals	169[a]	97	141	32	60	85	14
Percentage in peer groups		57.4	83.4	18.9	35.5	50.3	8.3

[a] Information on substance use was not available for one teenager.

on these data alone. What we can say is that it is only in the peer groups, in which substance use has occurred (ever use) or is currently occurring (current use) that peer influence in this complete network could occur. This is because weak components include every teenager who is connected through peer ties by paths of whatever distance. If there is no one in the peer group using the substance (ever or current), there is no source of peer influence in the peer group at this time. Unless relationships change, this situation does not change.

But these data are valuable for many reasons and can be examined further. Our results from dyadic peer ties have confirmed that teenagers were more likely to have ever smoked cigarettes and to be current users of cigarettes, alcohol and drugs if their peers were users. Our results on social position have confirmed that social position per se is unrelated to whether teenagers ever or currently use any of the substances. What is important to examine is the social position of the teenagers in peer groups in relation to other substance users. If the teenagers are members of peer groups with substance-using members, there is a source of peer influence there, but, even then, if teenagers do not have direct peer ties with those who are substance users, they are not likely to be influenced. Thus, their social position in relation to substance users in the peer group affects whether or not they are likely to be influenced. If they are members of peer groups with no substance-using members, there is no source of peer influence there.

Thus, what is important to examine is the substance use of the teenagers in the context of the peer groups in which they are embedded. Although the data on the complete network are cross-sectional, retrospective data were collected on the timing of the formation of peer ties and the timing of the first use of each substance by the teenagers. These data on timing can be used to examine the increasing similarity in substance use in peer groups and the relative impact of peer influence and selection on similarity. This question is examined in the next chapter using retrospective data for three different peer groups.

Conclusion

The selection of peers and the formation of peer groups and the complete network in this study were explained at the beginning of this chapter. Using the complete network data, rather than clique data as other researchers had done, this study found no association between the social position of teenagers among their peers and their ever or current use of any of the three substances. Social position was defined in this study as being a member of a peer group of any size, or being an isolate, with no peers in the population. This finding is contrary to much recent research, which was not based on complete network data, and defined social position somewhat differently, as being a member of a clique, a liaison or an isolate. Cliques and liaisons together would be comparable to a peer group in our study, but isolates were defined differently, as many isolates in other studies had friends. This study's findings did not support those of a number of researchers who found that isolates were more likely than clique members or liaisons to be current smokers (Ennett and Bauman, 1993: 231; Fang et al., 2003: 262), or Abel, Plumridge and Graham's (2002: 336), who found that loners, that is, those who were least well connected, were those least likely to smoke. Our findings were similar to those of Pearson and Michell (2000: 27), who found no association between social position and smoking and drug taking among 12–13-year-olds; but found small differences one year later with relative isolates being more likely than those in other social positions to smoke cigarettes ($p < 0.08$) and to take drugs ($p < 0.07$). This size of difference ($p > 0.05$) would have been accepted as not significant in most other studies and in mine.

This study's findings, based on dyadic data on teenagers and their peers, have confirmed that teenagers and their peers are likely to be similar in their ever use of cigarettes and in their current use of cigarettes, alcohol and drugs. These findings support those of numerous other researchers (Jessor and Jessor, 1978: 69; Kandel, 1978a: 24; Brook, Whiteman and Gordon, 1982: 1160; 1983: 276; Dembo, Schmeidler and Burgos, 1982: 376) for drug use, Grube and Morgan (1986: 77, 104, 126) for cigarettes, alcohol and drugs, and Akers et al. (1979: 638) for alcohol and drug use. This study's findings also confirmed that similarity in current drug use is more likely when the teenagers are close to their peers, supporting similar findings of Kandel and her associates (Kandel, Kessler and Margulies, 1978: 82, 87, 88; Kandel, 1978a: 25; 1980: 270).

This study has used complete network data to measure similarity in the use of the three substances in dyads, and in peer groups much larger, and sometimes much smaller, than cliques. The results have confirmed that similarity (at least two using the same substance) had occurred in numerous peer groups for ever use of cigarettes, alcohol and drugs, and in much fewer peer groups, for current use of cigarettes, alcohol and drugs. Similarity in substance use has been measured in other studies in dyads or in small cliques of teenagers. These studies usually focussed on just one substance, cigarettes, sometimes on two substances, but not on all three. This study's results support those of others that there is increasing similarity in the substance use of teenagers in cliques. Hunter, Vizelberg and Berenson (1991: 101) reported similarity in cigarette and alcohol use in cliques, while Ennett and Bauman (1994: 660) and Fang et al. (2003: 262) reported similarity in cigarette use in cliques.

When data on a complete network are used, peer groups can vary greatly in size, as they do in this study, making statistical comparisons difficult. But the real value of these data is to facilitate the examination of the teenagers' individual behaviour in the context of the peer groups in which they are embedded. Three examples of peer groups are used in Chapter 7 to demonstrate the value of combining the teenagers' individual attribute data (on gender, age, substance use, timing of peer selection and peer influence, and teenagers' reports of peer influence) with dyadic and peer group data to try to unravel the complex process of peer influence and selection at work in the increasing similarity of teenagers in their substance use. This process is examined further in Chapter 8, in which multilevel analyses are conducted on the three largest peer groups, to examine the chain reaction process.

7

Peer Influence and Selection in Peer Groups

Introduction

The findings given in Chapter 6 were based on cross-sectional, complete network data, so changes in the teenagers' substance use within their peer groups could not be attributed to peer influence or selection based on these data alone. But retrospective data were also collected on the timing of the formation of peer ties and the timing of the first use of each substance by the teenagers. These data are valuable in understanding the process of peer selection and peer influence which occurs among teenagers in their substance use. The retrospective data on timing are added in this chapter to illustrate the increasing similarity in substance use among teenagers in the peer groups in which they are embedded, and to examine the relative impact of peer influence and selection on their growing similarity.

The findings of this study have confirmed that social position per se was not associated with the teenagers' ever or current use of any of the three substances (Chapter 6). That is, whether the teenagers were in peer groups or were isolates, was unrelated to their substance use. These findings did not support those of Ennett and Bauman (1993: 231), who had found that isolates were most likely to have been current cigarette smokers, or Fang et al. (2003: 262), who found that isolates, in most of the school children they had studied, were most likely to have smoked cigarettes. Neither do they support Abel, Plumridge and Graham (2002: 336), who found the opposite: that loners, those least well connected, were least likely to have smoked cigarettes. They come closest to the findings of Pearson and Michell (2000: 27), who found no association between social position and smoking and drug taking among 12–13-year-olds and found a small, but not significant, association one year later for cigarettes ($p < 0.08$) and for drugs ($p < 0.07$), with isolates being more likely to be the users. But none of those analyses took into account the substance use of the peers with whom the teenagers were connected, or, in the case of the isolates, not connected.

So there is a need to find out what is happening in peer groups that results in more similarity in substance use among members, or no changes in similarity among members. Researchers who have examined similarity in substance use among members of peer groups have, to date, concentrated on small cliques. Their results have confirmed that similarity in substance use did arise in cliques and they attributed the growing similarity to peer selection or peer influence. This association was confirmed for cigarette use by Ennett and Bauman (1994: 660), Hunter, Vizelberg and Berenson (1991: 101), Cohen (1977: 239), Pearson and Michell (2000: 33) and Pearson and West (2003: 69); for alcohol use by Hunter, Vizelberg and Berenson (1991: 101) and Cohen (1977: 239); and for drug use by Pearson and Michell (2000: 33), Pearson and West (2003: 69) and Kandel (1978b: 436). In previous research, similarity was assumed to be due to selection if the teenagers were already similar in their use of a particular substance before they formed the peer tie, and similarity was assumed to be due to peer influence if teenagers became similar in their use of a substance after the peer tie was formed. The findings presented in this chapter confirm whether, or not, similarity in substance use occurred in the selected peer groups and whether that similarity could be attributed to peer selection or peer influence as previous researchers had suggested.

I will examine first some findings, presented previously in Kirke (1995), to demonstrate the growing similarity in drug use over time in one all-male peer group (Peer Group 4) and the evidence available to support the role of peer selection and peer influence on their growing similarity. This is followed by an examination of the similarity in the use of all three substances in two small peer groups, one all male (Peer Group 8) and one all female (Peer Group 9), and the evidence supporting the role of peer selection and peer influence in them.

Peer Group 4

Ideally, longitudinal data are needed to demonstrate the process of peer selection and change in peer group development and their connection with the growing similarity in drug use in peer groups. Such data are not available, but retrospective data are, dating back to the teenagers' early childhood. These retrospective data are used in this chapter to examine the question of peer selection and influence and their role in the teenagers' growing similarity in their drug use. When interviews were conducted in this study, teenagers were asked to state when (that is, month and year) they had formed each of the peer ties that they had at the time of interview and when they had first taken drugs. From these data it was possible to trace the formation and development of the peer groups from their inception, when the first peer tie was formed, to their structural composition in 1987, when the data were collected. Individual-level data relating to the timing of the teenagers' first drug use and the process through which drug influence had occurred were superimposed on these structural data. Selective findings for Peer Group 4, in which drug use had occurred and had apparently diffused to other members, are presented below as a case study in order to demonstrate how peer selection and peer influence contributed to the teenagers' drug use.

In this case study, the peer ties with people in the snowball sample are also included to give a more complete understanding of the network in which these boys were embedded. The peer group includes ten teenage males, who were interviewed in the population study, and six teenage males who were interviewed in the snowball sample. As explained earlier (Chapter 1), a five-digit identification number was used, with the first digit signifying the road number (0–9). In order to indicate that a teenager was interviewed in the snowball sample, the number 11 was entered in the space for the road number, resulting in a six-digit number for those in the snowball sample.

All 16 members of this peer group were teenagers of 15–19 years when interviewed in 1987. The 19-year-old (115761) was in the snowball sample and was, therefore, older than the 14–18-year-olds in the population study. Six of the 16 members (37.5 per cent) had taken drugs. Three (33851, 33961 and 43771) were current drug users and the other three (33971, 34191 and 115761) were previous users. The data presented trace the formation and development of this peer group over time and indicate when and how drugs were introduced to its members, resulting in growing similarity in their drug use.

Possible weaknesses of the data should be borne in mind. The first is that, while the analysis traces the historical formation and continuation of the peer ties that still existed in 1987, it does not trace all of the ties formed in each specific year which were subsequently broken. The second is that the teenagers who had taken drugs were not asked to name those who had given or sold the drugs to them, nor were they asked to name the people with whom they had taken drugs. They were, however, asked to state the relationship they had with these people and whether they were male or female. It is these data on relationship and gender, combined with the structural formation of the network at a particular time, which provide clues as to who had influenced whom into using drugs. This second weakness of the data may have resulted in the loss of data on the social context of drug influence, but it retained the strengths of having self-reported data from peers rather than perceived peer data, and retained the trust and rapport developed with the teenagers, thus ensuring the successful completion of the interviews in the community.

Data on the formation and development of the peer group and on the timing of the drug use of the teenagers are given in Figures 7.1–7.5. The direction of the peer ties is also taken into account as it allows for reciprocation in the peer ties to be demonstrated. The person at the head of the arrow has been named by the person at the tail of the arrow. When there is an arrow at the head and tail of the line, each person has mentioned the other and the peer tie is, therefore, reciprocated. The reader will note that many unreciprocated ties became reciprocated in subsequent years. Drug use is indicated in the figures by a 'd' beside the identification number in the year the teenagers started using drugs.

The first connections in this peer group were formed in 1970 when 34241 became friends with 43771 and 115761 (Figure 7.1). Note that these are unreciprocated ties at this time as neither 43771 nor 115761 had said that 34241 was their friend in 1970. New peer ties continued to be formed and just two of them were reciprocated over the years, so that by 1982 this network had 12 members (Figure 7.2). In 1982, a member of the peer group, 34191, who had joined in 1979, by naming 115761 as his friend, took drugs for the first time. The drugs, inhalants, had been given to him by members of his peer network. He had been given the drugs by his male friends, had taken the drugs with his male friends and

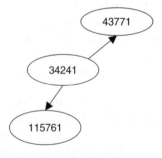

Figure 7.1   Peer Group 4: Peer ties in 1970.

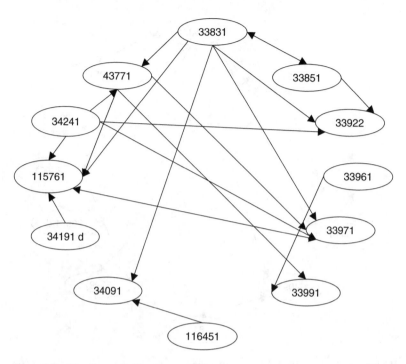

Figure 7.2 Peer Group 4: Peer ties in 1982.

said that he had used them because his friends in the neighbourhood were using drugs. Thus, he had been influenced, by the peers he had then, to use drugs. The friends who had influenced him do not appear in the peer group in 1982 because 34191 said that he had ceased being friends with them. From 1982, when this boy took drugs, the possibility of others, to whom he was directly connected, being influenced into using drugs existed.

During 1983 and 1984, new direct peer ties were formed between those previously indirectly connected (for example, 33961 and 33971) and previously unreciprocated ties were reciprocated (for example, 43771 and 33971). The result of these changes was that this peer group was becoming increasingly densely connected. Density in social network analysis refers to the ratio of the actual number of ties in the network to the number which would be present if all individuals were connected to all others (Scott, 1991: 74). The importance of the density of the network to similarity in the network is that drug use is more easily spread to others, through peer influence, when the network is more densely connected.

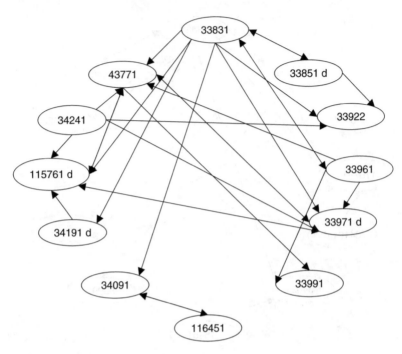

Figure 7.3   Peer Group 4: Peer ties in 1984.

In 1984 three teenagers, 33971, 115761 and 33851, took drugs for the first time (Figure 7.3). Their own replies indicate how they started to use drugs. Teenager number 33971 said that he had taken drugs because 'me friend had some'. That male friend had given him the drug, inhalants, and he had taken the drug in the company of that friend and other male friends. These findings confirm, therefore, that his peers had influenced him. He said that he was no longer friends with the person who had given him the drug, so that person was not in his peer group at the time of interview, but the other male friends may, or may not, have been in the peer group. Teenager number 115761 had bought the drug, marijuana, from a drug dealer who was not a friend then or later. He had taken the drug, however, in the company of his male friends, thus confirming that peer influence had occurred. Their peer ties in this peer group at that time (Figure 7.3) connected them to other drug users. Teenager number 33851 said that he had started taking drugs 'through friends'. It was not a friend, however, who had given him his first drug, marijuana. He had been given the drug by his 'friend's big brother' and had taken the drug with that person. Thus, peer influence had not occurred for this teenager, but indirect ties of his friends had facilitated his initiation into drugs. The structure of Peer Group 4, in 1984, confirms that this boy, 33851, had no direct peer connection with a drug user in this peer group at the time. The conclusion is that two of the three boys had been influenced by their peers. They had not been influenced by just one peer, however, as different people were involved in the supply and initiation into using the drug. The third teenager had not been influenced by peers but by a sibling of his peers.

Two members of the peer group stopped taking drugs in 1984. Teenager number 33971 started and stopped taking drugs during Easter 1984. On his second use of inhalants he had experienced a bad trip and had not used any drug since that time. Teenager number 34191 stopped taking drugs in December 1984 when he said that he had realised that it was 'stupid' using drugs. Their peer ties, it should be noted, were unaffected by their changed drug status. Both continued to be members of the peer group. This was a surprising finding as previous research had suggested that teenagers would break off their friendships, or change their drug use, to maximize similarity in their drug use (Kandel, 1978b: 433, 435).

In 1985, 43771 took drugs for the first time (Figure 7.4). His first drug was marijuana. He took it because his 'friends were taking it, I wanted to try it'. One of his male friends gave him the drug and he had taken it with a number of his male friends. He was still friends in 1987 with the person who gave him the drug and, since all of the friends he mentioned in 1987 were interviewed, the person who gave him the drug was one of the teenagers in this peer group. The structure of the peer group at the time linked him directly with two drug users (Figure 7.4). Thus, these findings confirm that peer influence had occurred and by peers in this peer group.

In 1986, four new peer ties were formed by 33851 (Figure 7.5). None was a drug user. No member of the peer group was initiated to drugs in 1986, but in 1987, 33961, took drugs for the first time. He started drugs because he was fed up and 'needed something to do'. He was given the drugs, marijuana and inhalants, by a male friend and had taken the drugs with his male friends. Peer influence had, therefore, occurred. Since he had taken the drugs for the first time in 1987 and the interview had been conducted in the same year, it can be assumed that his friendships had remained the same between the time he had first taken drugs in February 1987 and the time he had been interviewed in November 1987. Six of his seven male friends had been interviewed and

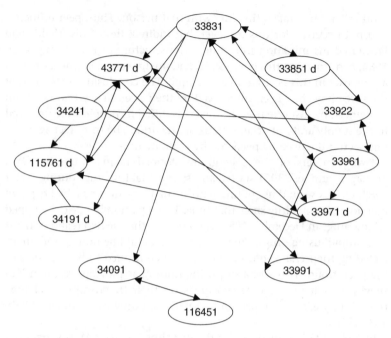

Figure 7.4   Peer Group 4: Peer ties in 1985.

were in this peer group. This information suggests that the male friends with whom he had first taken drugs were in this peer group. Since one of the seven friends had not been interviewed, the person who had given him the drug may or may not have been in the peer group when interviews took place. Since, however, three of his friends (33851, 43771 and 115761) who were in the peer group were current drug users at the time he was initiated into drugs, it seems quite likely that one of them may have given him the drug. One drug user stopped taking drugs in 1987. Teenager number 115761, who had started taking drugs during 1984, stopped taking drugs in May 1987. His reason for stopping taking drugs was related to a bad drug experience as a result of which he had 'ended up in hospital'.

These findings confirm that peer influence had resulted in the drug use of five of the six boys who had used drugs in this peer group. For two of the boys at least, peer influence appeared to have come from other boys in this peer group. For the others, peer influence may have come from within, or outside, the peer group. The data also demonstrate that peer influence is not a one-way process from peers to teenagers.

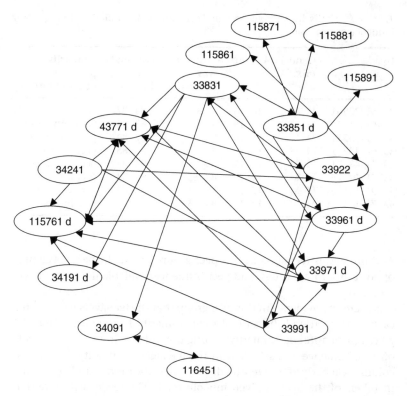

Figure 7.5 Peer Group 4: Peer ties in 1987.

The teenagers studied are peers to each other. Thus, a teenager may be influenced by peers at one point in time, and, at a later point in time, that teenager becomes the peer who influences other teenagers. The relationships between the teenagers do not seem to be based on a power base, in which there are some dominant teenagers influencing others, but on mutual trust, respect and tolerance of difference. The slowness of the drug diffusion process in this peer group, as well as in others examined in this study, suggests that there was no overt effort on the part of drug users to influence others to use drugs. The findings suggest that if teenagers wished to use drugs their drug-using peers would facilitate the process. Tolerance of difference in drug use was higher than expected. Some teenagers had peer ties with each other for years without ever becoming similar in their drug use. When teenagers, who had tried drugs, later stopped, the friendships with other drug users continued.

Table 7.1 Similarity in drug use in Peer Group 4: similarity through peer influence or selection

Dyad	Gender mix	Age mix	Year peer was selected	Year first used drugs	Similarity: peer influence or selection?
33851–33961	M M	16 15	– 87	84 87	Selection possibly
33961–115761	M M	15 19	– 87	87 84	Selection possibly
33961–33971	M M	15 16	83 –	87 84	peer influence
33961–43771	M M	15 17	83 –	87 85	peer influence
33971–43771	M M	16 17	83 77	84 85	peer influence
33971–115761	M M	16 19	83 83	84 84	peer influence
34191–115761	M M	17 19	79 –	82 84	peer influence
43771–115761	M M	17 19	83 83	85 84	peer influence

And numerous teenagers in this peer group, in which there was ample opportunity to use drugs, and peer influence available if wanted, never took drugs.

Is there any evidence in this peer group that the teenagers had selected each other as friends because of their similarity in drug use? Table 7.1 gives information on similarity in drug use in Peer Group 4 and the role of peer influence and selection in the teenagers' similarity. In the first column each dyad is identified. The identification numbers of the members of the dyad is given in Column 1. The reader will note that most of the boys lived on the same road (3) and that some of them lived very near each other. For example, families 396 and 397 (33961 and 33971) lived next door to one another. The second and third columns give the gender and age mix of the teenagers. The year the teenagers said they had selected each other as peers is given in Column 4 (87 means 1987). When there is a difference in the year given by the two teenagers, the first year is taken as the year the peer tie was first formed. The year the teenagers first used each substance is given in Column 5. The final column indicates whether the teenagers' similarity in their drug use was due to the selection of peers who were already similar in their drug use, or to peer influence after the selection of peers.

The results suggest that, in two dyads in Peer Group 4, similarity in the teenagers' drug use was possibly due to peer selection. In the first two dyads listed (33851–33961; 33961–115761), one teenager had taken drugs before the friendship was formed and the formation of the friendship occurred in the same year as the second teenager used drugs. Although similarity was possibly due to selection, the teenagers' own replies confirmed, however, that peer influence had also occurred for 33961 and 115761, but not for 33851. In none of the other six dyads between drug users was similarity due to selection. The friendship was formed before the drug use of either teenager in each of the dyads and each of them later used drugs. The teenagers in each of these dyads confirmed, during their interviews, that peer influence had occurred during their initiation to drugs.

These findings confirm that there was growing similarity in drug use in this peer group as the peer group developed and changed in structure over time. Peer influence explained the growing similarity in drug use for five of the teenagers. Peer influence came from peers within this peer group for four of the teenagers and from outside the peer group for the fifth (34191). The sixth teenager, 33851, had not experienced peer influence, nor was his similarity due to selection. Similarity may have been due to selection in the first two dyads listed, as 33961 had formed peer ties with 33851 and with 115761 (two drug users) in the same year as he had taken drugs for the first time. He confirmed in his interview, however, that peer influence had also occurred. Thus, the level of similarity in the peer group at the time of interview was explained by peer influence alone by teenagers within, or outside, this peer group for four of the six drug users, by peer selection and peer influence for one, 33961, and to neither peer selection nor peer influence for one of the teenagers, 33851.

Findings presented in Chapter 6 confirmed that, although much fewer teenagers would use drugs than cigarettes or alcohol, peer influence at initiation into substance use was most likely for drugs (Table 6.5). I will examine below whether similarity was likely to arise in the use of the three substances in two smaller peer groups, and whether the similarity could be attributed to peer selection or peer influence.

Peer Groups 8 and 9

Similarity in the use of all three substances is examined in Peer Groups 8 and 9 and the role of peer selection and peer influence is examined for all three substances. The first example is a small group of teenage boys, all of whom are aged either 14 or 15 (Peer Group 8). They were connected into one triad of all reciprocated ties, that is, the first three dyads listed, with one unreciprocated tie from 80411 to 80901 (Figure 7.6). The teenagers' substance use is indicated by 'c' for cigarette use, 'a' for alcohol use and 'd' for drug use beside their identification number. If the reader compares the year the peer was selected (Column 4) (Table 7.2) with the

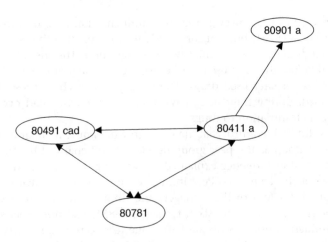

Figure 7.6   Peer Group 8: Pattern of peer ties.

year of first use of the substance (Column 5), the reader will note that each peer selection occurred before one, or both, of the teenagers had used the respective substances. Thus, the selection of peers was not based on substance use and the increasing similarity in substance use in this peer group was not attributable to peer selection for any of the dyads. Selection of their peers had occurred before either teenager in the dyad had taken any of the three substances (Column 6). Information in Column 6 also indicated that increasing similarity occurred in only two dyads (80411–80491 and 80411–80901) and both were for alcohol. Thus, peer influence apparently occurred in these dyads for alcohol use, if we assume, as other researchers have done, that the first person to use alcohol influenced the second person to use. The second person to use in both dyads is 80411. Although other researchers have assumed that peer influence has occurred under such circumstances, we did not assume peer influence had occurred. Instead, we asked the teenagers to tell us who had given them their first substance and with whom they had taken the substance. When 80411 had been asked these questions, he said that he had taken his first alcoholic drink with his family and relatives, and did not indicate which of them had given him the alcoholic drink. Thus, although peer influence by two different teenagers had apparently occurred for 80411's first alcohol use, no peer influence had occurred. The conclusion for this peer group, therefore, is that peer selection had occurred before their substance use for every dyad; only in two dyads did similarity occur, and when it did, it was not due to either peer selection or peer influence.

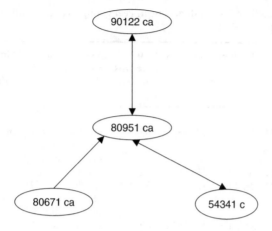

Figure 7.7 Peer Group 9: Pattern of peer ties.

The second example is a small peer group of teenage girls, aged from 16 to 18 years (Peer Group 9) (Figure 7.7). Three of the teenagers were connected to 80951 but not to each other. Two of the peer ties were reciprocated, and one was not (80951–80671). The teenagers' substance use is indicated by 'c' for cigarette use, 'a' for alcohol use and 'd' for drug use beside their identification number. The reader will note that, in this peer group too, the peer selection had occurred before one, or both, of the teenagers in the dyads had first used the respective substances (Columns 5 and 6) (Table 7.2). Thus, the selection was not based on substance use, and the increasing similarity in substance use was not attributable to peer selection in any of the dyads. Similarity in cigarette use and in alcohol use had occurred, nevertheless, and it appeared to be due to peer influence in three dyads for cigarette smoking and in two dyads for alcohol use. The second person to have smoked cigarettes in each of the three dyads was 80951. This would suggest that she had been influenced by three peers when she first smoked cigarettes. When asked who had given her the first cigarette she had smoked and with whom she had first smoked cigarettes, 80951 said that she had got her first cigarette herself and had smoked it alone. Thus, although peer influence appeared to have occurred for 80951's initiation to cigarettes, no peer influence had occurred.

Peer influence is assumed to have occurred for their first alcohol use, for 80951 and 80671 (both in 1986), and for 80951 and 90122 (both in 1986), because similarity in their alcohol use occurred after their

Table 7.2   Similarity in substance use in Peer Groups 8 and 9: Similarity through peer influence or selection

Dyad	Gender mix	Age mix	Year peer was selected	Year first used substance		Similarity: peer influence or selection?
Peer Group 8						
80491–80781	M M	14 15	87 81	cig. 84	no cig.	no similarity
				alc. 85	no alc.	no similarity
				drg. 85	no drg.	no similarity
80781–80411	M M	15 15	81 77	no alc.	alc. 87	no similarity
80411–80491	M M	15 14	82 82	no cig.	cig. 84	no similarity
				alc. 87	alc. 85	peer influence
				no drg.	drg. 85	no similarity
80411–80901	M M	15 15	82	alc. 87	alc. 86	peer influence
Peer Group 9						
80951–54341	F F	18 16	82 85	cig. 85	cig. 83	peer influence
				alc. 86	no alc.	no similarity
80951–80671	F F	18 17	83	cig. 85	cig. 84	peer influence
				alc. 86	alc. 86	peer influence
80951–90122	F F	18 17	74 83	cig. 85	cig. 79	peer influence
				alc. 86	alc. 86	peer influence

selection into the peer group. Their own replies support this assumption. All three teenagers said that they had taken their first alcoholic drink with friends. Two (80951 and 80671) said that they had bought the drink themselves and the third teenager (90122) said that she did not know who gave it to her. Thus, peer influence is confirmed for these three teenagers. Since we did not ask teenagers to identify the friends who had influenced them, the friends mentioned may, or may not, have been those identified in this peer group. Since these teenagers were among their friends at the time of their first use, they are likely to have been among the friends mentioned. Whether they were those friends or not, peer influence is confirmed, because they stated that they had taken their first alcoholic drink with friends.

Conclusion

Previous research has attributed the increasing similarity in substance use among teenagers in dyads or in cliques to either peer influence or selection (Cohen, 1977: 239; Kandel, 1978b: 436; Hunter, Vizelberg and Berenson, 1991: 101; Ennett and Bauman, 1994: 660; Pearson and West,

2003: 69). The conclusion by many researchers is that peer influence and selection contribute equally to similarity (Cohen, 1977: 239; Kandel, 1978b: 436; Hunter, Vizelberg and Berenson, 1991: 101; Ennett and Bauman, 1994: 660), while others suggest that selection seems to be more important than influence (Urberg, Degirmencioglu and Tolson, 1998: 703). In these studies peer influence was assumed to have occurred when one teenager used a particular substance later than their peer had done. In this study, on the other hand, two indicators of peer influence were used. These were whether peers had provided the substance and whether the teenagers had taken the substance in the company of their peers.

The findings discussed in this chapter confirm that increasing similarity in the substance use of teenagers in peer groups does occur and that it may be due to peer selection or peer influence, to both, or sometimes to neither. Peer influence and selection had been involved in increasing similarity in the drug use of one of the teenagers (33961) with members of Peer Group 4, peer influence only had been involved for four of the teenagers who had used drugs (33971, 34191, 43771 and 115761), and neither peer influence nor peer selection had been involved for the sixth teenager, 33851, who had used drugs in this peer group.

Peer selection had not been involved in increasing similarity for any of the teenagers in Peer Groups 8 and 9 for any of the three substances. Although peer influence had apparently occurred for alcohol use in Peer Group 8 and for cigarette use in Peer Group 9, the teenagers' replies confirmed that peer influence had not occurred. The increasing similarity was due to the influence of family and relatives for the alcohol use in Peer Group 8 and to the teenager's own actions for cigarette use in Peer Group 9. Peer influence was confirmed only for alcohol use in Peer Group 9, since all three teenagers confirmed that they had taken their first alcoholic drink with friends.

These findings support those which have suggested that increasing similarity in the substance use of teenagers is due to either peer influence or selection (Cohen, 1977: 239; Kandel, 1978b: 436; Hunter, Vizelberg and Berenson, 1991: 101; Ennett and Bauman, 1994: 660; Pearson and West, 2003: 69) but my findings have confirmed that selection, based on similarity in substance use, rarely explained the similarity. My findings have also confirmed that, even when peers became similar in their substance use over time, peer influence could not be assumed to have occurred. The teenagers' replies sometimes confirmed that peer influence had occurred (drugs, Peer Group 4; alcohol, Peer Group 9) and sometimes confirmed that people other than peers were those who had influenced (alcohol, Peer Group 8), and other times that no one had influenced (cigarettes, Peer Group 9). But, unlike other researchers, my findings have also indicated that sometimes both peer influence and selection are involved, and sometimes neither peer influence nor selection is involved.

These findings do not, therefore, support previous researchers' conclusions that, when teenagers become similar in their substance use, peer influence can automatically be assumed to have occurred. Sometimes, peers other than those who are similar will have influenced, and sometimes, people other than peers will have influenced, and other times, no one will have influenced. There was very little support for the conclusions of previous researchers that teenagers select each other as friends because they are similar in their use of a particular substance. Their peers were obviously selected for reasons other than substance use. Whether increasing similarity occurs in larger peer groups, and to what extent that similarity can be attributed to peer selection and peer influence, requires further exploration. These questions are examined in Chapter 8 using multilevel analyses and retrospective data. The purpose of the chapter is to explore whether similarity occurs, and when it does, whether peer selection or peer influence explain the similarity *between those who are similar,* and whether the structure, or patterning, of the peer ties in the peer group explain some of the similarity.

8
Chain Reactions in Teenagers' Substance Use

Introduction

Previous research has attributed the increasing similarity in substance use among teenagers in dyads or in cliques to either peer influence or selection (Cohen, 1977: 239; Kandel, 1978b: 436; Hunter, Vizelberg and Berenson, 1991: 101; Ennett and Bauman, 1994: 660; Bauman and Ennett, 1996: 187; Pearson and West, 2003: 69). The conclusion by many researchers is that peer influence and selection contribute equally to similarity (Cohen, 1977: 239; Kandel, 1978b: 436; Hunter, Vizelberg and Berenson, 1991: 101; Ennett and Bauman, 1994: 660), while others suggest that selection seems to be more important than influence (Urberg, Degirmencioglu and Tolson, 1998: 703).

But there has been some concern at the major inadequacies in the measurement of peer groups and peer influence, and researchers have highlighted the need to use social network analysis to identify peer groups directly and to examine individuals' drug use in the context of their peer groups (Bauman and Ennett, 1996: 191). There has been increasing recognition that the question of the relative impact of peer influence and selection cannot be adequately examined using small clique data and that complete network data are needed (Ennett and Bauman, 1993: 234; Haynie, 2001: 1023).

Findings presented in Chapter 7 called into question the conclusions reached in previous research that teenagers select each other as friends because they are similar in their use of a particular substance and that peer influence can be assumed to explain the increasing similarity between teenagers and their peers over time. My findings confirmed that increasing similarity in substance use did occur in the peer groups examined, that selection rarely explained the similarity, and that peer influence could not be assumed to have occurred when teenagers and their peers became similar in their use of the substances over time. The teenagers' replies sometimes confirmed that peer influence had occurred, sometimes that people other than peers were those who had influenced, and other times that no one had influenced. They also confirmed that sometimes peer influence and selection were involved, and sometimes neither peer selection nor influence were involved.

Two of the peer groups examined had four teenagers in each, about the size of the cliques in previous research. The question of the relative impact of peer influence and selection can be more adequately explored by examining larger peer groups taken from complete network data. The purpose of this chapter is to explore whether similarity occurs, and when it does, whether peer selection or peer influence explains the similarity *between those who are similar*, and whether the structure or patterning of the peer ties in the peer group explains some of the similarity. These questions are explored further in this chapter, drawing on results discussed in Kirke (2004). In order to place results for the case studies in context, findings are first presented for rates of substance use in the population of teenagers and in the case studies, similarity in substance use in dyads in the complete network, and peer influence in the population of teenagers.

Rates of substance use in population and in case studies

The rates of use of the three substances are given in Table 8.1 for the population of teenagers as a whole, for teenagers in all of the peer groups and for teenagers in Peer Groups 1, 2 and 3. Population rates vary between the substances, with rates of ever alcohol use (83.5 per cent) and current alcohol use (50.8 per cent) being higher that those for cigarettes and drugs. Rates of ever and current use of all three substances in all peer groups are very similar to those for the population as a whole. Rates of use vary between the three peer groups and between each of them and the population and all peer group rates. Nevertheless, rates of ever and current alcohol use remain higher than those for cigarette and drug use in all three peer groups.

Similarity in substance use in dyads in complete network

Similarity in substance use in the complete network of teenagers is explored in Table 8.2. These dyadic data are based on the peer ties among the teenagers in all of the peer groups in the complete network.

Table 8.1 Percentage of users of each substance in population, in all peer groups, and in Peer Groups 1, 2 and 3

	Population (%)	All peer groups (%)	Peer Group 1 (%)	Peer Group 2 (%)	Peer Group 3 (%)
Ever use					
Cigarettes	59.0	57.4	53.9	54.5	61.9
Alcohol	83.5	83.4	84.6	86.4	71.4
Drugs	16.9	18.9	26.9	4.6	19.0
Current use					
Cigarettes	38.3	35.5	23.1	36.4	33.3
Alcohol	50.8	50.3	57.7	45.5	38.1
Drugs	6.4	8.3	11.5	4.6	0
N	266	169	26	22	21

Table 8.2 Similarity in substance use in dyads/peer ties in all peer groups in the complete network

	Similar: Both users (%)	Dissimilar: One user (%)	Similar: No user (%)	No. of dyads	Significance
Ever use					
Cigarettes	42.1	41.0	16.9	278	$p < 0.03$
Alcohol	74.5	23.3	2.2	278	NS
Drugs	7.4	30.8	61.8	272	$p < 0.04$
Current use					
Cigarettes	25.2	25.5	49.3	278	$p < 0.001$
Alcohol	30.6	42.1	27.3	278	$p < 0.009$
Drugs	2.6	16.5	80.9	272	$p < 0.02$

Significant associations were found for ever cigarette and ever drug use, and for current cigarette, alcohol and drug use. These findings confirm that teenagers and their peers are likely to be similar in their use of these substances. The strength of the association was very weak except for current cigarette use. In Table 8.2, similarity based on both being users is distinguished from similarity based on neither being a user. It is those who are similar in their use of the substance who are of most interest in this analysis, because it is in these dyads that peer influence or selection might have occurred.

Peer influence in the population of teenagers

Peer influence has been discussed in Chapters 6 and 7 and is examined further in this chapter. Traditionally, researchers have assumed that peer influence has occurred within the peer tie if teenagers have changed their behaviour and become similar to their peers in their substance use. In this study, peer influence was not assumed under such circumstances. Instead, two indices of peer influence were used: whether the teenagers had been in the company of their peers and whether the teenagers had been provided with the substance by their peers. These indices are used for their first use and their current use of the respective substances. If their peers were involved in either way, or both ways, it was accepted that their peers had influenced. The findings from individual teenagers' replies have confirmed that peer influence had occurred for a large proportion of the teenagers in this study (Chapter 6; Table 6.5). Influence was more likely to have taken the form of being in the company of peers, however, than being provided with the substances by their peers for the teenagers' first and current use of each substance. Surprisingly, those who provided the substance and those with whom the teenager used the substance were frequently different people.

Rates of substance use, similarity in dyads and whether individual teenagers had experienced peer influence have been discussed above. These data cannot reveal, however, whether those who were similar had experienced peer influence from each other, whether they were similar due to selection of peers who had already taken the substance or to a peer group effect. These questions are examined in the three case studies.

Case studies of peer groups

Three case studies of the largest peer groups in the complete network are examined. The social network methods used to collect these data have already been explained (Chapter 3). These peer groups include all of the teenagers and their peers who are connected to each other through peer ties by paths of any distance. They combine each teenager's egocentric network of peers and all of the interlocks between those egocentric network members. These three peer groups have been selected because they have the largest number of teenagers in them, a mix of substance users and non-users, and, due to their size, the most complex patterning of peer ties. These peer groups, therefore, surpass the dyad or clique in terms of size and the complexity of the patterning of peer ties within them.

These case studies are used to examine three questions:

1. Whether there is any direct evidence in the teenagers' peer groups of similarity in their substance use and whether there is evidence of peer influence having occurred between those who are similar.
2. The relative impact of peer influence and selection on similarity in the substance use of the teenagers and their peers in the peer groups.
3. The contribution of the peer group to similarity in the substance use of teenagers and their peers.

In these case studies three levels of data are combined to examine these questions. Social network data are used to present graphically the patterning of the peer ties in each peer group, and individual-level data on the teenagers' use of the three substances are combined with the social network data in order to identify the location of the substance users in the peer groups. This process results in the identification of numerous chains of substance users in the peer groups, with dyads forming the links of the chains. These chains represent the teenagers who are similar in their substance use in each peer group. In the case studies a five-digit identification number is used for the teenagers (Chapter 1).

In order to examine the questions of peer influence, peer selection and the contribution of the peer group to similarity in the substance use of the teenagers, data on each link of the chains identified are presented in Tables 8.3–8.5. These tables combine dyadic data on each link of the chains (Column 1) with individual-level data on each teenager's gender (Column 2), age (Column 3), year peer tie was formed (Column 4), year of first use of the substance (Column 5), whether peer tie preceded first use (Column 6), whether peer influence had occurred at first use (Column 7), whether the teenagers were current users (Column 8) and whether peer influence occurred currently (Column 9).

Peer Group 1

Peer Group 1 is the largest network with 26 teenagers. The gender ratio is 17 males:9 females. Their ages range from 14 to 18 years, with a mean age of 16.2 years. The rates of use of the three substances have been given in Table 8.1. These confirm that 84.6 per cent of the teenagers in this peer group had ever used alcohol, while 53.9 per cent had ever smoked cigarettes and 26.9 per cent had ever used drugs. Fewer teenagers were current users of each substance. The extent to which there is similarity in the substance use of the teenagers, the relative impact of

Table 8.3 Peer Group 1: Substance use chains

Peer tie/link	Gender mix		Age mix		Year peer tie formed		Year first use		Peer tie < first use	Peer influence first use	Current use	Peer influence current
Chain 1: Cigarettes												
05502–15031	M	M	17	16	84		81	81	no	(pp)		
15031–15241	M	M	16	16	83		81	80	no	(pp)		
15031–14913	M	M	16	16	83	84	81	81	no	(pp)		
14913–15241	M	M	16	16	77	77	81	80	yes	pp		
15241–15211	M	M	16	15	84		80	83	no	(pp)		
14913–15211	M	M	16	15	72	77	81	83	yes	pp		
15211–15141	M	F	15	18	72		83	79	yes	p–	cc	–p
15141–62701	F	F	18	18	73	73	79	82	yes	–p	cc	pp
15141–14941	F	F	18	16	70	73	79	85	yes			
Chain 2: Cigarettes												
15122–15112	M	M	18	15	82		87	78	yes	pp	cc	pp
15112–15321	M	M	15	15	80		78	79	no	(pp)		
15321–05501	M	M	15	17	72	84	79	79	yes	pp		
15321–54491	M	M	15	18	72	84	79	79	yes	pp		
05501–54491	M	M	17	18	83	83	79	79	no	(pp)		
54491–54451	M	F	18	15	87		79	81	no	(pp)		
Chain 3: Alcohol												
15242–05502	M	M	17	17	81	82	86	84	yes	[–p]	cc	pp
15242–15031	M	M	17	16	80	83	86	85	yes	[–p]	cc	pp
15242–15271	M	M	17	18	80		86	87	yes	–p	cc	pp
05502–15031	M	M	17	16	84		84	85	yes	pp	cc	pp
15031–15271	M	M	16	18	83		85	87	yes	pp	cc	pp
15271–15241	M	M	18	16	80		87	84	yes	pp	cc	pp

ID												
15031–15241	M	M	16	16	83	84	85	84	yes	pp	cc	pp
15031–14913	M	M	16	16	83	77	85	85	yes	pp	cc	pp
14913–15241	M	M	16	16	77	77	85	84	yes	pp	cc	pp
14913–15211	M	M	16	15	72		85	83	yes	p⊢	cc	pp
15241–15211	M	M	16	15	84		84	83	yes	p⊢	cc	pp
15211–15141	M	F	15	18	72		83	81	yes			
15141–15131	F	F	18	18	68		81	84	yes	–p		
15131–15121	F	F	18	16	85		84	87	yes	pp		
15141–14941	F	F	18	16	70	73	81	82	yes			
15141–24832	F	F	18	18	73		81	87	yes	–p		
24832–24821	F	F	18	16	79	79	87	87	yes	pp	cc	pp
15141–62701	F	F	18	18	73	73	81	81	yes	–p		
Chain 4: Alcohol												
15122–15112	M	M	18	15	82		85	78	yes	pp	cc	–p
15112–15321	M	M	15	15	80		78	84	yes	pp		–p
15321–15111	M	M	15	15	72		84	86	yes	[p⊢]		pp
15321–05501	M	M	15	17	72	84	84	83	yes	pp	cc	pp
15321–54491	M	M	15	18	72	84	84	81	yes	pp	cc	pp
05501–54491	M	M	17	18	83	83	83	81	yes	pp	cc	pp
54491–54451	M	F	18	15	87		81	84	no	(pp)		
54451–54441	F	F	15	15	71	72	84	86	yes	pp		
Chain 5: Drugs												
05502–15031	M	M	17	16	84		86	86	yes	pp		
15031–15241	M	M	16	16	83		86	86	yes	pp		
Chain 6: Drugs												
15141–62701	F	F	18	18	73	73	85	83	yes	pp		
Chain 7: Drugs												
05501–54491	M	M	17	18	83	83	85	82	yes	pp	cc	pp

Table 8.4 Peer Group 2: Substance use chains

Peer tie/link	Gender mix		Age mix		Year peer tie formed		Year first use		Peer tie < first use	Peer influence first use	Current use	Peer influence current
Chain 8: Cigarettes												
80861–24582	M	F	17	17	87		80	84	no	(p–)		
24582–80551	F	F	17	16	87	87	84	85	no	(–p)		
80551–61381	F	F	16	15	83	84	85	NK	yes	pp	cc	pp
Chain 9: Cigarettes												
62551–80751	F	F	17	16	71		78	84	yes	pp	cc	pp
Chain 10: Cigarettes												
61291–61672	M	M	14	17	NK		85	82	NK	(pp)	cc	pp
61672–63301	M	M	17	17	85		82	83	no	(pp)	cc	pp
63301–62202	M	M	17	14	87		83	86	no	(pp)	cc	pp
62202–61672	M	M	14	17	80	81	86	82	yes	pp	cc	pp
62202–61331	M	F	14	16	80		86	85	yes	pp	cc	pp
Chain 11: Alcohol												
62702–80561	M	M	16	15	87		84	84	no	(pp)	cc	pp
80561–54282	M	M	15	15	72		84	85	yes	pp	cc	pp
80561–80861	M	M	15	17	72	80	84	86	yes	[p–]	cc	pp
80861–24582	M	F	17	17	87		86	85	no	(–p)	cc	pp
24582–80551	F	F	17	16	87	87	85	86	no	(p–)		
80551–24583	F	F	16	14	87	87	86	84	no	(–p)		

80551–61381	F	F	16	15	83	84	86	NK	yes	–NK
61381–43761	F	F	15	16	71	81	NK	87	yes	NKp
43761–62372	F	F	16	17	81		87	86	yes	pp
62372–62551	F	F	17	17	86		86	85	yes	p–
62551–80751	F	F	17	16	71		85	86	yes	–p
80861–80521	M	M	17	17	70	74	86	83	yes	[–p]	cc pp
24582–80521	F	M	17	17	87		85	83	no	(pp)	cc pp
80551–80521	F	M	16	17	86	86	86	83	yes	[–p]
80521–61672	M	M	17	17	83		83	84	yes	pp	cc pp
61672–63301	M	M	17	17	85		84	84	no	(pp)	cc pp
61672–61291	M	M	17	14	NK		84	86	NK	(pp)
63301–62202	M	M	17	14	87		84	86	no	(p–)
62202–61672	M	M	14	17	80	81	86	84	yes	[–p]
62202–61331	M	F	14	16	80		86	87	yes	
61331–61671	F	M	16	14	83		87	85	yes	[–p]
61671–62202	M	M	14	14	81		85	86	yes	[p–]
61671–61291	M	M	14	14	82	83	85	86	yes	pp

Table 8.5 Peer Group 3: Substance use chains

Peer tie/link	Gender mix		Age mix		Year peer tie formed		Year first use		Peer tie < first use	Peer influence first use	Current use	Peer influence current
Chain 12: Cigarettes												
43671–43581	M	M	17	18	75	75	82	81	yes	pp		
43581–43623	M	M	18	17	82		81	80	no	(p–)	cc	pp
43623–62522	M	M	17	17	77		80	84	yes	–p	cc	pp
43623–62523	M	M	17	18	87		80	83	no	(–p)	cc	pp
62523–61511	M	F	18	15	87	87	83	85	no	(pp)		
43581–43571	M	M	18	16	74		81	83	yes	pp		
43581–43791	M	M	18	18	82	84	81	82	yes	pp	cc	pp
43571–43623	M	M	16	17	82		83	80	yes	p–		
43571–43791	M	M	16	18	82	84	83	82	yes	pp		
43791–43623	M	M	18	17	82		82	80	yes	p–	cc	pp
43791–43582	M	F	18	16	74	82	82	84	yes	pp	cc	pp
43582–43591	F	F	16	17	74	75	84	82	yes	pp		
Chain 13: Alcohol												
54421–24822	F	F	15	15	76		87	85	yes	pp		
24822–43671	F	M	15	17	86	87	85	84	no	(pp)		
43671–43581	M	M	17	18	75	75	84	NK	yes	pp	cc	pp
43581–43791	M	M	18	18	82	85	NK	85	yes	pp	cc	pp
43581–43623	M	M	18	17	82		NK	81	NK	(pp)	cc	pp
43581–43571	M	M	18	16	74		NK	86	yes	pp		

									cc	pp
43791–43623	M	M	18	17	82		85	81	yes	pp
43791–43571	M	M	18	16	82	84	85	86	yes	pp
43571–43623	M	M	16	17	82		86	81	yes	pp
43623–62522	M	M	17	17	77		81	86	yes	[p–]
43623–62523	M	M	17	18	87		81	84	no	(pp)
62523–61511	M	F	18	15	87	87	84	85	no	(pp)
62523–61512	M	M	18	18	87	87	84	84	no	(p–)
62522–62091	M	F	17	15	85	85	86	76	yes	(p–)
62091–61511	F	F	15	15	87		76	85	no	(–p)
Chain 14: Alcohol										
71081–62291	F	F	16	17	86	86	84	86	yes	[p–]
Chain 15: Drugs										
24822–43671	F	M	15	17	86	87	87	85	yes	[–p]
43671–43581	M	M	17	18	75	75	85	85	yes	pp
43581–43791	M	M	18	18	82	85	85	85	yes	pp

peer influence and selection, and the contribution of the peer groups to similarity are examined in the following sections.

Similarity in Peer Group 1

The patterning of the peer ties, and the cigarette, alcohol and drug use of the teenagers in this peer group are given in Figures 8.1–8.3 respectively. The figures reveal that the patterning of the ties link the teenagers into two large, quite dense, clusters, which are linked by one teenager, 15092, who forms a cutpoint (see Glossary of Terms) between them. The remaining teenagers branch out in different directions from the two main clusters. The pattern formed is the result of selections made by individual teenagers of their peer ties. These selections result simultaneously in dyadic peer ties, the teenagers' egocentric peer networks and any interlocks formed between the egocentric networks to whom they are directly or indirectly tied.

When the substance use data for each of the teenagers are added to the social network data, the figures reveal two cigarette chains (Chains 1 and

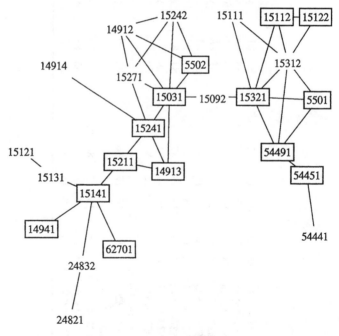

Figure 8.1 Peer Group 1: Cigarette use.

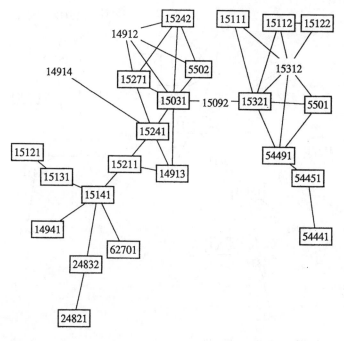

Figure 8.2 Peer Group 1: Alcohol use.

2; Figure 8.1), two alcohol chains (Chains 3 and 4; Figure 8.2) and three very short drug chains (Chains 5–7; Figure 8.3), which link up all of the substance users in the network (box surrounds identification number of substance users). These findings confirm that many teenagers adjacent to each other in the peer group are similar in their use of the respective substances. This is particularly so for alcohol since nearly all of the teenagers had taken alcohol. Whether the similarity of the teenagers is due to peer influence, selection or a peer group effect is explored in Table 8.3.

Peer influence at first substance use in Peer Group 1

Table 8.3 presents data on each peer tie/link in the seven chains of cigarette, alcohol and drug users in this network. The reader will note that chains usually linked teenagers of similar gender but frequently of different ages. In each peer tie/link, the teenagers were similar in their substance use. Column 4 gives the year that each teenager stated that the peer tie was formed and Column 5 gives the year that the teenagers said that they had first used the substance. Thus, peer influence

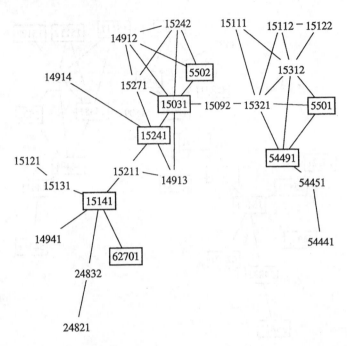

Figure 8.3   Peer Group 1: Drug use.

could have occurred between these peers if the peer tie had existed before the substance use of one or both teenagers ('yes' in Column 6) and that it *could not have occurred* between these peers if it had not ('no' in Column 6). The findings given in Column 7 indicate whether the teenagers in the peer tie/link said that their peers had influenced them (denoted by p, *p* or [p]).

In 42 of the 45 peer ties/links (93.3 per cent) (listed in Chains 1–7) peer influence had occurred. Peer influence had not, however, always been between the peers who were similar. In 31 links (68.9 per cent) peer influence had been between the peers who were similar in the chains (p or pp). In all of these links the peer tie had preceded the substance use of the teenagers (yes in Column 6). Their similarity is, therefore, explained by peer influence *between the peers who are similar* in the chains.

In eight peer ties/links (17.8 per cent) peer influence could not have been between the peers who were similar because the peer ties had been formed between them after the first substance use of both of them (no in Column 6; *pp* in Column 7). Their similarity is, therefore, explained by selection whereby teenagers, who were already similar in their substance use, selected each other as peers. All of the teenagers in these links had, nevertheless, been influenced by their peers but *not by the peers to whom they were now similar* in these chains.

Similarity in three (6.6 per cent) other peer ties had also occurred through peer influence but *not by the peers who were similar* in the chains (yes in column 6; [p] in Column 7). In each of these links one peer had not yet used the substance at the time that the other first used and could not, therefore, have influenced the other to use the substance. In the remaining three peer ties/links (6.7 per cent), one in Chain 1 and two in Chain 3, the teenagers had not experienced peer influence at all.

Peer influence in current substance use in Peer Group 1

If we turn now to Columns 8 and 9, chains of current users are formed when both teenagers in one or more peer ties/links are current users. There are two very small chains of current cigarette users in Chains 1 and 2, one large and two small current alcohol chains in Chains 3 and 4, and one small current drug chain in Chain 7. In all links between current users in the chains, peer influence was currently occurring, usually for both teenagers. Since these were the current peer ties, we can be confident that these were the peers with whom they were taking the substances or who were giving each other the substances.

Peer influence or selection in Peer Group 1

These findings confirm that many of the teenagers in this peer group are similar in their substance use and that peer influence and selection have both been at work in making them similar. In this peer group peer influence has occurred in 93.3 per cent of the peer ties but only in 68.9 per cent of the peer ties *between the peers who were similar* in the chains. Similarity in other peer ties was due to peer influence by peers outside these chains. Likewise, selection has occurred in all (100 per cent) of the peer ties. All teenagers (100 per cent) have selected each other as peers and they did so either before or after becoming similar in their substance use (through peer influence). Peer influence continued in all peer ties of current users of each substance.

Peer Group 2

Peer Group 2 is the second largest network with 22 teenagers. The gender ratio in this network is 11 male:11 female. Ages range from 14 to 17 years with a mean age of 15.7 years. The rates of use were similar to Peer

Group 1 for ever cigarette and ever alcohol use but were much lower for ever drug use (Table 8.1). They were higher than Peer Group 1 for current cigarette use and lower for current alcohol and drug use.

Similarity in Peer Group 2

The patterning of the peer ties and the cigarette, alcohol and drug use of the teenagers in this network are given in Figures 8.4–8.6. The figures reveal that the teenagers in this network are linked into two clusters, which are linked by a peer tie between one individual in each cluster, with the remaining teenagers branching out in three different directions from the smaller of these clusters. When the individual-level substance use data for each of the teenagers are added to the social network data, the figures reveal three cigarette chains (Chains 8–10; Figure 8.4) and one alcohol chain (Chain 11; Figure 8.5). The single drug user is indicated in Figure 8.6. There is, therefore, no drug chain in this network. These findings confirm that many teenagers adjacent to each other in the peer group are similar in their use of the respective substances. This is particularly so for alcohol, since nearly all of the teenagers had

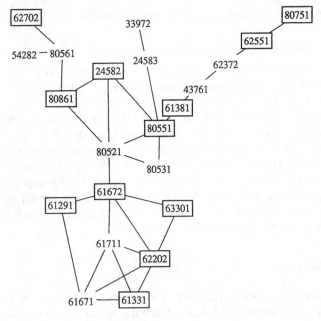

Figure 8.4   Peer Group 2: Cigarette use.

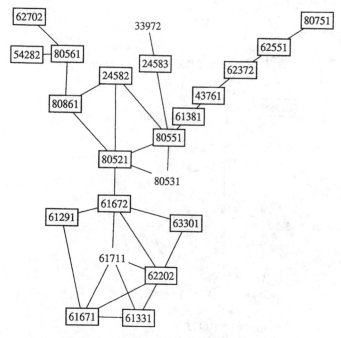

Figure 8.5   Peer Group 2: Alcohol use.

taken alcohol, and they are all connected in one continuous chain. Likely explanations for their similarity are discussed in the following section.

Peer influence at first substance use in Peer Group 2

Data on each peer tie/link in the chains of cigarette and alcohol users in this network are given in Table 8.4. The reader will note that, while these chains usually linked teenagers of similar gender, there were more mixed gender links than in Peer Group 1. As in Peer Group 1 the chains usually linked teenagers of different ages. In each peer tie/link the teenagers were similar in their use of the respective substances.

The findings given in Column 7 indicate whether the teenagers in the peer tie/link said that their peers had influenced them. These findings indicate that peer influence had occurred in 30 of the 32 peer ties/links (93.8 per cent) in Chains 8–11. Peer influence had not, however, always been between the peers who were similar. Only in 11 peer ties/links (34.4 per cent) had peer influence been *between the peers who were similar*

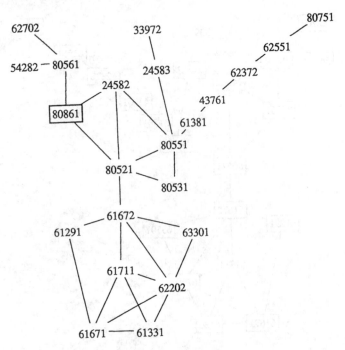

Figure 8.6   Peer Group 2: Drug use.

(p or pp in Column 7). In all of these links the peer tie had preceded the substance use of the teenagers (yes in Column 6). Their similarity is, therefore, explained by peer influence *between the peers who are similar* in the chains.

In 13 peer ties (40.6 per cent) peer influence could not have been between the peers who were similar because the peer tie had been formed between them after the first substance use of both of them (no in Column 6; *pp* in Column 7). Their similarity is, therefore, explained by selection because the teenagers were already similar in their substance use before being selected by each other as peers. All of the teenagers in these links had, nevertheless, been influenced by their peers but *not by the peers to whom they were now similar* in these chains.

Similarity in six other peer ties (18.8 per cent) had also occurred through peer influence but *not by the peers to whom they were similar* in the chains. In each of these links, one peer had not yet used the substance at the time that the other first used and could not, there-fore, have influenced the other to use the substance (yes in Column 6;

[p] in Column 7). In the remaining two peer ties, peer influence had not operated in one of them (3.1 per cent) and this information was not known for the other (3.1 per cent).

Peer influence in current substance use in Peer Group 2

In this peer group we find three small current cigarette chains in Chains 8–10 and one large current alcohol chain in Chain 11. We also find that peer influence was currently occurring for both teenagers in every link (100 per cent of the 14 peer ties/links) formed by current users. Since these were the teenagers' current peer ties, we can be confident that these were the peers who were influencing them.

Peer influence or selection in Peer Group 2

As in Peer Group 1, these findings confirm that many of the teenagers in this network are similar in their substance use and that peer influence and selection has operated in making them similar. Peer influence has occurred in this peer group in nearly all (93.8 per cent) of the peer ties but only in 34.4 per cent of the peer ties between the peers who were similar in the chains. In the others similarity was due to peer influence by peers outside these chains. Likewise, selection has occurred in all (100 per cent) of the peer ties. All teenagers (100 per cent) have selected each other as peers and they did so either before or after becoming similar in their substance use (through peer influence). Peer influence continued in all peer ties of current users of each substance.

Peer Group 3

This peer group is the third largest network with 21 teenagers (Figures 8.7–8.9). The gender ratio is 9 male:12 female. Ages range from 14 to 18, with a mean age of 16.3 years. The rates of use were higher for ever cigarette use than both Peer Groups 1 and 2; lower for ever alcohol use than both of the other two networks; lower than Peer Group 1 and much higher than Peer Group 2 for ever drug use; higher than Peer Group 1 and lower than Peer Group 2 for current cigarette use; much lower for current alcohol use than both other peer groups; and lower than both other peer groups for current drug use (Table 8.1).

Similarity in Peer Group 3

The patterning of the ties is given in Figures 8.7–8.9. The teenagers in this network are linked into three interconnected clusters, which are

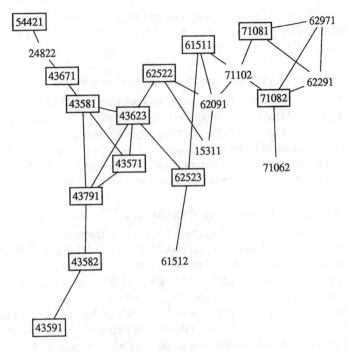

Figure 8.7   Peer Group 3: Cigarette use.

more dense than the rest of the network, with two less dense segments and two individual teenagers branching out in different directions from these clusters. When the substance use data are added to the pattern of peer ties given in the figures, we find that there is one cigarette chain (Chain 12; Figure 8.7), two alcohol chains (Chains 13 and 14; Figure 8.8) and one drug chain (Chain 15; Figure 8.9). Ten of the thirteen cigarette users are linked into the cigarette chain. Fourteen of the fifteen alcohol users are linked into the two alcohol chains and all of the four drug users are linked into the drug chain. These findings confirm that many teenagers adjacent to each other in the peer group are similar to each other in their use of the respective substances. Possible explanations are explored in the following sections.

Peer influence at first substance use in Peer Group 3

Table 8.5 presents data on each peer tie/link in the four chains of substance users in this network (Chains 12–15). Although there are more females than males in this network, the reader will notice that

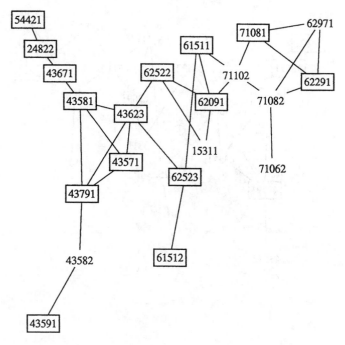

Figure 8.8 Peer Group 3: Alcohol use.

male–male peer ties predominate in the chains. As in the other two peer groups, teenagers of different ages are linked in the chains. In each peer tie/link, the teenagers were similar to each other in their substance use.

Peer influence had occurred in 30 of the 31 peer ties/links (96.8 per cent) in Chains 12–15 in this peer group (Column 7). Peer influence had not, however, necessarily been between the peers who were similar. In 18 peer ties/links (58.1 per cent) peer influence had been *between the peers who were similar* (p or pp in Column 7). In all of these links the peer tie had preceded the substance use of the teenagers (yes in Column 6). Their similarity is, therefore, explained by peer influence *between the peers who are similar* in the chains.

In nine other peer ties/links (29.0 per cent) peer influence could not have been between the peers who were similar because the peer tie had been formed between them after the first substance use of both of them (*pp* in Column 7). Their similarity is, therefore, explained by the selection of peers who were already similar to the teenagers in their substance use. Peer influence had occurred in each of these links for one

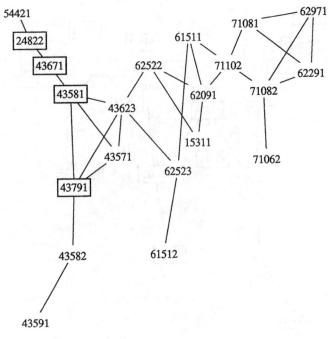

Figure 8.9   Peer Group 3: Drug use.

or both teenagers but *not by the peers to whom they were now similar* in these chains.

Similarity in three other peer ties/links (9.7 per cent) had also occurred through peer influence but *not by the peers to whom they were similar* in the chain ([p] in Column 7). In these peer ties/links one peer had not yet used the substance at the time that the other first used and could not, therefore, have influenced the other teenager to use the substance. In the remaining one peer tie (3.2 per cent) peer influence had not operated at all.

Peer influence in current substance use in Peer Group 3

There are just two chains of current users in this network. One chain links all of the current smokers in Chain 12 and another chain links all of the current alcohol users in Chain 13. As in the other two networks, peer influence was currently occurring for both teenagers in all links (100 per cent of the 10 links) between the current users of cigarettes and alcohol. Since these were the teenagers' current peer ties, we can be confident that these were the peers who were influencing each other.

Peer influence or selection in Peer Group 3

As in the previous two case studies, these findings confirm that many of the teenagers in this network are similar in their substance use and that peer influence and selection have led to their similarity. Peer influence has occurred in 96.8 per cent of the peer ties in this peer group but only in 58.1 per cent of the peer ties *between the peers who were similar* in the chains. In the other peer ties peer influence had been by *peers outside these chains*. Thus, the similarity of the teenagers in their substance use is due to peer influence but *not necessarily between the peers who are similar* in the chains. Likewise, selection has occurred in all (100 per cent) of the peer ties. All teenagers (100 per cent) have selected each other as peers and they did so either before or after becoming similar in their substance use (through peer influence). As in the other two peer groups peer influence continued in all peer ties of current users of each substance.

Conclusion

The findings from these three case studies have confirmed that teenagers adjacent to each other in these peer groups were likely to be similar in their substance use and to form chains of users of similar substances. These findings suggested, at first glance, that a chain reaction was occurring in these peer groups, in which peer influence was operating between peers who were adjacent to each other, resulting in chains of teenager users of similar substances.

When individual and dyadic data were added to the chain data and all were examined in the context of the peer group, the findings confirmed that peer influence had indeed occurred in nearly all of the peer ties (that is, links) in the chains. Thus, peer influence had occurred in 93.3 per cent of the links in Chains 1–7; in 93.8 per cent of the links in Chains 8–11; and in 96.8 per cent of the links in Chains 12–15. These findings support those of previous researchers who reported peer influence as a very potent source of influence on teenagers' substance use (for example, Akers et al., 1979: 644; Kandel, 1980: 269).

But do these findings support the apparent chain reaction effect? Is similarity in these chains due solely to peer influence and has peer influence occurred *between the peers who are similar?*

The findings from the case studies have confirmed that peer influence has occurred for these teenagers but *not necessarily between them and the peers to whom they were similar* in their substance use in the chains. The findings confirmed that similarity in peer ties had occurred through peer influence *between those who were similar* in 68.9 per cent of the links in Chains 1–7, in only 34.4 per cent of the links in Chains 8–11, and in 58.1 per cent of the links in Chains 12–15.

Similarity in other peer ties/links had occurred through selection. In all of these peer ties/links the teenagers had already taken their first substance before forming the peer tie/link. This was so for 17.8 per cent of the links in Chains 1–7, 40.6 per cent in Chains 8–11 and 29.0 per cent in Chains 12–15. Although similarity in these links was due to selection, however, peer influence had also occurred in all of these peer ties/links but it *could not have been between the peers who were similar* because their use of the substances had preceded the formation of their peer ties.

In some other peer ties similarity *could not have been between the peers who were similar* either, because the second peer had not used the substance in time to influence the other peer. This was so for 6.6 per cent of links in Chains 1–7, 18.8 per cent in Chains 8–11 and 9.7 per cent in Chains 12–15.

It has been suggested in the literature (Cohen, 1977: 239; Kandel, 1978a: 24; Bauman and Ennett, 1996: 187) that the impact of peer influence on similarity in teenagers' substance use will be exaggerated if the impact of selection on similarity is not taken into account. They have suggested that only half of the similarity in teenagers' substance use is due to peer influence and the other half is due to selection. The findings of this study have indicated that similarity was due to peer influence *between the peers who were similar* in proportions varying from 34.4 per cent to 68.9 per cent, and to selection for proportions varying between 17.8 per cent and 40.6 per cent in the three case studies examined. But the findings given in Tables 8.3–8.5 also confirmed that peer influence had occurred for one or both of the teenagers in all of the peer ties in which similarity was due to selection. The difference is that peer influence had, in these cases, come from peers *other than those to whom they were similar* in these chains. These findings support those of Bauman and Ennett (1996: 187), Kandel (1978a: 24) and Cohen (1977: 239) insofar as they confirm that peer influence by the peers who are similar will be exaggerated if selection is not controlled. But my findings add another dimension. They suggest that the role of peer influence will be underestimated if researchers do not find out who has influenced those who are selected when they are already similar in their substance use.

The findings from these case studies suggest, however, that it is more appropriate to conclude that similarity in the substance use of teenagers is due to *both peer influence and selection* rather than either peer influence or selection, as previous research has suggested. This study's findings have confirmed that similarity in the substance use of teenagers in peer ties in this study was due to peer influence in nearly all of the peer ties. The study has also confirmed that teenagers in all of the peer ties had selected each other as peers. Thus, similarity in the substance use of peers is due to both peer influence and selection. For some of the teenagers, peer influence *outside the chain* occurs first and selection as peers into the peer group follows; for other teenagers, their selection as peers into the peer group occurs first and peer influence *within the chain* follows. Chain reactions result from linking those who are similar with those who are not.

The findings are quite different for the current substance users. In every link of the chains between current users, peer influence is currently occurring and usually for both peers. Since the peers in the peer groups are their current peers, we can be confident that the peers in these current chains are those who are currently influencing. Thus, these chains of current users reinforce the substance use of the teenagers who form them in much the same way as Bauman and Ennett (1996: 188) suggested that they might, when they said that '... once friendships are formed they may reinforce common behaviors and, in that sense, operate as an influence among users'.

Finally, *is there evidence in these case studies of the contribution of the peer group (as a social network) to similarity in the substance use of teenagers and their peers?*

Peer ties are formed when teenagers select other teenagers as their peers (Chapter 6). The selection of one peer connects individual teenagers into a peer tie, which in turn indirectly connects them into a peer network. This peer network can be described as their peer group. The peer group might be very small with only a few members or it might be very large as in the case studies given in this chapter. All individuals in such a peer group will have selected those to whom they are adjacent as peers but they will be indirectly connected to many others whom they will not have selected. The particular pattern of the peer ties in the peer group is an unpredictable outcome of forming an individual peer tie. Nevertheless, that pattern of peer ties at the time the teenager forms a new peer tie is important to the individual's substance use as is the location of the peer whom the individual teenager has selected. Through the patterning of the peer ties an individual who forms a new peer tie may be connected to a chain of users of a particular substance or the individual may be connected to non-users.

As demonstrated in the case studies, the social network contributes to the similarity of the teenagers in their substance use by linking teenagers, who are already similar in their substance use, to teenagers who become similar through their continued association with their peers in the peer group. Thus, *the chain reaction results from linking those who are similar with those who are not.* By linking the teenagers through their peer ties in a pattern of ties, the peer group links up chains of users of similar substances. Some of those who are similar in these chains will have influenced each other; others will have been influenced by peers outside the chains. The outcome is the same: chains of similar users, in which the chain reaction has been brought about by the selection of peers, the patterning of their peers ties and peer influence.

The peer group contributes in a more straightforward way to the teenagers' current use. By linking the current users in chains in which peer influence occurs in every link of the chains, the peer group helps to reinforce and support their current substance use. Indeed, peers reinforced each other's current use even if they had not been involved in each other's initiation (see the current cigarette chain in Chain 12).

Peer groups, therefore, contribute to the similarity of teenagers' substance use in a profound manner by providing a pattern of peer ties in which peer influence can flourish. Chain reactions result from the pattern of peer ties, formed by peer selections, and from peer influence. Peer groups contribute to teenagers' current use by linking current users in chains, which enables them to reinforce each other's substance use. The role of gender in chain reactions is explored in Chapter 9.

9
The Role of Gender in Chain Reactions

Introduction

Findings given in Chapter 6 have confirmed the role of peers in the teenagers' substance use. Teenagers selected other teenagers from this population and formed peer ties with them and, in doing so, formed peer groups of various sizes. Teenagers who did not form peer ties with other teenagers in the population remained as isolates. The combination of peer groups and isolates comprised a complete network.

Using this complete network data, rather than clique data as other researchers had done, this study found no association between the social position of teenagers among their peers and their ever or current use of cigarettes, alcohol or drugs. These findings did not support those of other researchers who had found that isolates were more likely than clique members or liaisons to be current smokers (Ennett and Bauman, 1993: 231; Fang et al., 2003: 262). But it is not social position per se which is likely to have an impact on the teenagers' substance use but the teenagers' social position relative to other teenagers in their peer groups who have used the substances already and would, therefore, be able to influence them if they so wished. This question has been explored in Chapter 8. The findings in Chapter 8 have confirmed that teenagers adjacent to each other in peer groups were likely to be similar in their substance use and to form chains of users of similar substances. Their increasing similarity was explained by chain reactions which were due to a combination of peer selection, peer influence and the patterning of peer ties in the peer groups examined. Previous research had explained teenagers' increasing similarity in their substance use on peer selection or peer influence (Cohen, 1977: 239; Kandel, 1978b: 436; Hunter, Vizelberg and Berenson, 1991: 101; Ennett and Bauman, 1994: 660;

Pearson and West, 2003: 69), but not both, and had not discussed the importance of the patterning of peer ties in this process.

The role of gender in teenagers' substance use is rather complex and depends very much on the level of the data being analysed, that is, whether the data are on individual teenagers, dyads of teenagers and their peers, peer groups or a combination of those levels. A major advantage of having complete network data is that those data can be examined at all of those levels. This chapter explores the role of gender in chain reactions which result in increasing similarity in the substance use of teenagers and their peers and does so by examining data at a variety of levels. Traditionally gender is seen as an individual attribute but this chapter explores gender as an important social network variable that impacts on the substance use of teenagers in a subtle way. Gender plays a role in peer tie formation, the patterning of peer ties and in peer influence and, thus, impacts on the chain reactions evident in the social networks of teenagers.

Gender and the selection of peers

There were slightly more female than male teenagers in this community (52.1 and 47.9 per cent respectively) and the findings confirm that these teenagers selected their peers in the community very strictly along gender lines. Male teenagers formed peer ties predominantly with other males (89.4 per cent) and female teenagers formed peer ties predominantly with other females (88.9 per cent), with only a small percentage of mixed gender ties (21.7 per cent) ($p < 0.001$) (Table 9.1). Given the age of the teenagers (14–18 years) it was not surprising that only a small proportion of the teenagers had formed mixed gender peer ties. While there is no statistically significant association between the age of the teenagers and the formation of same gender or mixed gender peer ties, the findings given in Table 9.2 indicate that the tendency for mixed

Table 9.1   Gender of peer by gender of teenager

Gender of peer	Male teenager		Female teenager	
	No.	%	No.	%
Male	152	89.4	12	11.1
Female	18	10.6	96	88.9
	170	100	108	100

Table 9.2 Gender of dyad by age of the teenager

Gender of dyad	Age of teenager				
	14 (%)	15 (%)	16 (%)	17 (%)	18 (%)
Male/Male	47.2	63.9	62.1	50.7	46.2
Male/Female	7.5	9.8	5.2	16.4	15.4
Female/Female	45.3	26.2	32.8	32.8	38.5
N	53	61	58	67	39
Percentage	100	100	100	100	100

gender peer ties to be formed was greater among the 17- and 18- year-olds (NS). I will explore later why, and when, mixed gender peer ties are important to the teenagers' substance use and will discuss the importance of mixed gender peer ties for peer influence. Suffice to point out here that the younger teenagers were less likely than the older teenagers to have formed mixed gender peer ties.

So how did these peer ties differ by gender? The findings given in Table 9.3 confirm that the female dyads (FF) were most likely to be the strongest ($p < 0.0001$). Many more of the female dyads (63.5 per cent) than the male dyads (23.0 per cent) or the mixed gender dyads (6.7 per cent) were best friends. When closeness was used as a measure of the strength of the peer tie, results were similar. More of the female dyads (44.8 per cent) than the mixed gender (26.7 per cent) or the male dyads (19.2 per cent) were very close ($p < 0.001$) (Table 9.4). But the female dyads met least often. In the week prior to interview, the mixed gender dyads (96.7 per cent) were more likely than the male

Table 9.3 Strength of peer tie by gender of dyad

Strength of peer tie	Gender of dyad		
	MM (%)	MF (%)	FF (%)
Best friend	23.0	6.7	63.5
Friend	59.2	66.7	31.3
Pal	17.8	26.6	5.2
N	152	30	96
Percentage	100	100	100

134

Table 9.4 Level of closeness of teenager to peer by gender of dyad

Level of closeness	Gender of dyad		
	MM (%)	MF (%)	FF (%)
Very close	19.2	26.7	44.8
Close	64.4	60.0	45.8
Not close to ...	16.4	13.3	9.4
N	146	30	96
Percentage	100	100	100

Table 9.5 What did they do together when they met in the week prior to interview?

What they did together	MM (%)	MF (%)	FF (%)
Go to each other's houses	6.9	20.0	2.4
Visit/meet other friends	0.7	10.0	13.1
Talk/chat with each other	25.5	50.0	45.2
Watch TV or videos	5.5	6.7	4.8
Cinema/disco	4.8	16.7	20.2
Drinking alcohol	4.1	10.0	1.2
Smoking cigarettes	0	0	0.3
Babysat	0	0	1.2
At work	0.7	0	2.4
At school	1.4	3.3	3.6
A sport/sport's club	37.2	0	4.8
A hobby/a club	2.1	0	2.4
Listen to music	0	6.7	8.3
Go walking	6.2	13.3	15.5
Go shopping/to town	5.5	3.3	14.3
Played cards/games	13.8	3.3	2.4
Sit around inside house	0	6.7	2.4
Messing/hanging around outside	40.7	23.3	22.6
Listen to radio	0	0	4.8
Go out	0	3.3	7.1
Drink tea	0	0	1.2
Do homework/study	0	0	1.2
Parties	0	0	1.2
Go to Library	0.7	0	3.6
Robbing	0.7	0	0
Voluntary work	0	0	1.2
Other	1.4	0	0
N	145	30	84
Percentage	>100	>100	>100

dyads (90.0 per cent) and the female dyads (83.3 per cent) to have met at least twice that week ($p < 0.009$). All teenagers had been asked what they did with their peers when they met them in the week prior to interview, and the findings confirm that the teenagers spent their time together doing quite ordinary things, but pastimes were different in the different gender dyads (Table 9.5). The favourite activities in the male dyads were messing/hanging around outside (40.7 per cent), involvement in a sport/sport's club (37.2 per cent) and talking with each other (25.5 per cent). The main activities in the female dyads were talking with each other (45.2 per cent), messing/hanging around outside (22.6 per cent) or going to the cinema or disco (20.2 per cent). In the mixed gender dyads the favourite activities were talking with each other (50.0 per cent), messing/hanging around outside (23.3 per cent) and going to each other's houses (20.0 per cent). Did substance use appear among the pastimes? Very little, but it is notable that drinking alcohol together was mentioned by more teenagers in the mixed gender dyads (10.0 per cent) than in the male dyads (4.1 per cent) or the female dyads (1.2 per cent). Smoking cigarettes appeared only in female dyads and to a minimal extent (0.3 per cent) and drug use was not mentioned as something they had done together in any of the dyads in the week prior to interview.

Substance use among the teenagers by their gender

These analyses include the substance use of the individual teenagers by their gender, substance use by the teenagers when in dyads of single or mixed gender, and their substance use when the teenagers are in peer groups of single or mixed gender or are isolates. Previous research has usually compared the substance use of individual teenagers. The gender of the teenagers has been associated with substance use in previous research, with some variation between the substances in some studies. Results have consistently confirmed that males were more likely than females to use alcohol (Johnston, O'Malley and Bachman, 1984: 25, 29; Grube and Morgan, 1986: 96, 97) and drugs (Shelley et al., 1982: 255; Miller et al. 1983: 30; Johnston, O'Malley and Bachman, 1984: 25, 29; Grube and Morgan, 1986: 120, 122; Pearson and Michell, 2000: 27–29), while some studies have found that females were more likely than males to smoke cigarettes (Johnston, O'Malley and Bachman, 1984: 25, 29; Pearson and Michell, 2000: 27–29), and others have found that males were more likely than females to smoke cigarettes (Grube and Morgan, 1986: 72). In this study, statistical tests revealed that, unlike previous research, there was no statistically significant association between the teenagers' gender and either their ever or current use of any of the three substances (Chapter 4; Table 4.8). Although the associations were not significant, it is notable that male rates exceeded female rates for all but ever use of cigarettes (the ratio of 58.3 per cent for males to 59.7 per cent for females). But, even for cigarettes, our findings confirmed that more of the males than females were current smokers (the ratio of 40.9 per cent to 36.0 per cent). These findings were consistent with those of other researchers who found that male rates usually exceeded female rates of use of alcohol and drugs, and they supported the inconsistent results of other researchers for cigarettes, with sometimes male exceeding female rates and, other times, female exceeding male rates.

Although substance use did not appear to any great extent as a pastime in the week prior to interview, findings do confirm that the gender mix of the dyad was significantly associated with alcohol ($p < 0.004$) and drug use ($p < 0.002$), but not with cigarette use (NS). For this analysis, dyads of teenagers and their peers were analysed (N = 278). This analysis would not, of course, include isolates, as they had not formed dyadic ties with anyone in this population. The highest rates of ever and current alcohol and drug use were among teenagers in male only dyads, while the highest rates of ever and current cigarette use were among teenagers in mixed gender dyads (Table 9.6). Teenagers, who were in female only dyads, had the lowest rates of ever and current use of all three substances. These findings suggest, therefore, that the gender mix in the dyad has an impact on the substance use of the teenagers. Female

Table 9.6 Teenagers' substance use by gender in dyads

Substance use	Gender of teenagers in dyads		
	MM (%)	MF (%)	FF (%)
Cigarettes – ever	63.2	66.6	51.0
Alcohol – ever	88.8	86.7	80.3
Drugs – ever	30.1	26.7	9.4
Cigarettes – current	40.8	53.3	28.1
Alcohol – current	61.8	50.0	36.5
Drugs – current	17.1	16.7	2.1
N dyads	152	30	96

teenagers are least at risk of using all three substances when they are in female only dyads. When they are in mixed gender dyads, their risk of using all three substances increases. Male teenagers are most at risk of using alcohol and drugs when they are in male only dyads, and the risk decreases when they are in mixed gender dyads. Males are most at risk of being smokers, on the other hand, when they are in mixed gender dyads.

So how does the gender combination in the dyads transform into the peer groups and is substance use associated with peer groups of different gender composition? The findings given in Table 9.7 indicate whether the peer groups in this study were single gender or mixed gender, and

Table 9.7 Gender of teenagers in all peer groups and among isolates

Peer group identification number	Number of teenagers in group	Gender mix or single gender
1	26	17M:9F
2	22	11M:11F
3	21	9M:12F
12	3	1M:2F
29, 30	2 in each	1M:1F
35	2	1M:1F
4	10	all M
5, 6	7 in each	all M
8	4	all M
10	3	all M
14	3	all M
21–24	2 in each	all M
28	2	all M
34	2	all M
7	7	all F
9	4	all F
11	3	all F
13	3	all F
15–18	3 in each	all F
19, 20	2 in each	all F
25–27	2 in each	all F
31–33	2 in each	all F
Isolates	98	41M:57F
N in peer groups	169	
N of isolates	98	
N in complete network	267	

it gives the gender breakdown in the mixed gender groups and among the isolates. These findings confirm that the three largest peer groups and four very small ones (two or three members) were mixed gender. Twelve peer groups were all male: one of which had ten members, two of which had seven members, and the other nine were small (two to four members). Sixteen peer groups were all female: just one had seven members and the other 15 peer groups were small (two to four members). These findings confirm, therefore, that the mixed gender peer groups were most likely to be the largest, and the all-female peer groups were most likely to be the smallest, with the all-male peer groups in between with some medium size groups (seven to ten members) as well as smaller ones (two to four members). Isolates were more likely to be female.

Table 9.8 gives the rates of substance use among the male and female teenagers when they were in single gender peer groups, in mixed gender peer groups or were isolates. For this analysis the individual teenagers' substance use is examined, therefore, in the context of their social position in peer groups or as isolates. These findings confirm that the highest rates for ever and current use of all three substances were among the male teenagers. For ever alcohol use, males had the highest rate (87.0 per cent) when they were in male only peer groups. They had the highest rates for ever cigarette (63.4 per cent), ever drug use (24.4 per cent) and current alcohol (65.9 per cent) when they were in mixed gender groups, and the highest rate for current cigarette (48.8 per cent) and current drug use (14.6 per cent) when they were isolates. Although lower than the

Table 9.8 Teenagers' substance use by gender in peer groups and among isolates

Substance use	Gender in peer groups and among isolates					
	M only group (%)	M in mixed gender (%)	M as isolates (%)	F only group (%)	F in mixed gender (%)	F as isolates (%)
Cigarettes – ever	50.0	63.4	61.0	62.2	54.1	61.4
Alcohol – ever	87.0	85.4	85.4	80.0	81.1	80.7
Drugs – ever	23.9	24.4	14.6	8.9	18.9	12.3
Cigarettes – current	34.8	39.0	48.8	35.6	32.4	38.6
Alcohol – current	47.8	65.9	51.2	48.9	37.8	50.9
Drugs – current	10.9	12.2	14.6	4.4	5.4	10.5
N teenagers	46	41	41	45	37	57

male rates for all substances, the highest rates among the female teen-agers were when they were in female only peer groups for ever cigarette use (62.2 per cent), when they were in mixed gender groups for ever alcohol (81.1 per cent) and ever drug use (18.9 per cent) and as isolates for current use of cigarettes (38.6 per cent), alcohol (50.9 per cent) and drugs (10.5 per cent).

The question arises as to why isolates would have higher rates than those in peer groups. If peer influence is important to their substance use, who has influenced these isolated teenagers? These teenagers are isolates only in that they have no peer ties in this population of teenagers, but all but two of them have peer ties outside it. So peer influence was available to them, as it was to other teenagers in the ways indicated in Chapters 6 to 8, but not from peers within the population. A similar anomaly, although a more serious one, exists with the Ennett and Bauman (1993) definition of isolate. 'Isolates have few or no links to other adolescents in the network. This position category includes dyads ... and tree nodes (i.e., adolescents who are connected in a branching structure analogous to a tree, such that if any one link is removed the rest are separated from the network)' (Ennett and Bauman, 1993: 230). They follow the defin-ition of isolate given by Richards (1989) in the NEGOPY programme which they used to analyse social position. Thus, their isolates also had peer ties, but within the population studied, but the teenagers were considered to be isolates if they were in dyads or tree structures. This definition of isolate may have gender implications because my findings on patterns of peer ties in peer groups confirm that, in this study at least, females were more likely than males to be in dyads and, when in larger peer groups, to be in tree structures. Were I to exclude the female teenagers who are in tree structures from these peer groups, it would alter the naturally occurring patterning of the peer ties in the peer groups in my study. Whether clustered, as males usually are or in tree structures or dyads, as females usually are, they link into chains of substance users, thus contributing to the chain reaction effect, which I have described in Chapter 8. Artificially excluding these tree structures would mask the chain reaction which is occurring in these peer groups among those who are more clustered and those in tree structures.

Some previous research had found that social position was associated with substance use. The most notable was Ennett and Bauman's (1993: 231) finding that isolates were more likely than clique members or liaisons to be current smokers. But, as explained above, their definition of isolate is problematic, and particularly so when gender is taken into account. Their findings have not been consistently supported in the literature, however. Although Fang et al. (2003: 262) found that isolates were most likely to have smoked cigarettes in most of the school pupils they studied, they found the reverse situation among 10th grade boys. Nor were they supported by Abel, Plumridge and Graham (2002: 336), who found that those least well connected, whom they called loners, were those least likely to have smoked cigarettes. Pearson and Michell (2000: 27) found no association in the first year of their study but found a small association ($p > 0.05$) one year later with relative isolates being more likely to have smoked cigarettes ($p < 0.08$) or taken drugs ($p < 0.07$). As reported earlier in Chapter 6, this study's findings were that the social position of teenagers, that is, whether they were members of peer groups or isolates, was not associated with their substance use. Our findings on social position and gender add little to the explanation of how social position impacts on the substance use of teenagers but it allows us to examine the differences that do emerge and to suggest in what social positions teenagers appear to be more at risk of using the substances. Male teenagers appear to be more at risk overall of becoming substance users but the social position which leaves them most at risk varies from substance to substance. Female teenagers appear to be less at risk of becoming substance users but the social position which places them least at risk also varies from substance to substance.

The frustration of doing these analyses – examining the association between the gender of the individual teenagers and their substance use, the gender of their dyads and their substance use, and the gender of their peer groups, or the individuals as isolates, and their substance use – is that none of these analyses take into account the pattern of peer ties in which the teenager is located and the sources of influence to which he or she is exposed in that pattern. Analyses in Chapter 8 confirmed how important that pattern is to chain reactions in the teenagers' substance use. Before examining the role of gender in the patterning of those ties, let us first look at the association between gender and peer influence.

Gender and peer influence

Findings given in Chapter 6 confirmed that at their first use, and in their current use of all three substances, large proportions of the teenagers were influenced by their peers (Table 6.5). At their first use, many teenagers were provided with their first cigarette (70.7 per cent) and their first drug (62.2 per cent), and fewer of them with their first alcoholic drink (31.2 per cent) by their peers, and even more of them took their first cigarette (83.5 per cent), their first drug (88.9 per cent) or their first alcoholic drink (72.4 per cent) with their peers. In their current use of the three substances, peers provided them especially with drugs (58.8 per cent), alcohol (35.1 per cent) and cigarettes (25.7 per cent), and even more of them took the substances with their peers. Nearly all of the teenagers currently took alcohol (97.0 per cent) with their peers, and most of them took their drugs (88.3 per cent) and their cigarettes (87.1 per cent) with their peers. The disparities between the percentages of teenagers who were provided with a substance by their peers and took the substance with peers confirms that, for ever and current use of each substance, more than one peer may have been involved. This suggests that the pattern of peer ties in which the teenager is linked may be more important than just dyadic ties with peers.

When gender is added to the role of peer influence in the teenagers' substance use, the findings confirm that there are significant associations between gender and peer influence in all but being provided with alcohol and drugs during their current use (Table 9.9). In particular, what the findings establish is whether peer influence operated along gender lines or whether it crossed gender lines. If it operated along gender lines, single gender peer ties and peer groups would support it, but if it crossed gender lines, mixed gender peer ties and peer groups would be needed to support it. These findings were produced from teenagers' answers to questions about who had given them their substances, with whom they had taken their substances and the gender of the peers involved. For their first use of cigarettes, alcohol and drugs, male teenagers were most likely to have been influenced by other males. They were most likely to have been provided with each substance and to have taken them with their male peers. Thus, males with male only peers would be at risk of being initiated to all three substances.

Females, on the other hand, were most likely to have been influenced by female peers for their first cigarette use, but by a mix of male and female peers for their first alcohol and drug use. Their female peers were most likely to have provided the teenagers with their first cigarette, alcoholic drink and drug, but while they were most likely to have taken their first cigarette with female peers, they were most likely to have taken their first alcoholic drink and drug with a mix of males and female peers. Thus, female teenagers are at risk of initiation to cigarette use if their peers are female only, but they are more at risk of initiation to alcohol and drugs when they have male and female peers.

Results for current use are somewhat different. Males were most likely to have been influenced by male and female peers in their cigarette

Table 9.9 Influence by peers of the teenagers' substance use by gender of teenagers and peers

		Male peers (%)	Female peers (%)	Male + Female (%)	N	Significance
Company of peers						
First use						
Cigarettes	Male teens	77.4	3.2	19.4	62	$p < 0.0001$
	Female teens	0	79.1	20.9	67	
Alcohol	Male teens	67.9	0	32.1	78	$p < 0.0001$
	Female teens	0	33.8	66.2	77	
Drugs	Male teens	96.0	0	4.0	25	$p < 0.0001$
	Female teens	7.1	42.9	50.0	14	
Provided by peers						
First use						
Cigarettes	Male teens	92.5	7.5	0	53	$p < 0.0001$
	Female teens	5.2	93.1	1.7	58	
Alcohol	Male teens	91.4	5.7	2.9	35	$p < 0.0001$
	Female teens	17.6	76.5	5.9	34	
Drugs	Male teens	100.0	0	0	17	$p < 0.0001$
	Female teens	37.5	62.5	0	8	
Company of peers						
Current use						
Cigarettes	Male teens	44.2	4.7	51.2	43	$p < 0.0001$
	Female teens	0	33.3	66.7	42	
Alcohol	Male teens	61.5	0	38.5	65	$p < 0.0001$
	Female teens	4.9	19.7	75.4	61	
Drugs	Male teens	90.0	0	10.0	10	$p < 0.001$
	Female teens	0	0	100.0	4	
Provided by peers						
Current use						
Cigarettes	Male teens	37.5	12.5	50.0	16	$p < 0.006$
	Female teens	0	70.0	30.0	10	
Alcohol	Male teens	83.3	0	16.7	12	NS
	Female teens	55.9	11.8	32.4	34	
Drugs	Male teens	100.0	0	0	5	NS
	Female teens	40.0	40.0	20.0	5	

use. They were most likely to have been provided with cigarettes and to have taken them with male and female peers. Males, on the other hand, were most likely to have been influenced by other males in their current alcohol and drug use. Thus, males are most at risk of being current alcohol and drug users when they have male peers only, but they are most at risk of being current smokers when they have male and female peers.

Females were also most likely to have been influenced by males and females in their current cigarette use. They were most likely to have been given the cigarettes by other females but to have smoked them with a mix of males and females. They were also most likely to currently take all three substances with male and female peers, although they are more likely to be given alcohol by male peers and drugs by male or female peers. These findings suggest, therefore, that females would be most at risk of being current smokers, drinkers and drug users when they have male and female peers. To put this point another way, females are least at risk when they have only female friends. These findings have gone some way in establishing the role of gender in peer influence.

Gender and the patterning of peer ties

Table 9.7 gave information on the gender of teenagers in all peer groups and among the isolates. The patterning of the ties which isolates had outside this population are not discussed in this book, so the discussion of the patterning of peer ties will concentrate on the patterning of peer ties in the peer groups. The patterning of peer ties is obviously along gender lines in all of the single gender peer groups. Thus, males have peer ties only with other males in these groups and females have ties only with other females. If mixed gender ties were needed for influence, therefore, they would not be available in the single gender peer groups.

There were just seven peer groups with a gender mix and the ratio of males to females in these groups is given in the table. The small groups of two (Peer Groups 29, 30, 35) have obviously one link between the male and the female, so the pattern is at its most basic. In Peer Group 12, in which there are two females and one male teenager, there is one mixed gender peer tie and one single gender peer tie. The other three peer groups with a gender mix are the three largest peer groups in this study (Peer Groups 1–3), which featured extensively in Chapter 8. The patterning of the peer ties, the substance use of the teenagers and the chains of substance users formed have already been discussed in Chapter 8. When data were given in Chapter 8 on the substance use chains, the gender mix of the teenagers forming those chains was given in Column 2 of the tables and the reader may consult the details when necessary. Here, the patterning of the peer ties by gender is considered.

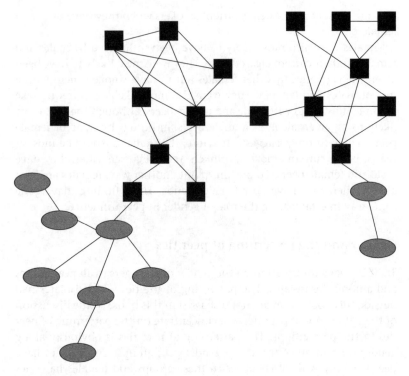

Figure 9.1 Peer Group 1 by Gender.

Figure 9.1 adds gender to the patterning of peer ties given for Peer Group 1 in Figures 8.1–8.3. The reader may consult the corresponding substance use chain data in Table 8.3. The shapes distinguish the teenagers by gender in Figure 9.1, with a square shape signifying male and an oval shape signifying female teenagers. The reader will note that there are just two mixed gender peer ties in this large peer group, between two different male and two different female teenagers. The male teenagers have formed into two rather dense clusters in this peer group, and the female teenagers form tree-like structures at the lower end of the figure.

Figure 9.2 gives the gender composition of Peer Group 2. This figure corresponds with Figures 8.4–8.6 and the corresponding details on substance use chains given in Table 8.4. The reader will note that there are nine mixed gender peer ties. These are between six different male and four different female teenagers. In this peer group the two clusters

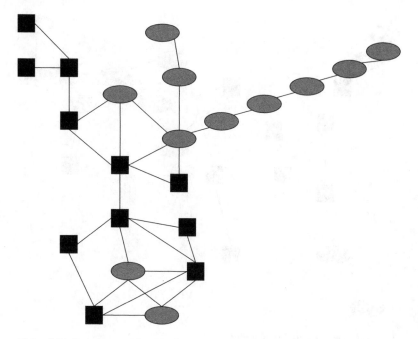

Figure 9.2 Peer Group 2 by Gender.

include males and females, but two of the three tree-like structures are female.

The gender composition of Peer Group 3 is given in Figure 9.3. This figure corresponds with Figures 8.7–8.9 and with the corresponding details on substance use chains given in Table 8.5. The reader will note that there are six mixed gender peer ties. These are between five different male teenagers and six different female teenagers. Females form a rather large dense cluster on the right of the diagram and males form a smaller dense cluster to the left of the diagram. Females are also in tree-like structures at the top left and the bottom left of the diagram, and males form tree-like structures at the bottom right and centre of the diagram.

What is notable is that in the entire complete network there are only 21 mixed gender peer ties, 17 of which are in the three largest peer groups, with one each in four very small peer groups. All other peer ties are single gender. The results, given in the figures for the largest peer groups (Figures 9.1–9.3), suggest that different patterns have emerged for male and female teenagers. When in single gender peer groups, males formed slightly larger groups than the females, which suggests more

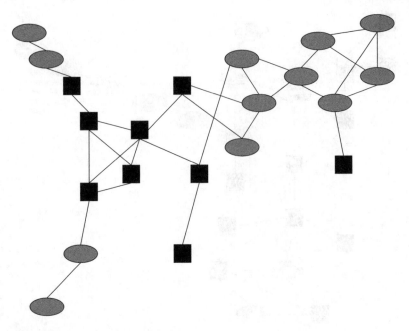

Figure 9.3   Peer Group 3 by Gender.

clustering among the males. When in mixed gender peer groups, especially in the three largest groups, males were more likely to be clustered
with other males and very few males formed tree-like structures. Females,
on the other hand, were very likely to form tree-like structures in all
three peer groups, with dense clustering of females only occurring in
Peer Group 2, and females were more likely to be isolates in the complete
network.

This kind of patterning could be important for peer influence. If single
gender peer ties are sufficient for peer influence to occur, the patterning
of peer ties in this complete network would facilitate it. If, on the other
hand, mixed gender peer ties are needed for peer influence to occur,
the patterning of peer ties in this complete network would hinder it. It
was shown earlier in this chapter that males were most at risk of being
current smokers when they had male and female peers, but they were
more at risk of initiation to all three substances and to current alcohol
and drug use when they had only male peers. The paucity of mixed
gender peer ties in this complete network would, therefore, only impede
the current cigarette use of males (Table 9.6). It was shown earlier in this
chapter that female teenagers were least at risk of ever and current use of

all three substances when they were in single gender dyads (Table 9.6). The paucity of mixed gender peer ties in this complete network would, therefore, impede the ever and current use of all three substances for females. Since their female peers primarily influenced their ever cigarette use, however, their cigarette use is least likely to be affected.

Gender in chain reactions

Chain reactions result from linking those who are similar in their substance use with those who are not (Chapter 8). By linking teenagers through their peer ties in a pattern of ties, the peer group links up chains of users of similar substances. Some of those who are similar in these chains will have influenced each other; others will have been influenced by peers outside the chains. The outcome is the same: chains of similar users, in which the chain reaction has been brought about by the selection of peers, the patterning of peer ties and peer influence. I have demonstrated in this chapter that gender impacts on all three: the selection of peers, the patterning of peer ties and peer influence. Peers are selected strictly along gender lines and very seldom across gender lines (Table 9.1). When mixed gender peers are selected it is usually when the teenagers are older (Table 9.2). The patterning of peer ties in this complete network was also, not surprisingly, along gender lines and not across gender lines, with different patterns emerging among males and females, and with only 21 mixed gender peer ties in the complete network. Peer influence, which had occurred in the teenagers' substance use, had not, however, always occurred along gender lines but had often crossed gender lines. For males, this mixed gender influence was only important for their current cigarette use, but for females it was important for all but their ever cigarette use (Table 9.9).

Gender, therefore, has an impact on the chain reactions which result. Single gender patterns will be sufficient for chain reactions to occur in all but current cigarette use for males, but female teenagers need mixed gender patterns to ensure that chain reactions occur for all substances other than their first cigarette use. Thus, the patterning of peer ties along gender lines, or across gender lines, will have a profound effect on whether, or when, chain reactions will occur for male and female teenagers. Since mixed gender peer ties are likely to be formed in the later teenage years, this may delay the substance use of female teenagers, who need mixed gender peer ties for all but their first cigarette use. Such a delay would not occur for male teenagers, who need mixed gender peer ties only for their current cigarette use.

Conclusion

It has been demonstrated in this chapter that the teenagers in this community selected their peers quite strictly along gender lines. Boys had selected boys as peers; girls had selected girls. Very few had selected peers of the opposite gender. Thus, the findings confirmed that gender played a role in peer tie formation. The gender composition of peer groups reflects the impact of gender on peer tie formation. Most of the peer groups in this community are composed of teenagers of one gender: 12 were all male, 16 were all female and just 7 peer groups were mixed gender.

When attributes of the actors are considered with their network data, this is known as the composition of the network (Wasserman and Faust, 1994: 21, 22). Thus, the composition of the peer groups was primarily single gender and more rarely mixed gender. But I am suggesting that the gender of the teenagers also affected the network structure. The structure of the network is the pattern of the relational ties in the network. In this book, it is the pattern formed by the peer ties in the different peer groups. The pattern which will result from the formation of the peer ties cannot be anticipated by the individuals forming those ties. Changes that occur in that pattern over time can also not be anticipated. When in mixed gender peer groups, especially in the three largest groups, males were more likely to be clustered with other males with very few males forming tree-like structures. Females, on the other hand, were very likely to form tree-like structures in all three peer groups, with dense clustering of females only occurring in one peer group (Peer Group 2). The females were also more likely than the males to be isolates in this complete network. Thus, the composition and structure of this complete network was affected by the gender of the teenagers. Single gender peer groups predominated with males more likely than females to form larger groups. This reflected more clustering among the males. In the very large mixed gender peer groups too, males were more inclined to be clustered with other males and to have a minimum of ties with females, while many females were in tree-like structures on the fringes of the peer groups.

Teenagers, who had used substances, confirmed that their peers had influenced them and findings given in this chapter have confirmed that peer influence was associated with gender. Males had been influenced predominantly by other males; females had been influenced predominantly by males and females. The structure and composition of this complete network, at the time interviews were carried out, would, therefore, enhance the likelihood of the male teenagers being influenced while, at the same time, would hinder the likelihood of females being influenced.

But chain reactions result from peer selection, the patterning of peer ties and peer influence. So changes in the pattern over time alter the likelihood of influence for both males and females. Tracing how these changes occur over time cannot be done in this book, but future research should tackle this issue and examine the theory of chain reactions put forward in this book and in Kirke (2004) in prospective longitudinal research projects. Only now is the computer technology available to do such research. Future research should examine whether chain reactions occur over time in the way suggested. The role of gender in chain reactions should be examined and the age of the teenagers should be monitored for its impact on the chain reactions and on the role of gender, since mixed gender peer ties are not usually formed until the later teenage years.

This book cannot definitively explain the role of gender in chain reactions in teenagers' substance use. Such an explanation would require a prospective longitudinal study, using complete network data, which would examine the dynamic influence of peer selection, the patterning of peer ties, peer influence, changes in substance use, changes in individual behaviour and the social networks formed over time. What was examined in this chapter, using the findings available from one complete network, was the way gender appears to impact on the different elements of the chain reaction process.

Rather than using gender as an individual attribute to examine its association with teenagers' substance use, I would suggest that gender can more beneficially be used as a social network variable which affects both the composition and the structure of the network. Findings discussed above suggest that it is not gender per se which is important in teenagers' substance use but the role gender plays in the selection of peers, in the patterning of peer ties, in peer influence and ultimately in the chain reaction process to which they contribute.

In the final chapter of this book, Chapter 10, the teenagers' substance use is placed within the context of the broader social networks in which their lives are embedded. These social networks include their peers, family and community. In Chapter 10 the findings presented throughout the book are drawn together to arrive at an explanation of teenagers' substance use in the context of the social networks and social environment in which it occurs.

10
Discussion and Conclusion

This book has been designed to examine the current research question of the relative impact of peer selection and peer influence on increasing similarity in the substance use of teenagers and their peers. The question has been approached differently to earlier research. While previous research has used dyadic or small clique data to examine this question (Cohen, 1977: 239; Kandel, 1978b: 436; Bauman and Ennett, 1996: 187), this book uses a population study of one community of teenagers and a complete network of their peer ties. The book examines the substance use behaviour of the teenagers in the context of the broader social networks in which their lives are embedded in order to get a comprehensive understanding of the impact of various social forces on their substance use. These social networks include their families and community, as well as their peers. A social network approach has been used, focussing on the network of relationships the teenagers have with their peers in the community, and various individual attributes and family variables have been added to get a comprehensive overview of the teenagers' lives and the influences that have affected their substance use. A complete network of peer relationships in this community has provided the peer network data and this has been used for single level and multilevel analyses. This chapter draws together the findings of the book and proposes a theoretical explanation for the teenagers' substance use based on chain reactions, which result from the selection of peers, the patterning of peer ties and peer influence. This explanation builds on earlier research on the role of peer selection and peer influence on similarity in teenagers' substance use and adds a new dimension – the patterning of peer ties in peer groups.

Discussion

The community of families provided the social environment in which the teenagers lived their lives. This community was working class with a high rate of unemployment. The families lived in houses in close proximity to one another. They were similar in race, religion and geographic location. Families with teenagers of 14–18 years were those covered by this study, but other families in the community were similar, in all but the age of their children. The families of the teenagers were, at the same time, the families of their peers in this study because the teenagers became peers to one another in the complete network covered.

Their parents had mixed effects on the teenagers' substance use, in some respects, resulting in the teenagers being more likely to have used cigarettes and alcohol and, in other respects, to have been less likely to have used them (Chapter 5). One result was very clear, however, parents did not support drug use. The families of the teenagers (that is, 14–18 years) were large but parents were actively involved with their teenage children. Parents advised their teenage children against using cigarettes, alcohol and drugs and they controlled their choice of friends and their free-time activities. Parents were, however, perceived by their children to have used cigarettes and alcohol (never drugs) and the effects on their teenage children were mixed. Parental smoking had no effect but parental drinking did have an effect. When mothers, fathers or parents were drinkers, their teenage children were more likely to have ever taken alcohol. But when their mothers or parents were drinkers, their teenage children were less likely to be current drinkers. Their fathers' drinking had no effect on the teenagers' current drinking. These findings seem to suggest that, if the teenager is in a home where there is parental drinking, the teenager is exposed to alcohol and is more likely to have ever used it. But parental drinking, especially their mothers' drinking, may deter them from continuing to drink alcohol. Findings also confirmed that a small proportion of parents influenced their children in their first use, and in their current use, of cigarettes and alcohol by providing them with the substances and by being in their company while their children were using. Such parents may have felt that it would be better to introduce their children to these substances at home, than have their children first use the substance in an environment where their parents would not be present. Whatever their reasons, parental influence at their first use and during their current use signifies parental support and approval of their children's smoking and drinking.

Their siblings affected the teenagers' substance use resulting in the teenagers being more likely to use cigarettes and alcohol, when their siblings did, and to use all three substances, when their siblings influenced them to do so (Chapter 5). These teenagers were surrounded by siblings in their large families and most of the teenagers had siblings whom they perceived were smokers and drinkers, and some siblings were, by their own admission, drug users. The teenagers were more likely to have ever used cigarettes and alcohol when their siblings did, but sibling use had no effect on their current use of either substance. Teenagers' drug use was unaffected by their siblings' drug use. Results also confirmed that their siblings had influenced a small proportion of the teenagers' first use and their current use of cigarettes and alcohol, and just one sibling influenced the teenagers' drug use. They did so by providing the teenagers with the substances or by taking the substances with them.

The main attribute of the teenagers which was associated with their substance use was their age, but this was only associated with ever and current use of cigarettes and alcohol and not with drugs (Chapter 4). Not surprisingly, older teenagers were more likely than younger teenagers to have ever used cigarettes and alcohol and to be current users of them. When examining the teenagers' substance use in the context of their peer groups, their age should be kept in mind, because even small differences in age (for example, one or two years), may mean that a younger teenager is exposed to the peer influence of an older teenager, who is more likely to be using these substances. A surprising result was that their gender was not associated with the teenagers' ever or current use of any of the substances in this study. Thus, gender, as an individual attribute, did not play a part in their substance use. But gender as a social network variable did seem to play a part and the impact of gender on chain reactions is discussed below.

The social networks provided for the teenagers, in their community and by their families, provided the social environment in which they could form their relationships with their friends and neighbours. They were the source of their peer ties. The single peer ties formed by the teenagers (dyads) connected them into larger social networks of peer groups, and into a complete network comprising all of the peer ties between all of the teenagers in this community of families. Analyses at each level of the dyad, the peer group and the complete network gave particular insights into the role of their peers in the teenagers' substance use (Chapters 6 and 7). Multilevel analyses gave new insights into a chain reaction process, which clarified the role of peers, in terms of selection, patterning of ties in peer networks and peer influence (Chapters 8), and gender was shown to affect the chain reaction process (Chapter 9). These results are discussed below, beginning with results from dyadic data.

Results based on dyadic data confirmed that teenagers were likely to be similar to their peers in their ever use of cigarettes and in their current use of all three substances, but not in their ever use of alcohol and drugs. Results from individual-level data confirmed that their peers had influenced most of the teenagers in their first and in their current use of all three substances (Chapter 6). These results contrasted with those in Chapter 5 which indicated that only a small proportion of the teenagers had been influenced by their parents or siblings in their first or current use of the substances. One large difference was that no parent and only one sibling had influenced the teenagers' drug use, while almost 90 per cent of the teenagers were influenced by their peers in their first and current drug use.

Results based on the complete network confirmed that the teenagers' social position per se, in terms of being in a peer group or being an isolate, was unrelated to their substance use (Chapter 6) although a number of studies in recent years had found an association between social position and cigarette use in particular. Previous studies had found that isolates were more likely than clique members to have smoked cigarettes (Ennett and Bauman, 1993: 231; Fang et al., 2003: 262) or that those most isolated, loners, were least likely to have smoked cigarettes (Abel, Plumridge and Graham, 2002: 336). Our findings were closest to those of Pearson and Michell (2000: 27), who found no association in the first year of their study and only very small associations one year later, between social position and smoking and drug taking. Complete network data, with naturally existing peer groups of various sizes, were likely to produce different results to the clique studies, but in what way they would differ was unpredictable. There are some problems of definition. In social network terms, defining a clique as a peer group is very restrictive (Wasserman and Faust, 1994: 256) and results in very small peer groups of 3 to 5 members, while in this study the number of teenagers in a peer group varied from 2 to 26 members. In this study the size of the peer groups had not been restricted by fixed choice questions or a rigid definition of peer group as used in the clique studies. The definition of isolate in these studies was also problematic since it included individuals who had no peer ties, with individuals who had peer ties, but who were in dyads or tree structures. Thus, when isolates were found to be those most likely to smoke cigarettes (Ennett and Bauman, 1993: 231), the findings called into question the importance of peers in such behaviour. If they were really isolates what peers would have influenced them? The definition of isolate used in the Kirke study was that isolates had no peer ties in the population covered. They could of course, and did, have peer ties with individuals outside the population. I also found that female teenagers were more likely to have been isolates and to be in dyads and tree structures. If this were so in the Ennett and Bauman (1993) data, the findings on isolates in their study would have masked a gender effect. The other important issue is that it is not social position per se, which is likely to be important to teenagers' substance use, but their social position among peers who use any of the substances under study. This question is addressed in substance use research in terms of similarity in substance use among teenagers and their peers and the role of peer selection and peer influence on their increasing similarity.

When the teenagers' substance use was placed in the context of the peer groups of which they were members, results confirmed that similarity in the substance use of teenagers and their peers (at least two using the same substance) had occurred, in numerous peer groups, for ever use of all three substances and, in fewer peer groups, for current use of all three substances (Chapter 6). These results confirmed, therefore, that similarity had occurred in these peer groups, but, because the data were cross-sectional, could not confirm whether similarity was due to the selection of peers, who were both already using the same substance, or to peer influence following the formation of the peer tie. Previous research, which had confirmed that similarity in substance use had occurred in dyads or cliques, had found that it was usually either peer selection or peer influence which explained the similarity (Cohen, 1977: 239; Kandel, 1978b: 436; Ennett and Bauman, 1994: 660; Urberg, Degirmencioglu and Tolson, 1998: 703).

In order to examine whether peer influence or selection were at work in the peer groups in this study, retrospective data on the timing of the peer selection and timing of the first use of each substance were combined with teenagers' reports of peer influence in a number of peer groups (Chapters 7). Using a multilevel analysis of three peer groups, it was confirmed that similarity had occurred (Chapter 7) and that peer selection and peer influence were involved, but not as previous researchers had suggested. My findings confirmed that similarity in their substance use was for some teenagers due to either peer selection or peer influence, for other teenagers to both peer selection and peer influence and, for others to neither. The findings also confirmed that, in these peer groups, peer selection rarely explained the similarity in the teenagers substance use, and the findings called into question the conclusion that other researchers had reached, that peer influence has occurred when two peers became similar in their substance use over time. Although peer influence appeared to have occurred when teenagers took substances after their peers, the teenagers' replies sometimes confirmed that peer influence had not occurred. For some of the teenagers, people other than their peers, such as family or relatives, had influenced them and for others no one had influenced.

A more complex multilevel analysis was conducted in Chapter 8 on the three largest peer groups. This analysis combined individual-level data, dyadic data and peer group data to reveal chains of substance users in each peer group. The findings revealed that similarity in substance use had occurred in these peer groups over time, but that similarity *between those who were similar* was due to peer influence between peers in proportions varying from 34.4 to 68.9 per cent of the links in the chains, and to selection in proportions varying from 17.8 to 40.6 per cent in these case studies, and for a small proportion of links to neither selection nor peer influence. These findings appear to support those of previous researchers that similarity is due to *either peer influence or selection*. But our findings add another dimension because they confirm that, when similarity was due to selection, it was also due to peer influence for one or both peers in all of those peer ties. Thus, although attributed to selection, their similarity was due to peer influence *but not by the peers to whom they were similar*. The conclusion is that similarity was due to peer influence for nearly all of the teenagers but not always by the peers to whom they were similar. Likewise, the findings also confirmed that the teenagers in all of the peer ties had selected each other as peers. Some had selected each other after they had already become similar in their substance use and others had selected each other before becoming similar through peer influence. Thus, the conclusion is that similarity in the substance of teenagers and their peers is due to *both peer influence and selection* and not *either peer influence or selection* as earlier thought. For some teenagers, peer influence *outside the chain of substance users* occurs first and selection as peers into the peer group follows; for others their selection as peers into the peer group occurs first and *peer influence within the chain* follows. Peer influence continues for all teenagers in their current substance use.

The explanation suggested, for increasing similarity in the substance use of teenagers and their peers, is that chain reactions result from linking those who are already similar in their substance use with those who become similar through their continued association in the peer group, that is, through peer influence. Thus, *the chain reactions result from linking those who are similar with those who are not.* The particular patterning of the ties which occurs in peer groups is part of this process. Peer ties (dyads) are formed when teenagers select other teenagers as their peers (Chapter 6). The selection of one peer connects individual teenagers into a peer tie, which indirectly connects them into a peer group. This peer group may be very small with only a few members or it may be very large. All individuals in such a peer group will have selected those to whom they are adjacent as peers but they will be indirectly connected to many others whom they will not have selected. The particular pattern of the peer ties in the peer group is an unpredictable outcome of forming an individual peer tie. Nevertheless, that pattern of peer ties at the time the teenager forms a new peer tie is important to the individual's substance use as is the social position of the peer whom the individual has selected. Through the patterning of the peer ties, an individual who forms a new peer tie may be connected to a chain of users of a particular substance or the individual may be connected to non-users. The social position of the selected peer is important in that he or she may be located centrally within a chain of substance users, peripheral to such a chain, or among all non-users.

If the new peer tie connects the individual teenager, who is a non-user, to a chain of users of a particular substance, that teenager is likely to experience peer influence to become similar. If the new peer tie connects the individual teenager, who is a non-user, to other non-users, no peer influence follows. If a new peer tie connects an individual teenager, who is a user, to a chain of users of a particular substance, no peer influence follows because they are already similar. If a new peer tie connects an individual teenager, who is a user, to other non-users, those non-users are likely to be exposed to peer influence by the teenager. When those, who are already similar in their substance use, are linked by a new peer tie into these peer groups, there is no change in similarity. But when those, who are not already similar in their substance use, are linked by a new peer tie in these peer groups, there is likely to be a change in similarity through peer influence. The chain reactions result from the formation of single peer ties, which in turn link the newly joining individual into a peer group, with a particular pattern of ties and a particular mix of substance users and non-users, which may, or may not, expose the individual to peer influence into substance use. Peer groups, therefore, contribute to the similarity of teenagers' substance use in a profound manner by providing a pattern of peer ties in which peer influence can flourish. It follows, of course, that for as long as teenagers remain isolated (that is, no friends or pals) from their peers, they are not exposed to peer influence. Likewise, if they have peer ties, but none of those peers use a substance, they are not exposed to peer influence. The chain reaction will continue as new peer selections are made which change the pattern of peer ties and the chains of substance users. The pattern of peer ties will change when new peer ties are added (through peer selection). The chains of substance users will increase when a new substance user is added (through peer selection or peer influence). Individual actions, therefore, of peer selection and peer influence change the peer group in the pattern of peer ties formed and in the chains of substance users formed. The peer group, in turn, is changed, as it then has a different pattern of peer ties and a different chain of substance users, and can, in turn, affect the substance use of other individuals. Those in the peer group may make new peer selections and those in the chains of substance users may influence others to use the substances. In this way, the chain reactions continue from individual to peer group to individual until all possibilities of change have been completed or the peer group is saturated with substance users. Time then becomes the important factor to further diffusion. New peer selections and peer influence will occur over time enabling the chain reactions to continue as more individuals who are similar in their substance use are linked with those who are not similar. To satisfactorily confirm these ideas requires studies using prospective longitudinal data. This will be discussed below in terms of future research.

Findings discussed in Chapter 9 have confirmed that gender impacts on all three aspects of the chain reaction process: the selection of peers, the patterning of peer ties and peer influence. Teenagers selected their peers strictly along gender lines, resulting in almost all single gender peer ties and peer groups. The patterning of peer ties in the complete network also reflected a gender influence, with different patterning emerging for males and females. Males clustered into larger more dense groups, while females generally were in smaller groups and less densely clustered, with many in dyads or tree-like structures. Peer influence, on the other hand, operated differently for males and females. For males, mixed gender influence was only important for their current cigarette use, but for females, it was important for all substance use other than their ever cigarette use (Chapter 9). Thus, single gender patterns of peer ties would be sufficient for chain reactions to occur in all but their current cigarette use for males, but female teenagers need mixed gender patterns to ensure chain reactions occur for all substances other than their first cigarette use. Thus, the patterning of peer ties along gender lines, or across gender lines, will have a profound effect on whether, or when, chain reactions will occur for male and female teenagers. Since mixed gender peer ties are likely to be formed later in the teenage years, this may delay the substance use of female teenagers, who need mixed gender peer ties for all but their first cigarette use. Such a delay would not occur for male teenagers who need mixed gender peer ties only for their current cigarette use.

The findings suggest, therefore, that gender impacts on the composition and structure of the networks that teenagers form with their peers. The gender composition of peer groups reflects the impact of gender on peer tie formation, which is usually single gender and rarely mixed gender. The structure of the networks, that is the patterning of peer ties in the peer groups, also appeared to vary by gender with males being more likely than females to form larger more dense patterns. Since male teenagers who were substance users had been influenced predominantly by other males, and females predominantly by males and females, the structure and composition of this complete network would have enhanced the likelihood of the male teenagers being influenced, while at the same time would have hindered the likelihood of females being influenced. Chain reactions result from peer selection, the patterning of peer ties and peer influence. So changes in the pattern over time alter the likelihood of influence for males and females. Further longitudinal research is needed to examine whether these findings on the gender impact on chain reactions are confirmed.

Despite the likelihood of peer influence by substance-using peers, some teenagers remain non-users even though they have substance-using peers (Chapter 8; Figures 8.1–8.9). They also continue in their peer ties and in their peer groups despite their dissimilarity in their substance use. Only in one of the 35 peer groups in this study have all teenagers in the peer group become similar in their use of all three substances (Peer Group 30), and only in one (Peer Group 28) has neither teenager used any of the three substances. In the other 33 peer groups, users and non-users of the different substances continue to interact and maintain their peer relationships, without the non-users becoming users. How can this be explained? The findings from this study suggest that peer ties do not discontinue due to dissimilarity in substance use. One reason seems to be that these peer ties were based on a much stronger footing than similarity in substance use. Similarities between these teenagers included age, gender, social class, geographical location, race, religion, education, their family life and their neighbourhood. Given this long list of similarities, substance use was just one more, and, on its own, did not merit losing friends, often lifelong friends. Another reason that explains the dissimilarity is that, while peer influence was apparently available, there was no overt effort to influence and, in response to questions as to why they did not use when they had an opportunity to do so, the teenagers usually simply did not want to, did not like the substance or did not agree with taking such substances. These teenagers were, therefore, exercising their individual choice not to use, although there was ample opportunity for them to use in their peer group.

Are peers the only influencers then? Results given in Chapter 5 have confirmed that parents and siblings influenced a small proportion of the teenagers into their use of cigarettes and alcohol in particular. And from other results, we are aware that relatives and other people have also influenced the substance use of the teenagers. They did so by providing the substance or being in the company of the teenagers when they used it. But it is not possible to know who has influenced particular teenagers without combining these data together. In order to place the teenagers' substance use in the context of the peer, family and other community influences, all of those who influenced them are combined in Table 10.1 for the 15 chains of substance users covered in Tables 8.4–8.6. Table 10.1 includes peer, family, relatives and other people who influenced the teenagers at their first use (Columns 2 and 3) and at their current use (Columns 5 and 6). These findings confirm that family members (f) have influenced the teenagers' cigarette use, sometimes in addition to their peers and sometimes instead of them (Chains 1, 2, 8, 10 and 12). For example, in link seven (15211–15141) of Chain 1, 15211 had been influenced by peers only for first use, while 15141 had been influenced by family only for first use. Numerous people, however, influenced the teenagers' alcohol use. Family (f), relatives (r) and other people (o) were involved with their peers, or sometimes replaced peers, to initiate the teenagers to alcohol use (Chains 3, 4, 11, 13 and 14). For example, in link one (15242–05502) of Chain 3, 15242 had been influenced by relatives and other people at first use, while 05502 had been influenced by peers (not 15242) and other people for first use. There was minimal involvement by people other than peers in the teenagers' drug use. Neither family nor relatives had been involved in their initiation to drug use and only in one chain (Chain 15) were other people (o) involved.

Family members, to a much lesser extent than peers, influenced the teenagers' current use of cigarettes (Chains 1, 10 and 12) and alcohol (Chains 3 and 11) and other people to a minimal extent influenced the teenagers' current use of alcohol (Chains 4 and 13) and drugs (Chain 7). These findings confirm that, at least in these three peer groups (Peer Groups 1–3), there has been considerable influence from family, relatives

Table 10.1 Substance use chains indicating influence by peers, family, relatives and others

Peer tie/link	Peer influence first use	Family, relatives and others influence first use	Current use	Peer influence current use	Family, relatives and others influence current use
Peer Group 1					
Chain 1: Cigarettes					
05502–15031	(*pp*)				
15031–15241	(*pp*)				
15031–14913	(*pp*)				
14913–15241	pp				
15241–15211	(*pp*)				
14913–15211	pp				
15211–15141	p–	–f	cc	–p	ff
15141–62701	–p	f–	cc	pp	f–
15141–14941		f–			
Chain 2: Cigarettes					
15122–15112	pp		cc	pp	
15112–15321	(*pp*)				
15321–05501	pp				
15321–54491	pp				
05501–54491	(*pp*)				
54491–54451	(*pp*)	–f			
Chain 3: Alcohol					
15242–05502	[–p]	ro o	cc	pp	f–
15242–15031	[–p]	ro–	cc	pp	f–
15242–15271	–p	ro o	cc	pp	f–
05502–15031	pp	o–	cc	pp	
15031–15271	pp	–o	cc	pp	
15271–15241	pp	o–	cc	pp	
15031–15241	pp		cc	pp	
15031–14913	pp		cc	pp	
14913–15241	pp		cc	pp	
14913–15211	p–	–f	cc	pp	
15241–15211	p–	–f	cc	pp	
15211–15141		ff			
15141–15131	–p	f–			
15131–15121	pp	–f			
15141–14941		ff			
15141–24832	–p	f fr			
24832–24821	pp	fr–	cc	pp	
15141–62701	–p	f–			
Chain 4: Alcohol					
15122–15112	pp				
15112–15321	pp	–o	cc	–p	o–
15321–15111	[p–]	o f			
15321–05501	pp	o–	cc	pp	

15321–54491	pp	o–	cc	pp	
05501–54491	pp		cc	pp	
54491–54451	(pp)	–o			
54451–54441	pp	o–			

Chain 5: Drugs

05502–15031	pp
15031–15241	pp

Chain 6: Drugs

15141–62701	pp

Chain 7: Drugs

05501–54491	pp		cc	pp	o–

Peer Group 2
Chain 8: Cigarettes

80861–24582	(p–)	–f			
24582–80551	(–p)	f–			
80551–61381	pp		cc	pp	

Chain 9: Cigarettes

62551–80751	pp		cc	pp

Chain 10: Cigarettes

61291–61672	(pp)		cc	pp	
61672–63301	(pp)		cc	pp	–f
63301–62202	(pp)		cc	pp	f–
62202–61672	pp		cc	pp	
62202–61331	pp				

Chain 11: Alcohol

62702–80561	(pp)		cc	pp	
80561–54282	pp	–f	cc	pp	
80561–80861	[p–]	–f	cc	pp	
80861–24582	(–p)	f–	cc	pp	
24582–80551	(p–)	–f			
80551–24583	(–p)	f–			
80551–61381	–NK	f–			
61381–43761	NK p				
43761–62372	pp	–o			
62372–62551	p–	o f			
62551–80751	–p	ff			
80861–80521	[–p]	f–	cc	pp	
24582–80521	(pp)		cc	pp	
80551–80521	[–p]	f–			
80521–61672	pp		cc	pp	
61672–63301	(pp)		cc	pp	–f
61672–61291	(pp)	–o			
63301–62202	(p–)	–r			
62202–61672	[–p]	r–			
62202–61331		r f			
61331–61671	[–p]	f o			
61671–62202	[p–]	o r			
61671–61291	pp	o o			

Table 10.1   (Continued)

Peer tie/link	Peer influence first use	Family, relatives and others influence first use	Current use	Peer influence current use	Family, relatives and others influence current use
Peer Group 3					
Chain 12: Cigarettes					
43671–43581	pp				
43581–43623	(p–)	–f	cc	pp	–f
43623–62522	–p	f–	cc	pp	f–
43623–62523	(–p)	f–	cc	pp	f–
62523–61511	(pp)				
43581–43571	pp				
43581–43791	pp		cc	pp	
43571–43623	p–	–f			
43571–43791	pp				
43791–43623	p–	–f	cc	pp	–f
43791–43582	pp		cc	pp	
43582–43591	pp				
Chain 13: Alcohol					
54421–24822	pp	–f			
24822–43671	(pp)	f–			
43671–43581	pp	–f	cc	pp	–o
43581–43791	pp	f–	cc	pp	o–
43581–43623	(pp)	f–	cc	pp	o–
43581–43571	pp	f–			
43791–43623	pp		cc	pp	
43791–43571	pp				
43571–43623	pp				
43623–62522	[p–]	–r			
43623–62523	(pp)	–o			
62523–61511	(pp)	o r			
62523–61512	(p–)	o f			
62522–62091		r fr			
62091–61511	(–p)	fr r			
Chain 14: Alcohol					
71081–62291	[p–]	– f			
Chain 15: Drugs					
24822–43671	[–p]				
43671–43581	pp	–o			
43581–43791	pp	o–			

and other people, as well as from peers, in the teenagers' substance use. This was particularly so for their alcohol use and may, in part, explain why the rate of alcohol use among the teenagers in this population was so high. There was minimal influence from people other than their peers for drug use and this may explain, in part, why the rate of drug use among the population of teenagers was so low. Their peers were, nevertheless, the main influencers in all 15 chains for the use of all three substances.

Conclusion

Social network analysis provides a very valuable framework for examining the individual behaviour of teenagers in the social context in which it emerges. It enables us to identify the social networks in which teenagers are located, to examine the pattern of relationships within them and to examine the impact of that pattern on the behaviour of the individual teenagers who form them (Wellman and Berkowitz, 1988: 3). Social network analysis has been used in this book to find and delineate the peer groups of teenagers in a complete network of teenagers in one community, and to examine the substance use of the individual teenagers in the context of the peer groups identified. The result has been the production of a chain reaction explanation, based on peer selection, the patterning of ties in peer groups and peer influence, for the teenagers' substance use. The explanation is strongly social network based. The social networks of particular relevance are the teenagers' peer groups because it is in these that the changes in behaviour, resulting in increased similarity in the substance use of teenagers, occur. Chain reactions, which are gender based, result from linking those who are similar in their substance use, with those who are not, in peer groups. Peer selections start the process. The peer group contributes in a profound manner by providing a pattern of ties in which peer influence can flourish. Within the peer group, those who are similar are linked with those who are not, and peer influence is available from those who are substance users, for those who have not yet used. Increasing similarity follows, with more teenagers becoming similar in their substance use over time. Some teenagers do not submit to peer influence because they do not want to use the substances.

When increased similarity does occur in the peer groups, following the chain reaction, the peer group itself changes. The chains of substance users in the peer group increase in size and thus provide more substance users in the peer group who may influence others. They may influence others through peer influence or they may select new peers who become part of the peer group and become exposed to peer influence. Thus, while the individual action of teenagers in selecting peers has a network effect, the network, in turn, has further effects on other individuals, by exposing them to peer influence, by selecting new peers and by continuing the chain reaction by linking those who are similar with those who are not similar in their substance use.

This chain reaction explanation for teenagers' substance use is consistent with research based on the homophily principle and on the tendency for those who are engaged in repeated interactions to become more similar over time. The homophily principle is the tendency for those who are similar in certain respects to form relationships (McPherson and Smith-Lovin, 1987: 370; McPherson, Smith-Lovin and Cook, 2001: 415). As explained above, the teenagers in this population had numerous similarities including their social class, geographical location, race, religion, education, their family life and their neighbourhood. Some were also similar in their substance use when they formed peer ties. This range of similarities made it likely that these teenagers would form peer ties. Through the formation of peer ties they were likely to increase their similarity and this is what the results of this study have confirmed. This is consistent with research which states that there is a tendency for those who engage in repeated interactions to become more similar to each other over time (Homans, 1950; Collins, 1988: 340). The teenagers in this study were engaging in repeated interactions numerous times a week in their neighbourhood. They were likely to become more similar. While the topic of interest in this book is their substance use, they were likely to have become similar in other ways too, for example the leisure time activities they liked, the kinds of films they liked or the music they liked.

Not only are teenagers in such peer groups likely to become similar, but social network theorists suggest that there are pressures towards similarity in the behaviour of individuals who form cohesive groups, such as peer groups (Friedkin, 1984: 236; Wasserman and Faust, 1994: 251). These pressures are due to social forces which operate in cohesive groups generally. Substance use research on teenagers has left little doubt that a strong social force at work in peer groups is peer influence. Thus, if teenagers are members of these cohesive peer groups, peer influence will be at work within them. The results of this study have confirmed that, indeed, there were pressures towards similarity in the substance use of teenagers in the peer groups identified in this study and that this operated in peer groups of all sizes and with a variety of patterns of peer ties. Despite these social forces, complete similarity was rarely observed in the peer groups. This is a valuable insight provided by this complete network study, which could not have been anticipated from previous research. Previous research was likely to find higher levels of similarity in dyads, or cliques of three to five members, than this study, or any other study, was likely to find in peer groups larger than cliques. Thus, previous research may have exaggerated the level of similarity likely to occur in peer groups of various sizes. These findings have, therefore, demonstrated that, while there is a tendency to similarity in peer groups in the teenagers' substance use, there is also a tolerance of difference in the same peer groups that is greater than might have been anticipated based on previous research on smaller peer groups.

The results of this study are also consistent with those of diffusion theorists. 'Diffusion is the process by which an innovation is communicated through certain channels over time among the members of a social system' (Rogers, 1983: 5). In this book, the innovation being diffused is substance use. The channels through which it is being diffused are the peer ties. It is, therefore, through the continued interactions in the peer relationships that the diffusion happens. The members of the social system are the teenagers and the social system is, in this case, the peer group and, at a broader level, the complete network. Diffusion theorists would suggest that, when an innovation is being diffused, there is uncertainty due to lack of knowledge about the innovation or the expected outcome. In the case of substance use, uncertainty would be based on not knowing from whom one could get the substance or not knowing the effect the substance would have on the teenager. These theorists suggest that successful diffusion depends on having others with whom one can communicate about the uncertainties of adopting the innovation (Rogers, 1983: 305; Burt, 1987: 1288; Valente, 1995: 12). Peers, who have already used the substance, can communicate with the teenagers about their uncertainties. These peers can provide the substance or help the teenager find someone who can provide it, demonstrate how to use it and provide a suitable environment, in the company of peers, in which the teenager can use the substance. Thus, their peers can deal with all of the uncertainties inherent in the teenagers' initiation to a new substance and ensure successful diffusion. The particular social conditions which lead to successful diffusion need to be addressed in future research. These include examining the relevance of threshold models (Valente, 1996: 70) in peer groups and complete networks and the importance of peer relationship timing and change (Moody, 2002: 25).

This book has used data from a complete network to examine teenagers' substance use in the social context in which it is embedded. A chain reaction explanation has been proposed, based on these data. While the data had some strengths, they also had weaknesses. Important strengths were that they were from a complete network of teenagers and that they were community, rather than school, based. This facilitated the examination of the teenagers' substance use behaviour in the context of the social networks of family, community and peers, in which it was embedded. But some limitations were that the data had been collected some time ago in one relatively small population in a Dublin suburb, and that they were cross-sectional. The population was similar on socio-demographic features to numerous other District Electoral Divisions in Dublin County Borough at the time it was selected (Chapter 3). So it was not unique. Nevertheless, it is not possible to gauge how similar this population would have been to others among whom it was selected in the social network features discovered within it. Nor is it possible to gauge how similar it is to other suburban working-class communities in other cities in other countries. So no claims are made as to the generalizability of the results from this study. Future research in similar communities in other cities and countries should explore this question.

The data were also cross-sectional and this limits the conclusions that can be made in terms of the relative impact of peer influence and selection on similarities in the substance use of teenagers. Ideally, longitudinal data are needed to arrive at definitive conclusions about this issue. In the absence of longitudinal data, this study has used retrospective data on the timing of the formation of peer ties and the timing of initiation to the use of each substance. These data were valuable as they could trace the teenagers' peer ties back to their early childhood and their substance use to their childhood or teenage years. They could not, however, provide any information on peer ties which had been dropped during that time and such information would be valuable in terms of understanding the relative impact of the formation of peer ties, the development of peer groups, changes in substance use among the teenagers, and the relative impact of individual behaviour on the peer groups and of the peer groups on the individual behaviour. Many of these questions cannot be satisfactorily answered without longitudinal data on individuals and social networks. Future research on teenagers' substance use in complete networks should, therefore, be longitudinal in design.

Ideally, complete network data, which are also longitudinal, are needed to provide full support for the theoretical explanation suggested in this book. Such data have not been found elsewhere in the literature. Future research should examine the chain reaction explanation suggested here with complete network, longitudinal data. What is needed is a study which can examine changes in individual behaviour, changes in the social networks in which that behaviour is embedded, including family and community, and the relative impact of one on the other over time. Important individual attributes, such as gender and age, must be included and their impact on the composition and structure of the changing networks monitored over time. Only with the use of such data can a definitive statement be made on the chain reaction explanation proposed in this book and on the relative impact of peer influence and peer selection on teenagers' substance use. There are huge methodological issues to be addressed in such research that researchers in the social network community have been trying to overcome for many years. In particular, the mathematical tools and computer technology needed for the analysis of the dynamic influence at work over time between individual action and social networks are crucial to this work and have only recently become available (Snijders et al., 2005). A longitudinal study, using complete network data, is planned by the author, which will combine a sociological approach with a social network perspective, and will use the newly available mathematical tools and computer technology to examine the dynamics of individual behaviour and social networks over time.

Ideally, researchers should do comparable research in different communities and in different countries to confirm the dynamic process of change which is at work among individuals in social networks, which I have suggested is a chain reaction process. Such innovative research would build on the achievements of researchers in recent years and would make a major contribution to sociological knowledge on the questions of peer influence, peer selection, the patterning of peer ties and the chain reaction process.

Appendix A
Questionnaire

[Gender of respondent: Male   Female]

1 Before we begin, could you tell me your age and date of birth?
   ____ years   Day ____ Month ____ Year ____
2 Are you living at home?   Yes   No

HAVE YOU PUT NAME ON CARD?

Adolescent social characteristics

3 Are you at school?
   At work?   GO TO Q16
   Not working?   GO TO Q16

IF AT SCHOOL

4 What is the name of your school?
5 What year are you in?   1st 2nd 3rd 4th 5th 6th
6 How many classes are in your year?
   1 2 3 4 5 6 7 8
7 Which class are you in?   Name of class:
8 Within your class would you say you are:
   one of the best students
   an average student or
   one of the worst at school work?
9 Have you done any State exam yet – like the: Inter Cert./group cert/other?

IF NO: GO TO Q11

10 What was your overall result in that exam?   Honours/pass/fail?
11 Overall, do you like or dislike school?   Like/dislike/don't know/other

IF DISLIKE: GO TO Q13

12 What do you like most about school?

NOW GO TO Q14

13   What do you dislike most about school?
14   At what age will you leave school?   15   16   17   18   19
15   Do you do any part-time work?   Yes   No

IF YES: GO TO Q25
IF NO: GO TO Q37
IF LEFT SCHOOL

16   What was the name of your last school?
17   What age were you when you left?   14   15   16   17   18
18   Why did you leave then?
19   Within your class in school would you say you were
        One of the best students
        An average student or
        One of the worst students at school work?
20   Had you done any State exam before you left school?
        Leaving cert/inter cert/group cert/other exam
21   What was your overall result in that exam?   Hons/pass/fail
22   Overall, did you like or dislike school?   Liked/disliked/don't know/other

IF DISLIKED: GO TO Q24

23   What did you like most about school?
24   What did you dislike most about school?

IF NOT WORKING GO TO Q30
IF AT WORK

25   Is your work part-time or full-time?
26   For how long have you been working?   < 1 year
                                            1 < 2 years
                                            2 < 3 years
                                            3 < 4 years
                                            4 < 5 years
27   What is your job?   Exact name?
28   Do you like your job?   Yes   No/Why not?
29   About how many miles from here is your work place located?
        <1   1   2   3   4   5   6   7   8   9   10+

NOW GO TO Q37
IF NOT WORKING

30   How long have you been out of work?   < 1 year
                                            1–2 years
                                            2–3 years
                                            3–4 years
                                            4–5 years
31   Have you had any job before now?   Yes
                                        No   GO TO Q34
32   What was that job?   Exact name:
33   Why did you leave?

34   Would you like to have a job?   Yes
                                     No   GO TO Q37
35   What job would you like?   Exact name:
36   Do you think you have: a good chance/a fair chance/no chance of getting
     such a job within the next year?

Family

I want to ask you some questions now about your family – first of all – your
parents
37   Are your parents alive?   Both parents alive
                               Mother only alive
                               Father only alive
                               Neither alive
38   Is your father working?   What is his job?
       Or unemployed?
     Does your mother work outside the home?   Yes   What is her job?
                                               No
39   For each of your parents would you say you are
                                       to your mother   to your father
       very close _____
       close _____
       not close _____
40   Within your family would you say that your mother and father
                                               Mother   Father
       Favour you _____
       Treat you the same as the others _____
       Treat you worse than the others _____
41   Do your parents give you   Mother   Father
       A lot of freedom _____
       A fair amount _____
       A little or _____
       No freedom _____
     To do what you want with your free-time when you are not at home?
42   Do you think they give you   Mother   Father
       Too much _____
       Enough _____
       Too little freedom _____
     To do what you want with your free-time when you are not at home?
43   Has either of your parents ever interfered with your choice of friends,
     that is, have they ever said they did not want you to be friendly with
     someone?
                                               Mother   Father
       Yes _____
       No _____

IF NO: GO TO Q46

44   Why did they object?
45   Did you do what they wanted?

46 Has either of your parents ever said that they did not want you to...

	Mother			Father		
	Yes	Not now	No	Yes	Not now	No
Go to a disco						
Smoke cigarettes						
Drink alcohol						
Take drugs						

47 Does your

	Mother		Father	
	Yes	No	Yes	No
Smoke cigarettes				
Drink alcohol?				

48 Have you ever

	Mother		Father	
	Yes	No	Yes	No
Smoked cigarettes with your				
Taken alcohol with your				

And now a few questions about your brothers and sisters

49 How many brothers   1   2   3   4   5   6   7
    and sisters have you?   1   2   3   4   5   6   7

PUT NAMES ACROSS TOP OF SHEETS

Starting with the eldest   Name   Name   Name   Name
                             Age   age   age   age
50   Who is living at home? _____

FOR ELDEST LIVING AT HOME AND WORKING

51   What is his/her job? _____
52   Are you very close/close/not close to _____
53   Who are you closest to? 1st/2nd/3rd _____
54   Do you pal around with any of
     them and their friends? _____
55   Do any of them pal around
     with you and your friends? _____
56   What do you do together? _____

ASK FOR ALL SIBLINGS

57   Does . . . smoke cigarettes? _____
58   Does . . . drink alcohol? _____

Just to finish this section . . .

59   How many evenings a week do you usually spend at home?
     0   1   2   3   4   5   6   7
60   How many evenings in the past week did you spend at home?
     0   1   2   3   4   5   6   7
61   How did you spend your evenings at home in the past week?

Associations with peers

This brings us to questions about your friendships and relationships with other people of your own age.

Before we start this section could I remind you again that everything you tell me is confidential . . . and if there is a question you don't want to answer just tell me . . . (Reasons names needed: easier to do the interview and as we want to work out friendship patterns from the results of the entire study we will only be able to do this if we know who is who!)

Could you tell me first about your friends – starting with your *best friend* – then *boyfriend* or *girlfriend* – then other *good friends* and then anyone else who is a *friend* of yours?

PUT NAMES ACROSS TOP OF SHEETS

Will you also tell me the other people of around your age that you *pal around with* (for example, in school or at discos) but who are not as close as friends? This list should cover all the people of your own age that you spend any free-time with?

PUT NAMES ACROSS TOP OF SHEETS
NOTE WHETHER PERSON IS BF (BEST FRIEND), BOYF (BOYFRIEND), GIRLF (GIRLFRIEND), GF (GOOD FRIEND), F (FRIEND) OR PAL

62   Name: _____
63   Age: _____
64   Gender: Male/female _____
65   How did you first get to know each of them? _____
66   When was that: Month/year? _____
67   Since when have you been BF, BOYF etc: Month/year ____
68   How often in the week do you usually meet? _____
69   How often did you meet last week? _____
70   How many of these meetings:
        did you arrange _____
        did he/she arrange _____
        did you both arrange? _____
71   What did you do together when you met? _____

ASK FOR ALL AFTER INDIVIDUAL QUESTIONS

72   Would you say you are very close/close or not close to? _____
73   Who are you closest to? 1st/2nd/3rd etc. _____
74   Going through the entire list again will you tell me which of them you go out with or spend time with in a group . . . and I want to keep the groups separate?

USE CAPITAL LETTERS TO LINK

. . . FOR EXAMPLE, AAA, BBB, CCC _____
FOR EACH GROUP

75   When did you start palling around together in a group?
     Month: ——   Year: ——

Smoking/drinking/drugs

I would like to ask you some questions now about smoking, drinking and taking drugs. We hope you will trust us with this information and answer honestly. Before we start I want to assure you again about the confidential nature of the interview.

Smoking

We will start with smoking cigarettes...

76   Have you ever smoked?   Yes   GO TO Q80
                              No
77   Have you ever had an opportunity to smoke?   Yes   No
78   Why did you not smoke?
79   Do you think you will ever smoke?   Yes   No

NOW GO TO Q103
IF HAVE EVER SMOKED

80   Have you smoked within the past month?   Yes   GO TO Q82
                                             No

IF NOT IN PAST MONTH

81   Have you smoked within the past year?   Yes   No

ALL WHO HAVE SMOKED

82   At what age did you first smoke a cigarette?   —— years
83   Did you continue to smoke from then?   Yes
                                           No... When did you start again?
84   How did you start smoking?
85   Who were you with when you took your first cigarette?
       On own
       With others: relationship then   male or female
86   Did you enjoy your first cigarette?   Very much/not at all/or was it just alright?
87   Did you feel all right afterwards or had you any ill-effects?
       All right   Ill-effects – Specify:
88   Did you buy or were you given your first cigarette or how did you get it?
       Buy   given   other

89   Who bought or gave it to you?   Relationship then   male or female
90   Did you pay for it?   Yes   Then?   Later?
                                    No

IF PAID: GO TO Q92

91   Did you buy or give . . . a cigarette in return?
        Yes   Then?   Later?
        No   Did you return the favour another way?
               Yes   How?   Then? Later?
               No

IF SMOKED IN PAST MONTH: GO TO Q94
IF NOT IN PAST MONTH

92   At what age did you last smoke a cigarette? —— years
93   Why did you not smoke since then?

FOR THOSE STOPPED SMOKING GO TO Q103

Current smokers/smoked in past month

94   How many cigarettes do you smoke a day?
95   When smoking, do you usually smoke . . . on your own
        With others: relationship   male or female
96   Would you say you enjoy smoking . . . very much/not at all/or is it just
     all right?
97   Do you feel any ill-effects from smoking cigarettes?
        Yes/Specify: No
98   When you want cigarettes now do you buy them or does someone give
     them to you or how do you get them?
        Buy always/buy . . . given sometimes/given always
99   Who buys or gives you cigarettes?   Relationship   Male or female
100 Do you pay for them?   Yes   Then?   Later?
                                    No

FOR EACH PERSON WHO BUYS OR GIVES CIGARETTES

101 Do you buy/give . . . cigarettes in return?   Yes   Then?   Later?
        No   Do you return the favour another way?
        Yes   How? Then? Later?
        No
102 Do you think you will continue to smoke?   Yes   No

Drinking

And now I would like to ask you about drinking alcohol, that is, any of the drinks
like cider, beer, wine or spirits.

103 Have you ever had a drink of
         Cider   Yes No
         Beer (lager, ale, stout etc.)   Yes No
         Wine   Yes No
         Spirits (vodka, whiskey etc.) Yes No

IF YES GO TO Q107
IF NEVER DRANK ALCOHOL

104 Have you ever had an opportunity to drink? Yes   No
105 Why did you not drink?
106 Do you think you will ever drink? Yes   No

NOW GO TO Q132
IF EVER DRANK ALCOHOL

107 Have you had an alcoholic drink within the past month?
         Yes   GO TO Q109
         No

IF NOT IN PAST MONTH

108 Have you had an alcoholic drink in the past year?   Yes   No

ALL WHO HAVE HAD AN ALCOHOLIC DRINK

109 At what age did you have your first drink? ____ years
110 Did you continue to drink from then?   Yes   No: When did you start
         again?
111 How did you start drinking?
112 Who were you with when you had your first drink?
         On own
         With others: Relationship then   Male or female
113 Did you enjoy your first drink... very much, not at all, or was it just all
         right?
114 Did you feel all right afterwards or did you experience any ill-effects?
         All right   Ill-effects... specify:
115 Did you buy or were you given your first drink or how did you get it?
         Buy   Given   Others
116 Who bought or gave it to you?   Relationship then: Male or female
117 Did you pay for it?   Yes   Then? Later?
                                       No
118 Did you buy/give... a drink in return?
         Yes   Then? Later?
         No   Did you return the favour another way?
                        Yes   How? Then? Later?
                        No

IF DID NOT DRINK IN PAST MONTH

119 At what age did you last take a drink? ____ years
120 Why did you not have a drink since then?

IF STOPPED DRINKING GO TO Q132

Current drinkers/drank in past month

121   Within the past month how many times/days have you had an alcoholic drink? Number: ____

122   For the most recent time you have been drinking, *what drink* did you have and *how many* drinks did you have?

      Drink   Number
      Cider   _____
      Beer   _____
      Wine   _____
      Spirits   _____

123   Have you ever been drunk?   Yes   How often?
                                 No

124   When drinking do you usually drink . . .
      On your own or   With others: relationship   male or female

125   Would you say you enjoy drinking
      Very much, not at all or is it just all right?

126   Have you ever felt any ill-effects from drinking alcohol?
      Yes   specify
      No

127   When you want a drink now, do you buy it yourself or does someone buy or give it to you or how do you get it?
      Buy always   Buy or given sometimes   Given always

128   Who buys/gives you drinks?   Relationship   Male or female

129   Do you pay for it?   Yes   No

For each person who buys/gives you drink

130   Do you buy/give . . . a drink in return?
      Yes   Then? Later?
      No   Do you return the favour another way?
              Yes   How?   Then?   Later?
              No

131   Do you think you will continue to drink alcohol?   Yes   No

Drug use

I'd now like to ask you about taking drugs – and again I hope that you will trust us with this information as it is vital to the study we are doing.

132   Have you ever used/or even tried any of these drugs?

USE SHOW CARD 1

Marijuana (cannabis, pot, hash, grass etc.)	Yes	No
Inhalants (glue, tippex, petrol, lighter fluid, solvents, gas etc.)	Yes	No
Hallucinogens . . .		
(LSD, acid, psilocybin-magic mushrooms, PCP, angel dust etc.)	Yes	No
Cocaine	Yes	No
Heroin	Yes	No

133 Drugs on this list are usually prescribed by a doctor – I want to ask you if you have used any of them at a time when they were *not* prescribed for you by a doctor...

USE SHOW CARD 2

Other opiates (codeine, cough syrup, painkillers, morphine etc.)	Yes	No
Stimulants (amphetamines, speed, uppers, ups, pep pills etc.)	Yes	No
Sedatives (Barbiturates, downs etc.)	Yes	No
Tranquillizers (valium, librium etc.)	Yes	No

134 Have you used any other drug that is not on these lists?
      Yes   Name of drug
      No

IF NEVER USED ANY DRUG   GO TO Q136

135 **For each drug ever used**

	Used in past month?		IF NOT PAST MONTH **Used in past year?**		IF NOT PAST YEAR **How often.. lifetime?**
	Yes (no. of times)	**No**	**Yes (no. of times)**	**No**	**No. of times**
Marijuana					
Inhalants					
Hallucinogens					
Cocaine					
Heroin					
Other opiates					
Stimulants					
Sedatives					
Tranquillizers					
Other					

[**Further references to this list in this Appendix will be reduced to marijuana to other**]

IF YES TO PAST MONTH/ PAST YEAR/ OR LIFETIME: GO TO Q140
IF NEVER USED ANY DRUG

136 Have you ever had an opportunity to use drugs? Yes   No
      IF YES: What drug?   When?   Where?
137 Why did you not use it/them?
138 Do you think you will ever take drugs? Yes   No
139 Do you think that taking drugs is good/all right/or bad?

IF NEVER USED ANY DRUG: END OF INTERVIEW

Thank you ...

We may want to talk to some of the teenagers we interview again – there would be no questionnaire – just talking. Before leaving, I'd just like to ask you if you would be willing to talk to one of the research team again? Yes   No

ALL WHO HAVE TAKEN A DRUG

140 Age when first used?   When was that?
                            Month: Year:
         Marijuana to _____
         Other _____
141 How did you start taking drugs? (Will you tell me a bit more about that?)
142 When taking/using your first drug were you . . .
         on your own
         With others: No names   relationship then   Male or female
143 Did you enjoy your first experience with drugs . . . very much, not at all or
     was it all right?
144 Did you feel all right afterwards or did you experience ill-effects?
         All right   Ill-effects . . . Specify:
145 Did you buy or were you given your first drug – or how did you get it?
         Buy   given   other
146 Did you get it from a friend ____ or some other person ____?
         No name   relationship then   Male or female
147 Are you (still) friends with this person now?   Yes   No
148 Did you pay for it?   Yes   Then? Later?
                           No
         IF NO: Did you buy/give . . . a drug in return?
                  Yes   Then? Later?
                  No
         IF NO: Did you return the favour another way?
                  Yes   How? Then? Later?
                  No

IF USED DRUGS IN PAST MONTH: GO TO Q151
IF DID NOT TAKE DRUGS LAST MONTH

149 What age were you when you last took a drug? And when was that?
         Name of drug: Age: Month: Year:
150 Why have you not taken drugs since then?

IF STOPPED TAKING DRUGS: GO TO Q176

Current drug users/used in past month

151 Each time that you take a drug, how much or what size of dose do you
     take? And is this more/same or less that when you took it first?
                                         How much?   More   same   less
         Marijuana to _____
         Other _____
152 For each drug taken – are the effects on you of taking . . . usually
                                              Pleasant   Unpleasant
         Marijuana to _____
         Other _____

IF MORE THAN ONE DRUG IS USED

153 Which of them do you most like taking?   Drug   Why?

154 When you want to get this (that is, your favourite) drug – and you have the money – can you always get it? Yes   No . . . what do you take instead?

155 What drugs are easiest for you to get?
Names of drugs:

156 What drugs are most difficult for you to get?
Names of drugs:

157 Have you ever taken more than one of the drugs you mentioned at the same time?
Names of drugs: FOR EACH MIX – Is effect usually
Pleasant or unpleasant?

_____

158 Have you ever taken alcohol with a drug?
Which drink(s) with which drug(s)?   FOR EACH MIX – Is effect usually
Pleasant or unpleasant?

_____

159 Have you ever got 'high' from drugs?
Yes   Which drug?   How often?

_____

IF NO: GO TO Q161

160 Will you describe the feeling of being 'high' . . . how you felt the last time you were 'high'? (WHICH DRUG – WHICH 'HIGH'?)

161 Have you ever had a bad experience from using a drug or a combination of drugs?
Yes   Which drugs?   What happened?
No

162 Have you ever had a bad experience because you could not get a dose of the drug(s) that you use?
Yes   Which drugs?   What happened?
No

163 When using drugs, do you usually take the drug(s)
On your own? With others? Relationship (no names)
Male or Female
Marijuana to _____
Other _____

164 When you want or need drugs now do you buy them yourself or does someone give them to you (that is, buy them for you)?
Buy always Buy/given sometimes given always
Marijuana to _____
Other _____

165 Do you buy/get them from a friend _____ or other person _____?
No name   relationship   male or female

166 You told me earlier who you got your first drug from – is this the same person or a different person?
Same person: Different person: why did you change?

167 Do you pay for the drug(s)?
Yes   Then?   Later?
No   GO TO Q169

168 Do you think that what you pay for your drugs now is . . . about right, too little or too much?

IF DON'T PAY

169   Do you buy/give ... drugs in return?
       Yes   Then? Later?
       No

IF YES: GO TO Q171

170   Do you return the favour another way?
       Yes   How? Then? Later?
       No

171   For how long can you manage without a dose of each drug used?
       How long?   Days Hours
       Marijuana to _____
       Other _____

172   Have you ever tried to stay off all drugs? How long did you stay off them?
                       Did try to stay off drugs   How long stayed off
                          Yes No   Days Hours
       Marijuana to _____
       Other _____

173   Have you ever had to go to – a doctor   Yes No
       Or a hospital – because of drugs?   Yes No

174   Why do you think you take drugs?

175   Do you think you will continue to take drugs? Which drugs?
                                                      Yes   No
       Marijuana to _____
       Other _____

To finish

176   Do you think taking drugs is ... good, all right or bad?

Thank you

We may want to talk to some of the teenagers we interview again – there would be no questionnaire – just talking. Before leaving, I'd just like to ask you if you would be willing to talk to one of the research team again? Yes   No

SHOW CARD 1

Marijuana (cannabis, pot, hash, grass etc.)
Inhalants (glue, tippex, petrol, lighter fluid, solvents, gas etc.)
Hallucinogens ...
(LSD, acid, psilocybin-magic mushrooms, PCP, angel dust etc.)
Cocaine
Heroin

SHOW CARD 2

Other opiates (codeine, cough syrup, painkillers, morphine etc.)
Stimulants (amphetamines, speed, uppers, ups, pep pills etc.)
Sedatives (Barbiturates, downs etc.)
Tranquillizers (valium, librium etc.)

Appendix B
Absolute Alcohol Consumption Index

Cider

1 litre = 35.2 fluid ounces × 3.5 per cent (absolute alcohol content, per cent volume) = 1.232 fluid ounces of absolute alcohol.

Beer

1 pint = 20.0 fluid ounces × 4.0 per cent (absolute alcohol content, per cent volume) = 0.8 fluid ounces of absolute alcohol.

Wine

1 glass = 4.0 fluid ounces × 11.5 per cent (absolute alcohol content, per cent volume) = 0.46 fluid ounces of absolute alcohol.

Spirits

1 glass = 1.25 fluid ounces × 40.0 per cent (absolute alcohol content, per cent volume) = 0.5 fluid ounces of absolute alcohol.

Appendix C
Drug Classes

Marijuana: other names include cannabis, hash, grass, pot or hashish. In the text it is spelt marijuana unless it is in a quotation which uses the spelling marihuana.

Inhalants: include sniffed glue, breathing the contents of aerosol spray cans or inhaling other gases or sprays as well as amyl or butyl nitrites (Johnston, O'Malley and Bachman, 1984: 454, 455) and solvents (Grube and Morgan, 1986: 115).

Hallucinogens: include LSD, that is acid, mescaline, peyote, psilocybin, which includes magic mushrooms (Grube and Morgan, 1986: 115), PCP or phencyclidine, that is, angel dust (Johnston, O'Malley and Bachman, 1984: 441) and DMT (Miller et al., 1983: answer sheet *8).

Cocaine: other names include coke or crack.

Heroin: other names include smack, horse, skag (Johnston, O'Malley and Bachman, 1984: 451). Since it is an opiate, some researchers may include it as an opiate rather than listing it separately.

Other opiates: include all opiates other than heroin. They include methadone, opium, morphine, codeine, demerol, paregoric, talwin, laudanum and morphine (Johnston, O'Malley and Bachman, 1984: 452), and painkilling drugs, such as darvon, percodan, demerol, dilaudid, tylenol with codeine, and codeine (Miller et al., 1983: Section F, questionnaire, answer sheet *6) and cough syrup.

Stimulants: include amphetamines and drugs such as benzedrine, dexedrine, methedrine, ritalin, preludin, dexamyl and methamphetamine, which are referred to as uppers, ups, speed, bennies, dexies, pep pills and diet pills (Johnston, O'Malley and Bachman, 1984: 444), biphetamine and desoxyn (Miller et al., 1983, Section F, questionnaire, answer sheet *5).

Sedatives: include barbiturates including phenobarbial, seconal, tuinal, nembutal, luminal, desbutal and amytal which are sometimes called downs, downers, goofballs, yellows, reds, blues and rainbows (Johnston, O'Malley and Bachman, 1984: 447), quaaludes, placidyl and sopor (Miller et al., 1983: answer sheet *3).

Tranquillizers: include valium, librium, benadryl, tranxene, equanil and libritabs (Miller et al., 1983: answer sheet *4), miltown, meprobamate, serax, atarax, and vistaril (Johnston, O'Malley and Bachman, 1984: 449).

Appendix D
The Patterning of Peer Ties in Peer Groups 6 and 7

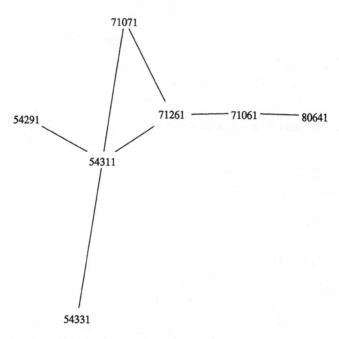

Figure A.1   Peer Group 6: Pattern of peer ties.

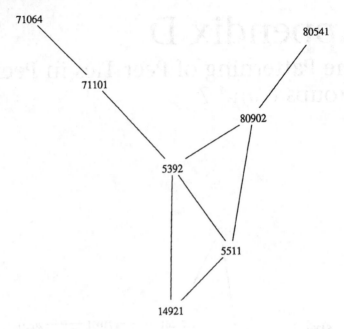

Figure A.2   Peer Group 7: Pattern of peer ties.

Glossary of Terms

Adolescents: usually refers to those who are in their teenage years (13–19) or a little younger; exact years are often not specified.

Alcohol use: refers in a general way to the individual's drinking of alcoholic drinks.

Cigarette use: refers in a general way to the individual's cigarette smoking.

Chains (of substance users): used to describe continuous links between dyads of substance users, who are connected to other dyads of users of the same substance, in a pattern similar to the links in a chain.

Chain reaction: used in this book to describe the process which results in chains of users of the same substance emerging in peer groups (Chapters 8 and 9). The chain reaction results from peer selection, the patterning of peer ties and peer influence.

Complete network: sometimes described as a whole network. A complete network is covered when all relationships existing between all actors within a particular population are identified (Knoke and Kuklinski, 1982: 17).

Composition of network: refers to measurements on actors in a network (Wasserman and Faust, 1994: 21). It is used in this book to refer to the gender composition of the peer groups (Chapter 9).

Current use (of substance): means use in the past 30 days or month prior to interview.

Cutpoint: a node (for example, an individual) is a cutpoint if the number of components in the graph that contains the node is fewer than the number of components in the subgraph that results from deleting the node from the graph (Wasserman and Faust, 1994: 112, 113).

Direct peer tie: peer tie linking two individuals, usually indicated by a line linking two nodes, which represent the individuals (see Figures).

Distance: is the length of the shortest path between individuals in a network (Wasserman and Faust, 1994: 110). Direct and indirect ties are counted to measure distance.

Drug classes: Marijuana, inhalants, hallucinogens, cocaine, heroin, other opiates, stimulants, sedatives and tranquillizers (Appendix C).

Drugs of abuse: Marijuana, inhalants, hallucinogens, cocaine, heroin, other opiates, stimulants, sedatives and tranquillizers (Appendix C).

Drug use: the use of any drug from the nine drug classes: marijuana, inhalants, hallucinogens, cocaine, heroin, other opiates, stimulants, sedatives and tranquillizers (Appendix C).

Dyad: a relationship between a pair of individuals, in this book usually between teenagers and their peers.

Dyadic peer tie: a relationship between a teenager and peer.

Early dropouts: leaving school before 16th birthday.

Egocentric peer network: an individual's peer ties and all of the peer ties between those peers (Knoke and Kuklinski, 1982: 16).

Ever use (of substance): means that the individuals have used a substance at some time in their lifetime.

Indirect peer tie: a tie which links two individuals, who do not have a direct peer tie with each other, but do have direct peer ties with one other individual (indicated by three nodes/individuals linked by two lines/relationships) (see Figures).

Interlocking egocentric networks: these networks form when individuals' egocentric networks share some of the same peers or when a relationship exists between members of two egocentric networks.

Link (between peers): a tie or relationship between two peers.

Mixed gender dyads or peer groups: male and female teenagers are members of dyads or peer groups.

Multilevel analysis: data at different levels of analysis are combined. For example, data on individual teenagers' substance use are combined with dyadic data on peer ties in peer groups (Chapter 8).

Path: direct and indirect ties are used to trace the path between individuals in a network. Path relates to distance, which is the length of the shortest path between individuals in a network (Wasserman and Faust, 1994: 110).

Pattern of peer ties: the structure or formation which the peer ties take in a network or peer group.

Patterning of peer ties: the structure or formation which the peer ties take in a network or peer group.

Peer(s): in research on substance use, peer usually refers to an adolescent's/teenager's friend. The type of friends included in this category often varies between researchers. In the Kirke data, peer is a generic term which includes best friend, boyfriend or girlfriend, good friend, friend or pal.

Peer group: this concept is used differently by different researchers. It may be used to describe a small clique of friends or as a generic term to include a range of friends. In the Kirke data, peer group includes all of the teenagers and their peers who are connected to each other through peer ties by paths of any distance (Kirke, 2004: 6). The peer group is defined as a weak component. This means that it is the maximum unique subset of points which are connected, directly or indirectly, to each other by lines (Harary, Norman and Cartwright, 1965: 405).

Peer influence: usually used to describe the tendency for similarity between adolescents or teenagers, whereby one individual is likely to change and become a substance user, at some time point after their peer has used a particular substance.

In this book, two criteria of peer influence are used: that the teenager was supplied with a substance by peers or that the teenager used the substance in the company of peers.

Peer network: may be used as a generic term to describe a network forming from the peer ties between individual teenagers/adolescents or with a more specific meaning. Researchers usually denote the type of network, that is, whether it is an egocentric peer network or a peer group of interlocking egocentric networks.

Peer tie: a relationship or tie between two individuals, usually used in relation to teenagers and their peers.

Peer selection: used to describe the process of choosing peers; used to describe the process by which teenagers and their peers become similar by choosing peers who are already similar to themselves in some respects.

Previous use (of substance): means that the individuals have used the substance at some time in their lifetime, but are not current users.

Relationship (between peers): tie or link between teenagers and their peers.

Selection (of peers): used to describe the process of choosing peers; used to describe the process by which teenagers and their peers become similar by choosing peers who are already similar to themselves in some respects.

Single gender dyads or peer groups: male teenagers only or female teenagers only in dyads or peer groups.

Size of social network: the number of nodes, or the number of individuals who have relationships or ties in a social network.

Size of peer group: the number of individuals who have peer ties in the peer group.

Social class: is based on the occupation of the principal wage earner in the family using the Classification of Occupations from the Census of Population (1986). The social classes range from Social Class 1: Higher professional workers to Social Class 6: Unskilled manual workers (Chapter 5).

Social network: consists of a finite set of actors and the relationships between those actors (Wasserman and Faust, 1994: 20). In this book, the peer groups and the complete network are social networks.

Social network analysis: social network analysis is a distinct research perspective in the social and behavioural sciences. It is based on the assumption of the importance of relationships among interacting units, and social network methods have been devised for the analysis of collections of individuals and the links between them (Wasserman and Faust, 1994: 4). Using this perspective in this book, teenagers are seen as interdependent, rather than independent, units; relational ties between the teenagers and their peers are seen as channels for the flow of resources, in this case, influence; the structure, or pattern, of peer ties in their peer groups are seen as providing opportunities for, or constraints against, peer influence; the structure and composition of the peer groups are examined in terms of gender; and peer network data are combined with individual-level data in multilevel analyses in order to explain the chain reaction process at work in their increasing similarity in substance use.

Structure of network: is the pattern of the relational ties in the network. In this book it is the pattern formed by the peer ties in different peer groups (Chapters 7–9).

Substance use: the use of any of the three substances, cigarettes, alcohol or drugs from any of the drug classes.

Teenagers: In this book teenagers of 14–18 years had been interviewed. When the concept teenager(s) is used in the book, to describe this study's data, it refers to teenagers in this age category.

Triad: ties between three nodes or individuals. In this book, triad would refer to peer ties between three teenagers.

Weak component: This means that it is the maximum unique subset of points which are connected, directly or indirectly, to each other by lines (Harary, Norman and Cartwright, 1965: 405). In the Kirke data, weak components are the peer groups.

Whole network: sometimes described as a complete network. A complete network is covered when all relationships existing between all actors within a particular population are identified (Knoke and Kuklinski, 1982: 17).

Bibliography

Abel, G., Plumridge, L. and Graham, P. (2002). 'Peers, networks or relationships: Strategies for understanding social dynamics as determinants of smoking behaviour', *Drugs: Education, Prevention and Policy*, 9(4): 325–338.

Adler, I. and Kandel, D. B. (1981). 'Cross-cultural perspectives on developmental stages in adolescent drug use', *Journal of Studies on Alcohol*, 42(9): 701–715.

Akers, R. L., Krohn, M. D., Lanza-Kaduce, L. and Radosevich, M. (1979). 'Social learning and deviant behavior: A specific test of a general theory', *American Sociological Review*, 44: 635–655.

Baerveldt, C. and Snijders, T. A. B. (1994). 'Influences on and from the segmentation of networks: Hypotheses and tests', *Social Networks*, 16(3): 213–232.

Bailey, S. L. and Hubbard, R. L. (1990). 'Developmental variation in the context of marijuana initiation among adolescents', *Journal of Health and Social Behavior*, 31(1): 58–70.

Bailey, S. L. and Hubbard, R. L. (1991). 'Developmental changes in peer factors and the influence on marijuana initiation among secondary school students', *Journal of Youth and Adolescence*, 20(3): 339–360.

Bailey, S. L., Ennett, S. T. and Ringwalt, C. L. (1993). 'Potential mediators, moderators, or independent effects in the relationship between parents' former and current cigarette use and their children's cigarette use', *Addictive Behaviors*, 18: 601–621.

Barnes, J. A. (1972). 'Social networks', *Addison-Wesley Modular Publications*, Module No. 26: 1–29.

Barnes, G. M., Farrell, M. P. and Banerjee, S. (1994). 'Family influences on alcohol abuse and other problem behaviors among black and white adolescents in a general population sample', *Journal of Research on Adolescence*, 4(2): 183–201.

Barrett, C. J. and James-Cairns, D. (1980). 'The social network in marijuana-using groups', *International Journal of the Addictions*, 15: 677–688.

Bauman, K. E. and Ennett, S. T. (1994). 'Peer influence on adolescent drug use', *American Psychologist*, 49: 820–822.

Bauman, K. E. and Ennett, S. T. (1996). 'On the importance of peer influence for adolescent drug use: Commonly neglected considerations', *Addiction*, 91(2): 185–198.

Becker, H. S. (1953). 'Becoming a marijuana user', *American Journal of Sociology*, 54: 235–242.

Bernard, H. R., Johnsen, E. C., Killworth, P. D., McCarty, C., Shelley, G. A. and Robinson, S. (1990). 'Comparing four different methods for measuring personal social networks', *Social Networks*, 12: 179–215.

Biernacki, P. and Waldorf, D. (1981). 'Snowball sampling: Problems and techniques of chain referral sampling', *Sociological Methods and Research*, 10(2): 141–163.

Brewer, D. D. (1993). 'Patterns of recall of persons in a student community', *Social Networks*, 15: 335–359.

Brewer, D. D. (2000). 'Forgetting in the recall-based elicitation of personal and social networks', *Social Networks*, 22: 29–43.

Brewer, D. D. and Webster, C. M. (1999). 'Forgetting of friends and its effects on measuring friendship networks', *Social Networks*, 21: 361–373.

Brook, J. S., Lukoff, I. F. and Whiteman, M. (1980). 'Initiation into adolescent marijuana use', *The Journal of Genetic Psychology*, 137(1): 133–142.

Brook, J. S., Whiteman, M. and Gordon, A. S. (1982). 'Qualitative and quantitative aspects of adolescent drug use: Interplay of personality, family and peer correlates', *Psychological Reports*, 51(3, 2): 1151–1163.

Brook, J. S., Whiteman, M. and Gordon, A. S. (1983). 'Stages of drug-use in adolescence – Personality, peer and family correlates', *Developmental Psychology*, 19(2): 269–277.

Brook, J. S., Whiteman, M., Brook, D. W. and Gordon, A. S. (1982). 'Paternal and peer characteristics – Interactions and association with male college-students' marijuana use', *Psychological Reports*, 51(3): 1319–1330.

Brook, J. S., Whiteman, M., Gordon, A. S. and Brenden, C. (1983a). 'Older brother's influence on younger sibling's drug-use', *The Journal of Psychology*, 114(1): 83–90.

Brook, J. S., Whiteman, M., Gordon, A. S. and Brook, D. W. (1983b). 'Paternal correlates of adolescent marijuana use in the context of the mother-son and parental dyads', *Genetic Psychology Monographs*, 108(2): 197–213.

Brugha, T. S. (Ed.) (1996). *Social Support and Psychiatric Disorder: Research Findings and Guidelines for Clinical Practice*, Cambridge, Cambridge University Press.

Burgess, R. L. and Akers, R. L. (1966). 'A differential association – reinforcement theory of criminal behavior', *Social Problems*, 14: 128–147.

Burt, R. S. (1984). 'Network items and the general social survey', *Social Networks*, 6: 293–339.

Burt, R. S. (1987). 'Social contagion and innovation: Cohesion versus structural equivalence', *American Journal of Sociology*, 92: 1287–1335.

Burt, R. S. (2000). 'Decay functions', *Social Networks*, 22(1): 1–28.

Campbell, K. E. and Lee, B. A. (1991). 'Name generators in surveys of personal networks', *Social Networks*, 13: 203–221.

Carrington, P. J., Scott, J. and Wasserman, S. (2005). *Models and Methods in Social Network Analysis*, New York, Cambridge University Press.

Census of Population (1981, 1986). Dublin, Central Statistics Office.

Clayton, R. R. and Voss, H. L. (1981). 'Young men and drugs in Manhattan: A causal analysis', *Research Monograph 39*, U.S. Dept. of Health and Human Services, National Institute on Drug Abuse.

Cohen, J. M. (1977). 'Sources of peer group homogeneity', *Sociology of Education*, 50(4): 227–241.

Collins, R. (1988). *Theoretical Sociology*, San Diego, Harcourt Brace Jovanovich, Inc.

Cotterell, J. (1996). *Social Networks and Social Influences in Adolescence*, London, Routledge.

Curran, P. J., Stice, E. and Chassin, L. (1997). 'The relation between adolescent and peer alcohol use: A longitudinal random coefficients model', *Journal of Consulting and Clinical Psychology*, 65: 130–140.

Dembo, R., Schmeidler, J. and Burgos, W. (1982). 'Processes of early drug involvement in three inner-city neighborhood settings', *Deviant Behavior*, 3(4): 359–383.

Dembo, R., Farrow, D., Des Jarlais, D. C., Burgos, W. and Schmeidler, J. (1981). 'Examining a causal model of early drug involvement among inner-city junior high school youths', *Human Relations*, 34(3): 169–193.

Donovan, J. E. and Jessor, R. (1983). 'Problem drinking and the dimension of involvement with drugs: A guttman scalogram analysis of adolescent drug use', *American Journal of Public Health*, 73(5): 543–552.

Elder, G. H. Jr. (1968). 'Adolescent socialization and development' in Borgatta, E. F. and Lambert, W. W. (Eds), *Handbook of Personality Theory and Research*, Chicago, Rand McNally and Company, 239–364.

Emirbayer, M. and Goodwin, J. (1994). 'Network analysis, culture, and the problem of agency', *American Journal of Sociology*, 99(6): 1411–1454.

Ennett, S. T. and Bauman, K. E. (1991). 'Mediators in the relationship between parental and peer characteristics and beer drinking by early adolescents', *Journal of Applied Social Psychology*, 21(20): 1699–1711.

Ennett, S. T. and Bauman, K. E. (1993). 'Peer group structure and adolescent cigarette smoking: A social network analysis', *Journal of Health and Social Behavior*, 34: 226–236.

Ennett, S. T. and Bauman, K. E. (1994). 'The contribution of influence and selection to adolescent peer group homogeneity: The case of adolescent cigarette smoking', *Journal of Personality and Social Psychology*, 67(4): 653–663.

Ennett, S. T. and Bauman, K. E. (1996). 'Adolescent social networks: School, demographic, and longitudinal considerations', *Journal of Adolescent Research*, 11(2): 194–215.

Ennett, S. T., Bauman, K. E. and Koch, G. G. (1994). 'Variability in cigarette smoking within and between adolescent friendship cliques', *Addictive Behaviors*, 19(3): 295–305.

Ennett, S. T., Bauman, K. E., Foshee, V. A., Pemberton, M. and Hicks, K. A. (2001). 'Parent-child communication about adolescent tobacco and alcohol use: What do parents say and does it affect youth behavior?', *Journal of Marriage and Family*, 63: 48–62.

Fang, X., Li, X., Stanton, B. and Dong, Q. (2003). 'Social network positions and smoking experimentation among Chinese adolescents', *American Journal of Health Behavior*, 27(3): 257–267.

Feld, S. (1981). 'The focused organization of social ties', *American Journal of Sociology*, 86(5): 1015–1035.

Fischer, C. S. (1982a). 'What do we mean by "friend"? An inductive study', *Social Networks*, 3: 287–306.

Fischer, C. S. (1982b). *To Dwell Among Friends: Personal Networks in Town and City*, Chicago, London, The University of Chicago Press, Ltd.

Flom, P. L., Friedman, S. R., Neaigus, A. and Sandoval, M. (2003). 'Boundary-crossing and drug use among young adults in a low-income, minority, urban neighborhood', *Connections*, 25(2): 77–87.

Fraser, M. and Hawkins, J. D. (1984). 'Social network analysis and drug misuse', *Social Service Review*, 81–97.

Freeman, L. C. (1992). 'The sociological concept of "group": An empirical test of two models', *American Journal of Sociology*, 98: 55–79.

Freeman, L. C., Webster, C. M. and Kirke, D. M. (1998). 'Exploring social structure using dynamic three-dimensional color images', *Social Networks*, 20: 109–118.

Friedkin, N. E. (1984). 'Structural cohesion and equivalence explanations of social homogeneity', *Sociological Methods and Research*, 12: 235–261.

Friedkin, N. E. and Cook, K., (1990). 'Peer group influence', *Sociological Methods and Research*, 19(1): 122–143.

Gaughan, M. (2003). 'Predisposition and pressure: Mutual influence and adolescent drunkenness', *Connections*, 25(2): 17–31.

Granovetter, M. S. (1973). 'The strength of weak ties', *American Journal of Sociology*, 78(4): 1360–1380.

Granovetter, M. S. (1976). 'Network sampling: Some first steps', *American Journal of Sociology*, 81(6): 1287–1303.

Granovetter, M. S. (1977). 'Reply to Morgan and Rytina', *American Journal of Sociology*, 83(1, 3): 727–729.

Grube, J. W. and Morgan, M. (1986). 'Smoking, drinking and other drug use among Dublin post-primary school pupils', *Paper No. 132*, Dublin, The Economic and Social Research Institute.

Harary, F., Norman, R. Z. and Cartwright, D. (1965). *Structural Models: An Introduction to the Theory of Directed Graphs*, New York, John Wiley and Sons, Inc.

Hawkins, J. D. and Fraser, M. W. (1985). 'Social networks of street drug users: A comparison of two theories', *Social Work Research and Abstracts*, 21(2): 3–12.

Hawkins, J. D. and Fraser, M. W. (1987). 'The social networks of drug abusers before and after treatment', *The International Journal of the Addictions*, 22(4): 343–355.

Haynie, D. L. (2001). 'Delinquent peers revisited: Does network structure matter?', *American Journal of Sociology*, 106(4): 1013–1057.

Haynie, D. L. (2002). 'Friendship networks and delinquency: The relative nature of peer delinquency', *Journal of Quantitative Criminology*, 18: 99–134.

Heckathorn, D. D. (1997). 'Respondent-driven sampling: A new approach to the study of hidden populations', *Social Problems*, 44(2): 174–199.

Homans, G. C. (1950). *The Human Group*, New York: Harcourt.

Hunter, S. MacD., Vizelberg, I. A. and Berenson, G. S. (1991). 'Identifying mechanisms of adoption of tobacco and alcohol use among youth: The Bogalusa heart study', *Social Networks*, 13: 91–104.

Jessor, R. (1979). 'Marihuana: A review of recent psychosocial research', in Dupont, R. L., Goldstein, A. and O'Donnell, J. (Eds), *Handbook on Drug Abuse*, National Institute on Drug Abuse, 337–355.

Jessor, R. (1987). 'Problem-behavior theory, psychosocial development, and adolescent problem drinking', *British Journal of Addiction*, 82: 331–342.

Jessor, R. and Jessor, S. L. (1977). *Problem Behavior and Psychosocial Development – A Longitudinal Study of Youth*, New York, Academic Press.

Jessor, R. and Jessor, S. L. (1978). 'Theory testing in longitudinal research on marihuana use', in Kandel, D. B. (Ed.), *Longitudinal Research on Drug Use – Empirical Findings and Methodological Issues*, New York, Hemisphere Publishing Corp. - Halsted Press, 41–71.

Jessor, R., Graves, T. D., Hanson, R. C. and Jessor, S. L. (1968). *Society, Personality and Deviant Behavior: A Study of a Tri-ethnic Community*, New York, Holt, Rinehart and Winston.

Johnson, T. P. and Mott, J. A. (2001). 'The reliability of self reported age of onset of tobacco, alcohol and illicit drug use', *Addiction*, 96(8): 1187–1198.

Johnston, L. D., O'Malley, P. M. and Bachman, J. G. (1984). *Drugs and American High School Students 1975–1983*, U.S. Dept. of Health and Human Services, National Institute on Drug Abuse.

Kandel, D. B. (1973). 'Adolescent marihuana use: Role of parents and peers', *Science*, 181: 1067–1070.

Kandel, D. B. (1974a). 'Inter- and intra-generational influences on adolescent marihuana use', *Journal of Social Issues*, 30: 107–135.

Kandel, D. B. (1974b). 'Reaching the hard-to-reach: Illicit drug use among high school absentees', *Addiction Diseases: An International Journal*, 1: 465–480.

Kandel, D. B. (1975). 'Stages in adolescent involvement in drug use', *Science*, 190: 912–914.

Kandel, D. B. (1978a). 'Convergences in prospective longitudinal surveys of drug use in normal populations', in Kandel, D. B. (Ed.), *Longitudinal Research on Drug Use: Empirical Findings and Methodological Issues*, New York, Hemisphere Publishing Corp. - Halsted Press, 3–38.

Kandel, D. B. (1978b). 'Homophily, selection, and socialization in adolescent friendships', *American Journal of Sociology*, 84: 427–436.

Kandel, D. B. (Ed.) (1978c). *Longitudinal Research on Drug Use: Empirical Findings and Methodological Issues*, New York, Hemisphere Publishing Corp. - Halsted Press.

Kandel, D. B. (1980). 'Drug and drinking behavior among youth', *Annual Review of Sociology*, 6: 235–285.

Kandel, D. B. (1986). 'Processes of peer influences in adolescence', in Silbereisen, R. K. (Ed.), *Development as Action in Context – Problem Behavior and Normal Youth Development*, Berlin, Springer-Verlag, 203–227.

Kandel, D. B. and Adler, I. (1982). 'Socialization into marijuana use among French adolescents – A cross-cultural comparison with the United States', *Journal of Health and Social Behavior*, 23(4): 295–309.

Kandel, D. B. and Andrews, K. (1987). 'Processes of adolescent socialization by parents and peers', *The International Journal of the Addictions*, 22(4): 319–342.

Kandel, D. B. and Davies, M. (1991). 'Friendship networks, intimacy, and illicit drug use in young adulthood: A comparison of two competing theories', *Criminology*, 29(3): 441–469.

Kandel, D. B. and Faust, R. (1975). 'Sequence and stages in patterns of adolescent drug use', *Archives of General Psychiatry*, 32: 923–932.

Kandel, D. B. and Yamaguchi, K. (1993). 'From beer to crack: Developmental patterns of drug involvement', *American Journal of Public Health*, 83(6): 851–855.

Kandel, D. B., Kessler, R. C. and Margulies, R. Z. (1978). 'Antecedents of adolescent initiation into stages of drug use: A developmental analysis', in Kandel, D. B. (Ed.), *Longitudinal Research on Drug Use: Empirical Findings and Methodological Issues*, New York, Hemisphere Publishing Corp. - Halsted Press, 73–99.

Kirke, D. M. (1990). *Teenage Drug Abuse: An Individualistic and Structural Analysis*, Ph.D. Thesis, University College Dublin.

Kirke, D. M. (1995). 'Teenage peer networks in the community as sources of social problems: A sociological perspective', in Brugha, T. S. (Ed.), *Social Support and Psychiatric Disorder: Research Findings and Guidelines for Clinical Practice*, Cambridge, Cambridge University Press, 174–194.

Kirke, D. M. (1996). 'Collecting peer data and delineating peer networks in a complete network', *Social Networks*, 18(4): 333–346.

Kirke, D. M. (2004). 'Chain reactions in adolescents' cigarette, alcohol and drug use: Similarity through peer influence or the patterning of ties in peer networks?', *Social Networks*, 26(1): 3–28.

Klovdahl, A. S. (1985). 'Social networks and the spread of infectious diseases: The Aids example', *Social Science and Medicine*, 21(11): 1203–1216.

Knoke, D. and Kuklinski, J. H. (1982). 'Network Analysis', *Sage University Paper Series on Quantitative Applications in the Social Sciences*, Beverly Hills and London, Sage Publications: Series No. 07-028.

Kobus, K. (2003). 'Peers and adolescent smoking', *Addiction*: 98(Suppl. 1): 37–55.

Laumann, E. O. (1973). *Bonds of Pluralism: The Form and Substance of Urban Social Networks*, New York, Wiley.

McPherson, J. M. and Smith-Lovin, L. (1987). 'Homophily in voluntary organizations: Status distance and the composition of face-to-face groups', *American Sociological Review*, 52: 370–379.

McPherson, J. M., Smith-Lovin, L. and Cook, J. M. (2001). 'Birds of a feather: Homophily in social networks', *Annual Review of Sociology*, 27: 415–444.

Malvin, J. H. and Moskowitz, J. M., (1983). 'Anonymous versus identifiable self-reports of adolescent drug attitudes, intentions and use', *The Public Opinion Quarterly*, 47(4): 557–566.

Marsden, P. V. (1990). 'Network data and measurement', *Annual Review of Sociology*, 16: 435–463.

Michell, L. and Amos, A. (1997). 'Girls, Pecking Order and Smoking', *Social Science & Medicine*, 44(12): 1861–1869.

Michell, L. and West, P. (1996). 'Peer pressure to smoke: The meaning depends on the method', *Health Education Research: Theory and Practice*, 11: 39–50.

Miller, J. D., Cisin, I. H., Gardner-Keaton, H., Harrell, A. V., Wirtz, P. W., Abelson, H. I. and Fishburne, P. M. (1983). *National Survey on Drug Abuse : Main Findings 1982*, U.S. Dept. of Health and Human Services, National Institute on Drug Abuse.

Miller, R. L., Acton, C., Fullerton, D. A. and Maltby, J. (2002). *SPSS for Social Scientists*, Houndmills and New York, Palgrave Macmillan.

Moody, J. (2002). 'The importance of relationship timing for diffusion', *Social Forces*, 81(1): 25–57.

Newcomb, M. D., Huba, G. J. and Bentler, P. M. (1983). 'Mothers influence on the drug-use of their children – Confirmatory tests of direct modeling and mediational theories', *Developmental Psychology*, 19(5): 714–726.

Nie, N. H., Hull, C. H., Jenkins, J. G., Steinbrenner, K. and Bent, D. H. (1975). *Statistical Package for the Social Sciences*, 2nd Ed., New York, McGraw-Hill Inc.

Oetting, E. R. and Donnermeyer, J. F. (1998). 'Primary socialisation theory: The etiology of drug use and deviance', *Substance Use and Misuse*, 33(4): 995–1026.

O'Malley, P. M., Bachman, J. G. and Johnston, L. D. (1983). 'Reliability and consistency in self-reports of drug-use', *The International Journal of the Addictions*, 18(6): 805–824.

Pearson, M. and Michell, L. (2000). 'Smoke rings: Social network analysis of friendship groups, smoking, and drug-taking', *Drugs: Education, Prevention and Policy*, 7(1): 21–37.

Pearson, M. and West, P. (2003). 'Drifting smoke rings: Social network analysis and Markov processes in a longitudinal study of friendship groups and risk-taking', *Connections*, 25(2): 59–76.

Rice, R. E., Donohew, L. and Clayton, R. (2003). 'Peer network, sensation seeking, and drug use among junior and senior high school students', *Connections*, 25(2): 32–58.

Richards, W. D. (1989). *The NEGOPY Network Analysis Program*, School of Communication, Simon Fraser University, Burnaby, BC, Canada.

Robbins, C. and Martin, S. S. (1993). 'Gender, styles of deviance, and drinking problems', *Journal of Health and Social Behavior*, 34: 302–321.

Rogers, E. M. (1979). 'Network analysis of the diffusion of innovations', in Holland, P. W. and Leinhardt, S. (Eds), *Perspectives on Social Network Research*, New York, Academic Press, 137–163.

Rogers, E. M. (1983). *Diffusion of Innovations*, 3rd Ed., New York, The Free Press.

Scott, J. (1991). *Social Network Analysis: A Handbook*, London, Sage Publications Ltd.

Shelley, E. B., Wilson-Davis, K., O'Rourke, F. and O'Rourke, A. (1982). 'Drugs – a study in Dublin post-primary schools', *Irish Medical Journal*, 75(7): 254–259.

Shrout, P. E. and Kandel D. B. (1981). 'Analyzing properties of dyads: Determinants of similarity of marijuana use in adolescent friendship dyads', *Sociological Methods and Research*, 9(3): 363–374.

Single, E., Kandel, D. B. and Johnson, B. (1975). 'The reliability and validity of drug use responses in a large scale longitudinal survey', *Journal of Drug Issues*, 5: 426–443.

Snijders, T. A. B. (2001). 'The statistical evaluation of social network dynamics', in Sobel, M. E. and Becker, M. P. (Eds), *Sociological Methodology – 2001*, Boston and London, Basil Blackwell, 361–395.

Snijders, T. A. B. (2005). 'Models for longitudinal network data', in Carrington, P. J., Scott, J. and Wasserman, S. (Eds) *Models and Methods in Social Network Analysis*, New York, Cambridge University Press.

Snijders, T. A. B., Steglich, C. E. G., Schweinberger, M. and Huisman, M. E. (2005). *Manual for SIENA Version 2.1*, Groningen, ICS.

Sprenger, C. J. A. and Stokman, F. N. (Eds) (1989). *Gradap: Graph Definition and Analysis Package*, Groningen, ProGamma.

Tudor, C. G., Petersen, D. M. and Elifson, K. W. (1980). 'An examination of the relationship between peer and parental influences and adolescent drug use', *Adolescence*, 15(60): 783–798.

Urberg, K. A. (1992). 'Locus of peer influences: Social crowd and best friend', *Journal of Youth and Adolescence*, 21(4): 439–445.

Urberg, K. A., Cheng, C. and Shyu, S. (1991). 'Grade changes in peer influence on adolescent cigarette smoking: A comparison of two measures', *Addictive Behaviors*, 16(1–2): 20–28.

Urberg, K. A., Degirmencioglu, S. M. and Pilgrim, C. (1997). 'Close friend and group influence on adolescent cigarette smoking and alcohol use', *Developmental Psychology*, 33(5): 834–844.

Urberg, K. A., Degirmencioglu, S. M. and Tolson, J. M. (1998). 'Adolescent friendship selection and termination: The role of similarity', *Journal of Social and Personal Relationships*, 15(5): 703–711.

Urberg, K. A., Shyu, S. and Liang, J. (1990). 'Peer influence in adolescent cigarette smoking', *Addictive Behaviors*, 15(3): 247–256.

Urberg, K. A., Luo, Q., Pilgrim, C., and Degirmencioglu, S. M. (2003). 'A two-stage model of peer influence in adolescent substance use: Individual and relationship-specific differences in susceptibility to influence', *Addictive Behaviors*, 28(7): 1243–1257.

Valente, T. W. (1995). *Network Models of the Diffusion of Innovations*, Cresskill, New Jersey, Hampton Press, Inc.

Valente, T. W. (1996). 'Social network thresholds in the diffusion of innovations', *Social Networks*, 18(1): 69–89.

Valente, T. W. (2003). 'Social network influences on adolescent substance use: An introduction', *Connections*, 25(2): 11–16.

Valente, T. W., Gallaher, P. and Mouttapa, M. (2004). 'Using social networks to understand and prevent substance use: A transdisciplinary perspective', *Substance Use and Misuse*, 39(10–12), 1685–1712.

Van der Poel, M. G. M. (1993). 'Delineating personal support networks', *Social Networks*, 15(1): 49–70.

Wasserman, S. and Faust, K. (1994). *Social Network Analysis: Methods and Applications*, New York, Cambridge University Press.

Wasserman, S. and Galaskiewicz, J. (Eds) (1994). *Advances in Social Network Analysis: Research in the Social and Behavioral Sciences*, Thousand Oaks, California, Sage Publications.

Watters, J. K. and Biernacki, P. (1989). 'Targeted sampling: Options for the study of hidden populations', *Social Problems*, 36(4): 416–430.

Wellman, B. (1979). 'The community question: The intimate networks of East Yorkers', *American Journal of Sociology*, 84: 1201–1231.

Wellman, B. (1988). 'Structural analysis: From method and metaphor to theory and substance', in Wellman, B. and Berkowitz, S. D. (Eds), *Social Structures: A Network Approach*, Cambridge, New York, Cambridge University Press, 19–61.

Wellman, B. (Ed.) (1999). *Networks in the Global Village: Life in Contemporary Communities*, Boulder, Colorado, Westview Press.

Wellman, B. and Berkowitz, S. D. (1988). 'Introduction: Studying social structures' in Wellman, B. and Berkowitz, S. D. (Eds), *Social Structures: A Network Approach*, Cambridge, New York, Cambridge University Press, 1–14.

Wister, A.V. and Avison, W. R. (1982). ' "Friendly persuasion": A social network analysis of sex differences in marijuana use', *The International Journal of the Addictions*, 17(3): 523–541.

Yamaguchi, K. and Kandel, D. B. (1984a). 'Patterns of drug use from adolescence to young adulthood: II. Sequences of progression', *American Journal of Public Health*, 74(7): 668–672.

Yamaguchi, K. and Kandel, D. B. (1984b). 'Patterns of drug use from adolescence to young adulthood: III. predictors of progression', *American Journal of Public Health*, 74(7): 673–681.

Yamaguchi, K. and Kandel, D. B. (1985). 'On the resolution of role incompatibility: A life event history analysis of family roles and marijuana use', *American Journal of Sociology*, 90(6): 1284–1325.

Index